LINDAU'S PLACE

GREEN'S APARTMENT

GAS COUNTRY

ED FISHER JR

ADELINE GOES TO THE LAWYER

NORTHWICKS' RESIDENCE

IN CANADA

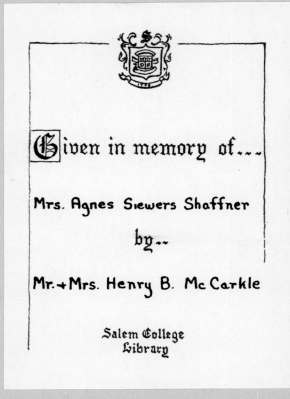

The Realist at War

Edwin H. Cady

THE
REALIST AT WAR

THE MATURE YEARS 1885–1920

OF

William Dean Howells

SYRACUSE UNIVERSITY PRESS

LIBRARY OF CONGRESS CATALOG CARD NO.: 58–13106

© 1958 SYRACUSE UNIVERSITY PRESS

*Manufactured in the United States of America
by The Colonial Press Inc.*

To Norma

Preface

AS THE SECOND HALF OF THE FIRST INTERPRETIVE BIOGRAPHY OF William Dean Howells, this unavoidably assumes a reader's knowledge of the first volume, *The Road to Realism*. That book mainly recounted Howells' growth; it was essentially a history of the man and artist's becoming. This, on the other hand, concentrates on his mature achievement and its significance. Though there was a last, triumphant growth into greatness in the period covered by this volume, it remains largely a story of being.

In the roughly twenty years between *The Rise of Silas Lapham* and *The Son of Royal Langbrith* fell the creative, artistic, critical, philosophic, and tutorial accomplishments in which Howells' life attained its major proportions. Yet these years, 1885–1904, have on the whole been the least studied, least comprehended part of his career. To illuminate the work and activities of those years therefore became the crowning task of this biography, and the weight of emphasis through space as well as through strategy falls upon that period.

In dealing with a life so long, so complex and interesting as Howells', the temptation to run interminably to length is almost irresistible. It has been resisted as well as possible, however, and partly by the device of not dwelling longer than necessary on aspects specially covered in other books either in print or known to be forthcoming in close sequence with this. Miss Mildred Howells' *Life in Letters* is particularly rich and illuminating on her father's twentieth-century years and has been reduplicated as little as could be. Everett Carter's *Howells and the Age of Realism*, 1954, and the soon to be published books by Walter Meserve on Howells' plays and by Clara and Rudolph Kirk on his criticism have been gratefully left to their fields. The one place in which it proved hardest to economize on space was in the elucidation of the major novels and other books. In the interplay between an author's other life and his literature lies his true biography. Since new insights into Howells' writing seemed to flow from contemplation of it in the whole biographical context, it seemed necessary to explain them. And that need was complicated by the unhappy truth that even the ordinary cultivated and serious reader must at this moment be assumed to be ignorant of these masterly writings. That is a condition one hopes this and associated books by other historians and critics may soon obviate. On the other hand, none of the explications makes any pretense of completeness. Much more could, and has been or will be, said about each of Howells' major works, especially the novels.

Once again it is a privilege to thank great institutions and libraries for their help as well as to thank individuals. In addition to the John Simon Guggenheim Memorial Foundation, I must again thank Syracuse University and its officials for that generosity in repeated subsidized research leaves which was renewed in the fall term of 1957–58. For materials particularly helpful to this volume I must express again my gratitude to Mr. William Jackson and his staff of the Houghton Library, Harvard University, as well as to the Widener Library of the same institution; to the Syracuse University Library, and especially Mr. Lester Wells; to the Newberry Library and its staff; to the Ohio State Historical Library in Columbus and the Rutherford B. Hayes Library in Fremont, Ohio. To the libraries of Columbia, Leeds, Oslo, Uppsala, and Yale Universities; the libraries of the University of Pennsylvania and the University of Wisconsin. To the Library of Congress, the British Museum, the New York Public Library, and the Huntington Library—to all my thanks are renewed. And to the libraries of the University of California at Los Angeles and the University of Southern California for the first time.

Again I have incurred debts to individuals whom it is a pleasure to name: Professor and Mrs. William White Howells, William M. Gibson, Louis Budd, Clara and Rudolph Kirk; Albert J. George, Jack Lunn Mowers, David Owen, Roy Harvey Pearce, and Antonio Pace; William Pearson Tolley, Finla G. Crawford, Eric Faigle, and Sanford B. Meech; Lars and Erna Åhnebrink and Clarence Clausen; Edwin Laird Cady. But most especially Norma Woodard Cady, to whom it is all most properly dedicated.

Edwin H. Cady

Acknowledgements

THE THANKS OF AUTHOR AND PUBLISHER ARE OFFERED FOR the following permissions to quote privileged or copyrighted materials:

To Professor William White Howells, literary executor of the estate of William Dean Howells and to the Committee of the Houghton Library on the Howells Papers, chaired by Mr. William Jackson, for quotations from unpublished letters, notebooks, and other materials from the Howells Papers, and for quotations from *The Son of Royal Langbrith* and *The Leatherwood God.*

To Miss Mildred Howells for quotations from *The Life in Letters of William Dean Howells.*

To Appleton-Century-Crofts for quotations from Edith Wharton, *A Backward Glance;* and Allan Nevins, ed., *The Letters . . . of Brand Whitlock.*

To Harper and Brothers for quotations from Joseph Henry Harper, *I Remember.*

To the Rutherford B. Hayes Library for quotations from *The Diary of Rutherford B. Hayes.*

To the Houghton Mifflin Company for quotations from *Passages from the Journal of Thomas Russell Sullivan;* Robert Grant, *Fourscore;* Arthur S. Hardy, *Things Remembered;* Kate D. Wiggin, *My Garden of Memory;* Ferris Greenslet, *Life of Thomas Bailey Aldrich.*

To Alfred A. Knopf, Inc., for quotations from Carl Van Doren, *The Roving Critic;* Robert W. Stallman, ed., *Stephen Crane Omnibus.*

To the Macmillan Company for quotations from *The Autobiography of William Allen White.*

To the Oxford University Press for quotations from William Lyon Phelps, *Autobiography with Letters.*

To Charles Scribner's Sons for quotations from Augustus Thomas, *Print of My Remembrance.*

To Robert Wooster Stallman for graciously waiving his interest in excerpts from the correspondence of Howells and Crane.

Contents

"BANGING THE BABES
OF ROMANCE ABOUT"

WILLIAM DEAN HOWELLS WAS THE FIRST TO SEE CLEARLY THAT the important writers of his generation, almost all of them his friends, had joined with him to produce a new kind of literature, the American realistic novel. And for participating in that achievement Howells found himself under bitter attack after the publication of *The Rise of Silas Lapham* in 1885. Formidable efforts were being made to attach the labels of "atheism," "poison," and "dirt" to his writings. Was an effort on foot to direct, or silence, or, if need be, destroy him? Well, then, he would fight back. Without having intended it, he found himself in the midst of a major literary war. Soon, as he wrote a friend, he was "banging the babes of Romance about" with gusto. He warred with the critics and defied the powers and lived to win a creative success deeper and weightier than could have been predicted from his earlier work.

I

Fortunately for Howells at war, he acquired just at the outset of hostilities a strong new financial base of operations and a potent journalistic weapon at one stroke. In the spring of 1885, after years of strain, his publisher James R. Osgood finally "broke" and fell into bankruptcy. He was apparently able to meet his creditors, so that Howells lost nothing—but there was the question of what to do now that Osgood's weekly salary arrangement could no longer go on. Almost immediately Howells found that he was in demand.

Ticknor and Company, successors to Osgood, negotiated persistently but, as it turned out, much too cautiously to inherit him along with the novels Osgood had published. Scribner's of New York bid high—20 per cent royalties on all books, with advances to

1

keep a regular income flowing to Howells. But it was Osgood, assisted by Howells' old Belmont friend, Charles Fairchild, who negotiated for the star of his old stable of authors a record-breaking contract with what was then the biggest and richest publishing house in America. Osgood had gone to work for Harper and Brothers after his own smashup. No doubt he was glad to be able to serve as liaison between the house and Howells. They began by proposing to "the Harpers," as the firm was always called, an idea Howells had thought up for conducting a magazine of serious, international realistic writing to be called *The World of Fiction*. The counterproposal took Howells' breath away.

After the contract was signed on October 6, 1885, Howells described it as "incredibly advantageous for me." It was indeed a literary bonanza, especially in consideration of the purchasing power of the then almost untaxed dollar. For agreeing to offer all his work to the Harpers, Howells received $10,000 a year. He agreed to write one novel per year the size (roughly 100,000 words) of *The Undiscovered Country*. The $10,000 paid for the serial publication of the novel; on book publication Howells received a 12½ per cent royalty. Three thousand of the ten were to be paid for writing three to five pages per month of a new *Harper's Monthly* department to be called "The Editor's Study." Aware of increasing powers and public appeal, Howells, perhaps the best literary businessman among the standard American authors, never hesitated to renegotiate. His correspondence with the various representatives of the Harpers throughout this period, and indeed from time to time for the rest of his life, shows him constantly rearguing his case and using his leverage to raise his take. The history of the arts is replete with sad stories of how immature and necessitous creators were fleeced by rapacious publishers and promoters. That did not happen to Howells.

Certainly he now had his "basis" again, and with a vengeance. Such security was previously undreamt of for an American author; and it is worth noting that, in spite of all the strain Howells put on the Harpers by his pugnacity in the succeeding years, it was he, not they, who eventually broke off the arrangement. More immediately, Howells' proposal to the Harpers that he earn part of his keep by founding a magazine devoted to nothing but fiction was met by them with the counterproposal that he continue to put the major part of his energy into fiction but, if he wished, take up an equal place beside the ancient and honorable "Editor's Easy Chair" in *Harper's Monthly*—long conducted with distinction by George W. Curtis. Howells was to write, with an entirely free hand, his own department, distinguishing it from Curtis' by devoting it strictly to subjects of current literary interest. Thus "The Editor's Study" was born, the first essay written and accepted in October to be printed in the January 1886 number. Howells was back in journalism, and the potency of the weapon now put in his hand was well attested by the frequent screams from opponents in the literary war which followed.

The Harpers contract did, of course, cut one of Howells' ties to Boston, and when the autumn announcement of his arrangement caused a small newspaper sensation, "the New York papers were filled with editorials announcing that Mr. Howells' removal to the metropolis would deal a blow to Boston's literary supremacy." The fact that the joint inability of his daughter Winifred and her mother to cope with a winter of Boston social life caused Howells to let his Beacon Street house and move out to a hotel in Auburndale, Massachusetts, for the season may have given countenance to rumors. But in April he let it be known at a reception for him at the Author's Club in New York that he was not ready to cast loose from the Hub. The feature of the occasion was much gay chaff about his decision, climaxed by the solemn reading of a note from Aldrich: "Come back to Boston and all will be forgiven."

II

There was perhaps a little more than met the eye in Aldrich's burlesque of the prodigal's return because Howells, undeterred by the attacks on *Lapham,* had finished (by February 9, 1886) and begun to print in the February *Century* a new novel which was one of his acts of war. It was a redevelopment of some of the insights from *Lapham,* one of the last installments in the saga of "Boston-Torn-to-Tatters," and he called it *The Minister's Charge; or, The Apprenticeship of Lemuel Barker.*

Actually Howells was now in a mood less satiric and more compassionate than he had been for any of his previous Boston novels. It was still true that "the sympathies of Howells the artist (but also the aspiring democrat) were all on the side of the newcomers" as his friend the Proper Bostonian novelist Robert Grant later observed. But in this variation on the conventional-unconventional conflict, the Coreys, the Bellinghams, and their friends are handled more kindly. Howells had been treasuring "insights into the lying, suffering, sinning, well-meaning human soul." He had been accusing himself of cowardice and falseness—not, as he wrote S. Weir Mitchell, because he never spoke the truth, but because he was not bold enough to speak it frequently.

The ironies of *The Minister's Charge* are therefore more indulgent. The Bostonians are permitted a warmth and breadth of sympathy previously denied them. Indeed, the true movement within the novel would have been revealed if Howells had called it "Lemuel Barker; or, The Education of Proper Boston." On the surface the hero's story is as close to Horatio Alger as Howells ever came. Lem Barker, a back-country farm boy, comes to Boston with high hopes for a literary career because the vacationing Rev. Mr. David Sewell has disingenuously praised his bad poetry. Sewell, of course, had hoped only to spare his feelings and is nonplussed when he stays in Boston to become a moral charge on the minister.

But Howells' means of placing Barker on the minister's account was to run Lem through a series of scenes so unprecedented in Howells' fiction and so daringly aggressive as a move in his warfare that they left many of his readers and critics gasping. In a swift but excellently detailed and well-articulated succession of scenes, he had Lem swindled by a pair of counterfeiters on the Common, wandering homeless and starved among the dregs of Boston, arrested, jailed on a false charge, tried in court and discharged, and rescued from the streets by a charity flophouse before Sewell could catch up with him. The personalities, conversations, humor, and atmosphere of all these scenes Howells studied at length. No doubt he drew on his experiences as a visitor for the Boston Associated Charities. Also he had spent hours during the steaming weather of July 1 and 2 visiting (and recording in his notes without a trace of the old neurotic shrinking) the scenes, smells, voices, and personalities on tap at the Joy Street Police Station and the City Lodging for Tramps in Hawkins Street.

He was out to shock readers with a clear view of that other side of Boston life which he had scanted in *Lapham*. But, quite naturally, he was out to use the shock for something serious. He had hinted both in *A Modern Instance* and in *Lapham* that something important could be gained by examining both the ideological and the practical futilities of the charity approach to Boston's increasingly horrible problems of slums and poverty. Now, using characters and thematic patterns to which his readers were already accustomed, he proposed to draw them into just that examination which the majority of politicians, social thinkers, and churchgoers of his time had determinedly avoided making.

The apprenticeship of Lemuel Barker, which started out to be literary, soon became sociological. By putting Lem in jail and a flophouse, Howells started him out at the bottom of Boston and then moved him up to the place of janitor and personal servant to various of Sewell's friends and parishioners—including Bromfield Corey. This gave Howells a chance to work on a theme which had concerned him in *Out of the Question* and was to recur frequently in the social-centered writings of his next years. Were the American upper classes right in condemning to eternal subservience those who had once worked with their hands or acted as personal servants? Or was that an untenable, undemocratic, unrealistic kind of snobbery? Barker's granitic Yankee integrity, his natural intellectuality and his innate sensitivity make great growth possible to him, so that Bromfield Corey is moved to say to a delightedly agreeing Bellingham: "Why the boy's an Ancestor ! . . . All you have to do . . . is to give him time, and he'll found a fortune and a family, and his children's children will be cutting ours in society. Half of our great people have come up in that way. Look at the Bluebook, where our nobility is enrolled; it's the apotheosis of farm boys, mechanics, insidemen, and I don't know what !"

Thus the unconventional man and the tradition of the natural gentleman are vindicated again—there is even the somewhat weary hint at the end of the book that Lem eventually marries Miss Vane, Sewell's parishioner who has befriended, educated, and employed him. Howells takes a few pages to suggest that this might have happened within the confines of the novel had Miss Vane not been a victim of the feminine self-sacrifice bugaboo. But the real, fresh questions of the book were left unanswered by such familiar developments. It is in the education, the ethical evolution, of the Rev. Mr. David Sewell that Howells contemplates both the implications of the Boston in which Lem has had his shocking adventures and the fundamental uselessness of the well-meaning efforts Sewell, his parishioners, and people like them have put forth to cope with it. Sewell, often humiliated, learns much from his charge—and profits in the way of several fine sermon inspirations. Properly enough, the last, the one on which the novel essentially closes, is the best—and represents the best of Howells' own ethical thought to date.

It may well be that Howells made a minister one of the centers of his book in order to have a spokesman he need not feel artistically awkward about. Originally the planning novelist had proposed to himself that Barker, by thinking how one character "depresses" but another "elevates" him, was to become "dimly conscious of the notion of elevating others. (Complicity.) In this way he is to escape from all that's sordid in his own life." From that germ there grew one of Howells' pivotal moral insights—one of such magnitude that it was much more fittingly expressed in a cultivated minister's sermon than in Barker's laconic talk.

Sewell's last sermon is called "Complicity" and takes off from the Pauline text: "Remember them that are in bonds as bound with them":

'Those who were aware of his habit of seeking to produce a personal rather than a general effect, of his belief that you can have a righteous public only by the slow process of having righteous men and women, knew that he meant something much nearer home to each of his hearers when he preached the old Christ-humanity to them, and enforced again the lessons that no one for good or for evil, for sorrow or joy, for sickness or health, stood apart from his fellows, but each was bound to the highest and lowest by ties that centered in the hand of God. No man, he said, sinned or suffered to himself alone, his error and his pain darkened and afflicted men who never heard his name. If a community was corrupt, if an age was immoral, it was not because of the vicious, but the virtuous who fancied themselves indifferent spectators. . . . The gospel—Christ—God, so far as men had imagined him,—was but a lesson, a type, a witness from everlasting to everlasting of the spiritual unity of man. As we grow in grace, in humanity, in civilization, our recognition of this truth would be transfigured from a duty to a privilege, a joy, a heavenly rapture. . . . Only those who had had the care of others laid upon them, lived usefully, fruitfully. . . . The wretched, the foolish, the ignorant whom we found at every turn were something more, they were the messengers of God, sent to tell his secret to any that would hear it. Happy he in whose ears their cry for help was a perpetual voice. . . . In his responsibility for his weaker brethren he was Godlike, for God was but the impersonation

of loving responsibility, of infinite and never-ceasing care for us all.'
And so the tale of the apprenticeship of Lemuel Barker climaxes
in the minister's charge—to his people, a charge Howells would
make to all the world.

Having poured himself out in this, the best of his thought, the
inmost cry of his conscience, Howells found that he had stirred up
yet more controversy. Young Hamlin Garland, converted by reading
Howells in order to confute and attack him, found his books very
hard to get at the Boston Public Library. There was huge demand
for them. And when Garland went to volunteer a review of *The
Minister's Charge* for the Boston *Transcript,* its literary editor accepted and promised Garland an introduction to Howells: ". . . but
not now. Wait a while. War is being made upon him and if you
were to meet him at this time your criticism would have less weight.
His enemies would say that you had come under his magnetic influence."

The tactic of the enemies was characteristic of literary wars.
They simply ignored the point and purpose of the novel to concentrate on something prejudicial, though in this case it was certainly
not irrelevantly so. As Howells complained to Henry James, who
liked and had been moved by it:

'. . . in many quarters here the book
meets with little but misconception. If we regard it as nothing but an
example of work in the new way—the performance of a man who won't
and can't keep on doing what's been done already—its reception here
by most of the reviewers is extremely discouraging. Of all grounds in
the world they take the genteel ground and every "Half-bred rogue that
groomed his mother's cow," reproaches me for introducing him to low
company. This has been the tone of "society" about it; in the newspapers
it hardly stops short of personal defamation.'
There was nothing to do but go on fighting.

III

Though it probably can never be determined exactly what influence
the event had upon the thought which produced *The Minister's
Charge,* there can be no doubt that Howells was stiffened against
his opposition by a major discovery in the autumn of 1885. Sometime while he was working on the problems of Lemuel Barker, he
picked up a copy of *The Cossacks* which had lain on his shelf for a

long time and all at once came upon the last of his great literary passions—Lyof Tolstoi. As Howells read eagerly on past *Anna Karenina*, which he sometimes thought the greatest of all novels, into the body of Tolstoi's work and discovered the theoretical writings as well, he underwent an experience so profound as to be comparable to a religious conversion. He was, of course, ripe for such an event, with all his susceptibilities whetted by the experience associated with that recent moment when "the bottom dropped out."

Deliberately making the last, climactic chapter of *My Literary Passions* an extraordinary testament to Tolstoi, Howells described his experience of the great Russian with a care and a precision which have not always been sufficiently attended to by Howells' readers. Tolstoi, he said, was at his best the perfect artist, who conveys reality with utter transparency and with a power of genius which "has a method which not only seems without artifice, but is so." The esthetic paradox there employed can probably only be explained as one might the paradoxes of a metaphysical poet: it hints at the ineffable. Certainly, however, Howells felt confirmed by Tolstoi in his devotion to realism.

But the great force of Tolstoi was ethical: "I can never again see life in the way I saw it before I knew him," Howells wrote. Tolstoi made Christianity quicken into life in Howells' heart for the first time since his boyhood. He "gave me heart to hope," reads the testament, "that the world may yet be made over in the image of Him who died for it, when all Caesar's things shall finally be rendered unto Caesar, and men shall come into their own, into the right to labor and the right to enjoy the fruits of their labor, each one master of himself and servant to every other. He taught me to see life not as a chase of a forever impossible personal happiness, but as a field for endeavor towards the happiness of the whole human family; and I can never lose this vision, however I close my eyes, and strive to see my own interest as the highest good."

Yet "conversion" to these ideas was much more a reawakening— of the ideas and sentiments of his father, William Cooper Howells, in the long ago scenes of Hamilton and Eureka Mills, Ohio—than the turning of a pagan to the good news of Christ. In January 1886, Howells sent Tolstoi's "My Religion" to his father, recognizing how cordially the old Utopian would receive it: and from about that period forward to the father's death in 1894 their correspondence reveals a sympathetic mutuality far stronger than any which had united them since young Howells' departure for Venice in 1861. This Howells recognized in another paradox, as he continued: "[Tolstoi] gave me new criterions, new principles, which, after all, were those taught us in our earliest childhood, before we came to the evil wisdom of the world." For the rest of his life, though most especially for the next decade or so, the unfolding of these ideals awakened by Tolstoi was among the most powerful of Howells' experiences. It strengthened and heartened him to fight where he thought he should and must. It sensitized his responses to the world he lived in and drove his imagination to grapple with its evils.

Behind the fighting Howells of these years, then, lay the truly religious experience which had culminated in his devotion to Tolstoi. His moral and humanitarian tenderness, his surprising acts of fortitude for the right as he saw it, and much of his unique creative achievement in these years must be credited to a blend of three factors: his personal store of temperament and talent; the wisdom both in art and thought which his half-century of carefully examined life and work had lent him; the continuing, recurring impulses from a living religious experience of which "Tolstoi" was the symbol and symptom, not the single, simple "cause."

At the same time, it should not be forgotten that Howells never became, in the ordinary churchly sense, a Christian. Theologically, metaphysically, intellectually, even perhaps spiritually, he remained an agnostic. He could commit himself, could give himself away, only sporadically and impermanently. That gave him certain advantages both in life and art. It kept him from saintly arrogance, the fanatic pride of formal humility and absolute knowledge. It kept him focused on persons and their troubles, kept him tolerant and humane. It also probably denied him great rewards of personal consolation and the creative potency of assured faith. As a realist he was deprived of the romantic's faith in the sublimity of his ego, and as an agnostic deprived of the believer's faith in the support of the cosmos.

Temperamentally, as well as agnostically, Howells avoided having his religion institutionalized. He wrote of Tolstoi and talked him so persuasively that he was instrumental in having a Tolstoi Club founded in Boston. But he was not active in it himself. The closest he came to religious affiliation was to subscribe to the Church or Brotherhood of the Carpenter begun in 1890 as a mission in Boston by the ardent Christian Socialist clergyman, the Episco-palian W. D. P. Bliss. It seems unlikely either that the "church" had any permanent existence or that Howells' relation to it was more than nominal, even then. His joining, in fact, was taken to be "an effort to exalt the life of Jesus above the creeds of the churches. . . ."

IV

Loudly publicizing their capture of the famous author nation-wide, the Harpers went Howellsian with a bang. Through some untrace-able arrangement, they were able to serialize *Indian Summer,* be-tween July 1885 and February 1886, although Ticknor and Company published the book, as it did *The Minister's Charge* which *Century* serialized. For the December 1885 number, *Harper's Monthly* could add one of the best of Howells' farces, "The Garroters," thus solid-ifying what had become (beginning with "The Sleeping Car" in *Harper's Christmas* in 1882) almost a national institution through which young people turned to *Harper's* at Christmas time for a Howells farce eminently suited to gay amateur performance as part of the holiday festivities. And in January 1886 there appeared the first "Editor's Study."

Its advent was greeted by Curtis from his magisterial "Editor's Easy Chair" with what truly was, as Howells wrote in thanking him for it, a "very sweet and gracious welcome." The Magazine not only wished its readers a Happy New Year, said Curtis, but undertook to guarantee it by adding this "new room" to its Club for readers. The Study had for its *"genius loci"* one "whose fine and penetrating power has at once charmed [the reader's] fancy and touched his character and refined his life." Curtis promised that expert selections from the horde of books being published would be discussed in that "true modern taste and style, which . . . is a happy blending of the best of the old with the best of the new." Suppose, once upon a time, "a Study had been furnished in which Faraday could have told us every month in pleasant chat something about science, or Edmund Burke, let us say, had talked of politics, or Coleridge of philosophy . . . ," *that,* suggested flattering Curtis, is what "the Editor's Study" will be like.

Since the tradition of "The Editor's Easy Chair" and "The Edi-tor's Drawer" which bracketed the "Study" in *Harper's* demanded a playful pose of anonymity, the *genius loci* had fun introducing himself as "the unreal editor" who inhabited a fabulous room. "Heavy rugs silence the foot upon his floor; nothing but the costliest masterpieces gleam from his walls; the best of the old literatures, in a subtly chorded harmony of bindings, make music to the eye from his shelves, and the freshest of the new load his richly carved mahogany table. His vast windows of flawless plate look out upon the confluent waters of the Hudson and the Charles, with expanses in the middle distance, of the Mississippi, the Great Lakes, and the Golden Gate, and in the background the misty line of the Thames, with reaches of the remoter Seine, and glints of the Tiber's yellow tide. The peaks of the Apennines, dreamily blending with those of the Sierras, form the vanishing point of the delicious perspective." There he proposed, "the airy, elusive abstraction who edits the Study," to sit "at fine ease" and talk over with the reader, as "a symposium of one," whatever "matters of literary interest may come up from time to time, whether suggested by the new books of the day or other accidents of the literary life." He promised to have opinions to express—which dissident readers might think "prejudices and grudges"—but pledged that "the editor will try to keep his temper, and to be as inconclusive as possible."

For all the great charm of style and fancy, there is a bite of potential asperity here new to Howells' occasional writing. A sensitive reader might have predicted that there would be times when the editor did lose his temper and become not only conclusive but dogmatic about his "prejudices and grudges." The reader had, in fact, only to turn to page two of this first "Editor's Study" to find an open militancy which well reflected the mood of the real creator of the unreal editor. This was the opening gun of a great battle in Howells' war. He was, somewhat amazingly, not only in a fighting mood but enjoying it. The militancy is not so surprising; he had honestly been forced to the attitude he expressed to Thomas Wentworth Higginson on August 31 while meditating if not writing this first Study: "After your liking my story I ought to be willing you should dislike my literary creed, or my preaching it. But I can't. . . . I mean that no reader of mine shall suppose that the true and natural way of writing fiction which is now universal, wherever fiction is worth reading, is any longer to be taken on sufferance. It has come to stay."

But the romanticists not only roused Howells' ire, their "foolish old superstition" tickled his risibilities (with all their native Western scorn of foofaraw). Young William Lyon Phelps visited him once to discuss literature and was amazed. "I never saw him or any one else laugh more unrestrainedly than he did while discussing 'romantic fiction,'" said Phelps. "He laughed till the tears ran down his face." Such feelings make a critic a dangerous adversary. Recording to Gosse the newspaper reaction to the first Study, Howells said, "the small fry of critics swarm upon me." But he didn't care. "It's fun," he wrote, "banging the babes of Romance about. . . . There hasn't been so much honest truth aired in this country since Columbus's second mate shouted 'Land ho !' and Columbus retorted 'What a lie ! It's clouds.'"

Therefore, the first Study hits hard. Howells is humorous and humane, but tough. He leaves little doubt that his attitudes will be strongly favorable to realism, democracy, and patriotism. "It is well to call things by their names, even if they are spades," he announces, and proceeds to distinguish between "the bad school we were all brought up in" and the "admirable" among the latest novels. The good novel shows "a disposition to regard our life without the literary glasses so long thought desirable, and to see character, not as it is in other fiction, but as it abounds outside of all fiction. . . . It is what relates American fiction to the only living movement in imaginative literature, and distinguishes by a superior freshness and authenticity this group of American novels from [any also random] . . . group of English novels, giving them the same good right to be as the like number of recent Russian novels, French novels, Spanish novels, Italian novels, Norwegian novels."

The Editor praised Mary Noailles Murfree's *Prophet of the Great Smoky Mountain* for its faithfulness to observed locale and character, for the artistry of her method ("there is little comment; the people speak for themselves"), for the skill with which she communicated a fresh point of view. He spanked her for copying Dickens with occasional special atmospheric and plot effects but ended on a note of praise for her and glad hope for the future of Southern fiction.

Less qualified praise went to S. Weir Mitchell's *In War Time* for its "two or three thoroughly well represented people" who "represent in two extremes" something Howells himself had been much intrigued by: "the decay of Puritanism; in one the moral nature almost paralyzed, in the other, hysterically active—a conscience divided from reason, working automatically, with a sort of stupefied helplessness." The way Mitchell handled local color, Howells said, "is most valuable; more valuable still is the artistic quiet of the book, which takes at once a high level, and keeps it without the emotional foolishness of manner or the contorted pseudo-dramaticism of method which cause the compassionate to grieve over so much of our fiction, especially our lady-fiction."

Here and in the swiftly paraded accompanying contents were, at least by implication but in large part expressed either through direct statement or a dry, hard irony, most of the main elements of what Howells would develop in the Study during the next six years as his realistic creed. He insisted that the realist not only "look at life" but "look at it keenly and closely in the right American manner, and . . . question the results with the last fineness for their meaning and value." In other words, the realistic vision was of necessity a moral one, dominated by "conscience and purpose." And so he brushed away "the make-believe 'Greek' theory of art for art's sake—as if the Greekest of the Greek art were not for religion's sake, as the Greeks understood it." From the start Howells was aware of that neoromanticism which would be called "the decadence" and became its unsparing—and unspared—enemy. With that enmity went his devotion to Americanism in art. Not chauvinism—no major American author or critic has been more easily and readily international than Howells—but an Americanism which insisted on the fundamental goodness of democracy and decentralization for the arts. The "great American novel" was a chimera like "a literary centre," the Editor pointed out. Neither can ever really occur in the United States so long as it remains true to its best tradition of an "intense localism" like that which made the art of old Italy glorious—when "every rock-built or sea-girt provincial city exulted to be the home of the letters and the arts."

And, lastly, let the American novelist take heart, turn away the pedants, ignore the carping British, and write from the treasury of American English "freshened and revived from the native sources which literary decentralization will help to keep open." Languages do not belong to grammarians and purists: "God apparently meant them for the common-people—whom Lincoln believed God liked because He had made so many of them." American novelists would be dismally wrong to "try to write Americanly, from any motive." But they should simply and naturally write the language that strikes their native ears. So, "When their characters speak, we should like to hear them speak true American, with all the varying Tennessean, Philadelphian, Bostonian, and New York accents." There is really nothing for the American to worry himself about but his honesty. "We have only to leave our studies, editorial and other, and go out into the shops and fields to find the 'spacious times' again; and from the beginning Realism, before she had got a name or put on her capital-letter, had divined this near-at-hand truth along with the rest."

This was all banging the babes of romance about with gusto. With certain most essential differences, it was the bold voice of Emerson heard again. And, for all the angry swarm of little critics, perhaps even in part through the publicity the small fry gave it, the "Editor's Study" took well with the public. As soon as the first one was submitted in October 1885, Osgood spoke his own delight and the Harpers' acceptance. The whole thing was "charming," he wrote, "filled with your happiest touches. The Introduction is the most graceful and most adroit bit of writing which I have met with in a long time. If the public doesn't meet you more than half-way," he concluded, "the public is a d—d fool."

Certainly in "The Editor's Study" the public was treated to a "column" which approached as near greatness as any in the history of that journalistic genre. Many of those dozens of little essays which appeared in clusters of four, five, or six in each of the seventy-five Studies are admirable. Serious of purpose and important in content, they shine with Howells' practised humanity and lightness of touch. They are packed, strong, able, often funny, often penetrating. It is a pity that most readers know them only in the often heavy and awkward polemic Howells hastily selected from them and threw together as *Criticism and Fiction*. No future anthologist of his criticism should choose from that volume, but always directly from the Studies. The results would be far more sparkling—and more truly representative of the author.

Howells wrote his series, each about four months in advance of publication, doing in September 1885 what would appear with his forty-ninth birthday the following March, and penning his last probably in November 1891, throughout a period of great turbulence in both his inner and outer lives. There he recorded his response to the most profoundly challenging period of his life. He placed in the Study the intellectual product of that last, magnificent burst of growth in his mind and personality which went forward between his forty-seventh and fifty-fourth years, at a time when most men have long since settled, at least psychologically, into slippered and more or less cynical ease.

One of the ways of making the Study lively and important for himself as well as his readers was to exercise in it the bite of his growing heresies. Let the critics yap or roar, Howells had fun and, what was better, told the truth as he saw it. Realism is better than romance, he said, especially when romance becomes "romanticistic" by pretending to reality. *Madame Bovary,* Zola, Dostoevsky, Turgenev, Palacio Valdés, Hardy, Ibsen, Tolstoi, and Henry James are great; Scott, Dickens, Thackeray, and their followers are inferior. English criticism and most English literature therefore lies benighted while America and the Continent surge forward into the light of modernity, reality, and truth. "Literosity" and adherence to convention poison art, but a direct and personal relation to life, as life is available to contemporary thought, makes art free and great. Genius does not exist; the idea of genius is a romantic superstition. The novel is a serious business. It exists not to pander to the reader's appetite for cheap thrills or irresponsible oblivion but to provide him with sharpened insights into the nature of things through the responsible magic of art. The writer should never flirt with the reader or even admit overtly that the reader is there. In the long run good morals and good art are identical, and vice versa. Only character and characterization really count in fiction, all else is subordinate. Therefore historical fiction must be bad: since the author can know character only through personal observation, his historical characterizations can't escape anachronism.

A last, and for many readers baffling and infuriating, set of heresies ran from esthetics to social ethics. Serious literature, which must be realistic to be esthetically and intellectually respectable, must also be democratic because it must focus on individual and common character. It must be humane because it must enter sympathetically into the problems of the individual in contemporary life. When it is democratic and humane, it will find that in the political and social, but especially in the economic circumstances of contemporary life many people suffer and are stultified. Therefore the ideas of Tolstoi and the socialists merit conscientious consideration.

To the support of these and other heresies Howells rallied all his gifts of literary charm. His lifelong grace of humor was reinforced by a power never before so ready to his journalistic hand: the impact of the perfectly aimed, clean, hard phrase, often finished off with a re-echoing ironic twist. Uniting all his main ideas, he said, "If America means anything at all, it means the sufficiency of the common, the insufficiency of the uncommon. It is the affirmation in political terms of the Christian ideal, which when we shall affirm it in economic and social terms will make us the perfect state. . . ."

He could not for himself accept Tolstoi's attempt to become a peasant; it violated common sense, he felt. Yet he would not evade, nor if he could avoid it permit his readers to evade, the force of Tolstoi's demonstration. What if this rich ruler, also "the greatest living writer, and incomparably the greatest writer of fiction who has ever lived," should be right? "In that case, how many of us who have great possessions must go away exceeding sorrowful ! Come, star-eyed Political Economy ! come, Sociology, heavenly nymph ! and soothe the ears tortured by this echo of Nazareth. Save us, sweet Evolution ! Help, O Nebular Hypothesis ! Art, Civilization, Literature, Culture ! is there no escape from our brothers but in becoming more and more truly their brothers?" The mangled bodies in the ditch behind him could have been labeled Gospel of Wealth, Social Darwinism, Art for Art's Sake, or Average Cultivated Citizen.

A lifetime of amateur joke-smithing, much of it in the swiftest company, also lent Howells weapons. Some of the jokes were mainly for their own sakes: "Publishers, with all their virtues, are as distinctly made a little lower than the angels as any class of mortals we know. They are, in fact, a tentative and timid kind, never quite happy except in full view of the main chance. . . ." Lowell, he noted, knew enough to stop being antislavery when the question had been settled. He "was not of those who belabor a dead dog, to give him a realizing sense that there is a punishment after death."

Other jokes had more mordant intent. "French plays," wrote the realistic critic, are noted for "their carpentry, and their carefully adjusted and brilliantly varnished sections, which can be carried to any climate, and put together and taken apart as often as you like, without making them less representative of anything that ever was in the world." A perfect target, of course, was "the bold Mr. Rider Haggard," author of the best-selling *She:* "The kind of novels he likes, and likes to write, are intended to take his reader's mind, or what the reader would probably call his mind, off himself; they make one forget life and all its cares and duties. . . . No sordid details of verity here, if you please; no wretched being humbly and weakly struggling to do right and to be true, suffering for his foibles and his sins, tasting joy only through the mortification of self, and in the help of others; nothing of all this, but a great, whirling splendor of peril and achievement, a wild scene of heroic adventure, and of emotional ground and lofty tumbling, with a stage 'picture' at the fall of the curtain, and all the good characters in a row, their left hands pressed upon their hearts, and kissing their right hands to the audience, in the good old way that has always charmed and always will charm, Heaven bless it !"

Very wisely, Howells was by no means always superior and magisterial in his conduct of the Study. If readers wrote in direct and relevant objection to him, he would print their letters and argue his case beside theirs. When one caught him up on the "sinuous obscurantism" into which his style could fall when he nodded, Howells good-humoredly ate "humble-pie" in the columns. He had said, "One must be slow to deny that the writer could fail of the highest effect she aimed at." Now he blushingly admitted that he had meant praise. Yet of course it did him no harm to be humanely fallible with his readers on occasion. No doubt that helped reconcile them to his distinction as well as his frequent didacticism.

The very best of the Studies are perhaps the seven (the number is not magic, one wishes it could fairly be fewer) which appeared in *Harper's Monthly* in April 1886; December 1887; July 1888; December 1888, November 1889; December 1890; and November 1891. These represent Howells at the peak of his powers as a major American magazinist. They contain some of the finest literary criticism he wrote. They show why and how he became involved in a critics' war, the Realism War, and demonstrate how he conducted his side of it. They are certainly prime candidates for the shears of the anthologist. For all these reasons, they merit brief exploration here.

Six more or less interlocking essays make up the April 1886 Study in which Howells, earth-shakingly in many quarters, first publicly announced his allegiance to Tolstoi. He begins by reviewing the two short volumes by his old friend John Fiske, *The Destiny of Man as Viewed in the Light of his Origin* and *The Idea of God as Affected by Modern Knowledge*, which were cornerstones in the structure of that "soft" Darwinism which reconciled science and theology in Howells' time. Reasoning, as Howells said, from "fact scientifically ascertained" and "as an induction from the Darwinian theory," Fiske argued that the modern evolution of man emphasized "psychical," not "physical variations." This has established "the gradual predominance of the soul over the body" and points to the time when "war must cease," and, to quote Fiske, " 'a stage of civilization will be reached in which human sympathy shall be all in all, and the spirit of Christ shall reign supreme through the whole length and breadth of the earth.' "

That naturally led Howells to a discussion of Tolstoi's *My Religion* and its proposal to live the Sermon on the Mount in all seriousness. Summarizing Tolstoi, Howells points out that he thinks like an early Quaker or Moravian afflicted by "the vast, passive Asiatic melancholy which seems to tinge all Russian character." Then he proceeds to an analysis of *Anna Karenina,* in which Tolstoi's convictions are given "dramatic" not "hortatory expression." And this gives Howells scope for one of his earliest and most effective definitions of realism.

"After one has lived a certain number of years, and read a certain number of novels," he reflects, "it is not the prosperous or adverse fortune of the characters that affects one, but the good or bad faith of the novelist in dealing with them. Will he play us false or will he be true in the operation of this or that principle involved? We can not hold him to less account than this: he must be true to what life has taught us is the truth, and after that he may let any fate betide his people; the novel ends well that ends faithfully." Informed by "this conscience," *Anna Karenina* tells "that saddest story of guilty love, in which nothing can save the sinful woman from herself. . . . It is she who destroys herself, persistently, step by step, in spite of all help and forebearance. . . ." All the mixed good and evil, folly and virtue of ordinary life are acted out by recognizable people, never commented on. "As you read on you say, not, 'This is like life,' but, 'This is life,' " said Howells. ". . . It is a world, and you live in it while you read, and long afterward; but at no step have you been betrayed, not because your guide has warned or exhorted you, but because he has been true, and has shown you all things as they are."

Continuing, Howells quotes from Tolstoi and Gogol to show the development of Russian realism and opines that American criticism of it in 1886 is just where Russian criticism had been in 1836. Gingerly he analyses *Margaret Kent*, a deservedly obscure American novel, revealing its mixture of romantic and realistic tendencies, and then lavishes praise on Armando Palacio Valdés for his *Marta y Maria*. Finally, in an anticlimax that probably deliberately glossed over his militancy with a tone of genial literary gossip, he dashed off a quick casserole of comment on a mixture of historical, biographical, and travel books, and ended with a return to the tone and character of the avuncular "unreal editor."

Equally devoted to fighting realism, the much briefer December 1887 issue used an entirely different, but brilliant strategy. Summarizing the view of John Addington Symonds' *The Renaissance in Italy*, Howells held it to show that, in spite of all changing fads and fancies, in the arts of all epochs "What is unpretentious and what is true is enduringly beautiful and good, and nothing else is so." He quotes Edmund Burke *On the Sublime and the Beautiful* to deny "the foolish old superstition that literature and art are anything but the expression of life" and is then ready to explode his mine. The mine is one of the most effective tropes ever coined for critical controversy.

Young writers, says Howells, who attempt to "report the phrase and carriage of everyday life," are always being shamed by a "wretched pedantry" into "idealizing" their work. Says the pedant: " 'I see that you are looking at a grasshopper there which you have found in the grass, and I suppose you intend to describe it. Now don't waste your time and sin against culture in *that* way. I've got a grasshopper here, which has been evolved at considerable pains and expense out of the grasshopper in general; in fact, it's a type. It's made up of wire and cardboard, very prettily painted in a conventional tint, and it's perfectly indestructible. It isn't very much like a real grasshopper, but it's a great deal nicer, and it's served to represent the notion of a grasshopper ever since man emerged from barbarism. You may say that it's artificial. Well, it *is* artificial; but then it's ideal too; and what you want to do is to cultivate the ideal. You'll find the books full of my kind of grasshopper, and scarcely a trace of yours in any of them. The thing that you are proposing to do is commonplace; but if you say that it isn't commonplace, for the very reason that it hasn't been done before, you'll have to admit that it's photographic.' "

Though this was appearing at a time when Howells' name had

become notorious across the nation for his daring defense of the Chicago Anarchists, he had no hesitation in following up his polemic advantage ruthlessly. Obsolete people, he said, will make the young artist suffer if he chooses "the real grasshopper. The people who have been brought up on the ideal grasshopper, the heroic grasshopper, the impassioned grasshopper, the self-devoted, adventureful, good old romantic cardboard grasshopper, must die out before the simple, honest, and natural grasshopper can have a fair field." These people are well-intentioned but "destitute of the documents" of modern literature. "They suppose that Balzac was the beginning of realism, and that Zola is its wicked end; they are quite ignorant, but they are ready to talk you down, if you differ from them. . . . The horror, the resentment, with which they receive any question of their very peccable literary saints is to be matched only by the frenzy of the *Saturday Review* in defending the British aristocracy; you descend at once very far in the moral and social scale, and anything short of offensive personality is too good for you. . . ."

Yet, reflected Howells, it does no good to blame these nice, old folks. It is "part of their intellectual mission to represent the petrifaction of taste, and to preserve an image of a smaller and cruder and emptier world than we now live in." The important thing is to rally to "the standard of the arts which we all have in our power, the simple, the natural, and the honest." In its time and place that was strong meat, but it was soon to be nourishing such babes as Stephen Crane, Harold Frederic, and Frank Norris.

By no means all of the great Studies were given to problems of realism. After theorizing at a distance, Matthew Arnold had come to lecture in America with the predetermined conviction that he would find little or no culture in the democracy. He left again, smugly announcing that, quite as he had thought, America was all very well in its way but there was really no hope for it because it was devoid of distinction. Howells, who had suffered a good deal from professional snobbism on both sides of the Atlantic, took thought. Arnold's recent death, he wrote in the July 1888 Study, had restored him to perspective. American resentment of his works and the national horselaughter which Arnold's personal sillinesses while here had engendered were both quieted.

Now "we can freely admit his greatness in literature and his good-will toward a perverse generation." And "even while we perceive that his observation of our life wanted breadth and depth and finality, we must acknowledge that in its superficial way, and as far as it went, it was mainly just." Arnold's strictures against American boastfulness, the irresponsibility and vulgarity of our press, and our lack of picturesqueness and splendor were correct. He might have said much worse things about the dishonesty and inefficiency of our political system in practice and the violence in "the relations of capital and labor . . . ; we have wasted the public lands which we won largely by force and fraud, and we are the prey of many vast and corrupting monopolies. . . . If the future is still ours, the present is by no means without its danger and disgrace," wrote Howells.

But many of Arnold's critics as well as Arnold have been all wrong about the question of distinction: ". . . it is his only stricture upon our conditions which we should gladly accept as true," said the penetrating democrat. "If we have really got rid of distinction of the sort he seems to prize, we have made a great advance on the lines of our fundamental principles." Insofar as Arnold is right, we have cast out snobbishness. A nation which has "produced such varied types of greatness in recent time as Lincoln, Longfellow, Emerson, John Brown, Mrs. Stowe, Hawthorne" and avoided "distinction," might give way to "self-gratulation" and "a serene complacency" in the fact that "our conditions, which we have always said were the best in the world, have evolved a type of greatness in the presence of which the simplest and humblest is not abashed." The realization of the American idea tends toward "identification" not "distinction."

One can see the point, Howells goes on, in contrasting Franklin, the man of the people, with Gouverneur Morris as he appears in Theodore Roosevelt's biography. Brilliant as Morris was, America could spare him much better than Franklin. The man of distinction "has somewhere in his soul . . . the spark of contempt for his fellow-men," and if America's civilization is unfavorable to that, then there is hope for it.

And there is a unique hope, Howells could not help ending, in the American arts. Bereft of "distinction," the American artist must turn to "common beauty, common grandeur." And "these conditions invite the artist to the study and the appreciation of the common, and to the portrayal in every art of those finer and higher aspects which unite rather than sever humanity. . . . The talent that is robust enough to front the everyday world and catch the charm of its work-worn, care-worn, brave, kindly face, need not fear the encounter, though it seems terrible to the sort nurtured in the superstition of the romantic, the bizarre, the heroic, the distinguished, as the things alone worthy of painting or carving or writing. The arts must become democratic, and then we shall have the expression of America in art."

Here for his generation Howells had produced a unique democratic manifesto. It prescribed for many of the worst antidemocratic ills a difficult age was heir to. It deserves a permanent place in the American pantheon.

Like other magazines, *Harper's Monthly* tried to make a big splash at Christmas, and Howells' December farce had become a fixture in the holiday issue. Like many another columnist before and since, however, Howells in the Study was beset by the problem of how to be adequate to the great topical occasions—especially of how to be adequate to Christmas. At least twice, in 1888 and 1890, he was thoroughly successful. In 1888 he chose a very delicate subject for the realist—Christmas literature—and managed triumphantly to treat it in an appropriate mood and yet to say something worth reading.

The age of Dickens had given way, he said, to "a gentle superstition" meant to "console the race for the formidable phase which the dismal science of political economy was then beginning to assume": the laws of Nature decreeing that the poor must ever increase and increasingly starve. Christmas literature was invented as an opiate for "well-to-do people-of-heart." But "political economy exists, like other sciences, to learn from time to time that it is mistaken. It has come to recognize that circumstances alter cases; that conditions affect and annul infallible laws. . . ."

Thus, in the past, Christmas literature featured a kindly but bootless "bestowal of turkey upon the turkeyless," of wassail feasts in the great hall "while the upper servants carouse in their hall, and the scullions carry out the fragments of the second table to the dogs and the poor." But now Christmas literature, "oddly enough after a period of scientific exaltation in which it seemed as if man might really live by the nebular hypothesis alone if he could have a little help from the missing link," has become good for all year round because it restores Christ to Christmas.

To almost no one's surprise, it turned out that this literature was best typified by Tolstoi's *What to Do?* But Ruskin, William Morris, and Victor Hugo are also listed as among those who show that "Art indeed is beginning to find out that if it does not make friends with Need it must perish." Romance had by no means always been blind to need. Its "error was to idealize the victims of society, to paint them impossibly virtuous and beautiful; but truth, which has succeeded to the highest mission of romance, paints these victims as they are, and bids the world consider them not because they are beautiful and virtuous, but because they are ugly and vicious, cruel, filthy, and only not altogether loathsome because the divine can never wholly die out of the human." Among these victims are not only the hopeless poor but also the sated, aimless, despairing, selfish rich.

Let us be merry on Christmas, Howells concludes, and do all the good deeds we can. But then let us take thought for the healing of "the plague that luxury and poverty, that waste and want, have bred together in the life-blood of society."

The December 1890 Study celebrates Christmas in altogether a different mode and mood. This time Howells wrote a sportive, mocking little fable. Peering through the beautiful frostwork on its windows at "the witching Christmas time," the Study saw the festive procession on the first Christmas since "the former imperfect republic of the United States of America had given place to the ideal commonwealth, the Synthetized Sympathies of Altruria in the future time." In that harmonious state he saw, among others, the literary parade, led by "Dramatic Critics wreathed with rose-buds, and led in flowery chains by a laughing band of Playwrights," all now united "in the endeavor for the beautiful." They were followed by "the Literary Critics, accompanied each by the poet, novelist, historian, or essayist whom he had most deeply injured"—and to whom he was linked by a band of violets "as best expressive of the critics' modest and shrinking character." The authors were nobly doing their best to assure the critics "that they too had their uses in the literary world, in noting and classifying its phenomena."

On the flanks of the procession (like the clowns in the circus) came, in fantastic dress, two unreformed characters, "the Last of the Romanticists, telling the same old story; and the . . . Anonymous Critic, firing blank-cartridges at authors." While the new Altrurians wait for that great ceremony of Restitution to foreign authors of the profits from pirated books which will be the center of the literary Christmas, The Real and The Ideal and then The True and The Beautiful put on vaudeville acts of melting into each other. "This was not so difficult as it seems when put in words," remarks the Study; "for The True and The Beautiful are one and the same; only The True is the one, and The Beautiful is the same." This and predictable nonsense from the Last of the Romanticists and the Anonymous Critic (who at one time wipes the sweat from beneath his mask with a black, skull-and-crossbones flag) lead up to the great moment when Perpetual Copyright is declared, the mountain of pirated editions is set afire, and the foreign authors, their widows, orphans, and descendants fully recompensed. Utopian Christmas has come to the literary world.

The remaining two of the best Studies concern themselves with major problems of literary history. What has happened to the English novel? asks the November 1889 Study. Specifically, why have the English so wholly lost contact with the greatness of Jane Austen? Having once known "the simple verity, the refined perfection of Miss Austen," how could "those poor islanders" reconcile themselves to Scott and his successors? To answer, Howells had recourse to his own translations of the preface to Palacio Valdés' *La Hermana San Sulpicio,* a somewhat sly stratagem, since Howells had made a substantial contribution to the motivation of Valdés' essay. He lets the Spaniard differentiate between neutral, simple realism and "the French naturalism . . . characterized by sadness and narrowness." He quotes Valdés' attack on "the vice which has been very graphically called effectism, or the itch of awaking at all cost in the reader vivid and violent emotions, which shall do credit to the invention and originality of the writer."

Ultimately Howells comes around to paying off his scores across the water. Why indeed has English literature lost its opportunity to stay at the forefront in the nineteenth century by failing to improve on Austen's immortal discovery of realism? Because the English "taste has been perverted by their false criticism." Their critics like "to be melted, and horrified, and astonished, and blood-curdled, and goose-fleshed, no less than to be 'chippered up' in fiction" rather than attend to honesty like that of "the divine Jane and her novels." And so the critics have "warped" Trollope and ignored Hardy and kept their nation in darkness "even at this late day, when all continental Europe has the light of aesthetic truth." So "we must await the gradual advance of civilization among them.

Then they will see that their criticism has misled them; and that it is to this false guide they owe, not precisely the decline of fiction among them, but its continued defacement as an art."

After those bold and bitter words, Howells had little or nothing to lose with English criticism. So that, when he took up the long-vexed question of a unique American literature in the November 1891 number, he was free to speak on the subject with an objectivity and wisdom rarely matched. With historical justice, Howells treats ironically the fact that agitation of the question has generally come as "a voice across the sea, asking us in varied terms of reproach and entreaty, why we have not a national literature." The voice is usually ignorant of American affairs but it is persistent: "there is nothing mean about Englishmen when it comes to advice and censure."

In reply to that voice, says Howells, certain considerations helpful to clarity of understanding might be urged. With a language, institutions, and people still essentially British, our literature must be "American-English literature, just as English literature is English-European." Further, at the present stage of civilization, "there is no such thing as nationality in the highest literary expression; but there is a universality, a humanity, which is very much better." If America has come on the stage too late to invent any of the basic literary forms, she can at least learn to use literature to express her own true qualities and aim at that human universality which leaves mere nationalism in the benighted past.

Naming the special American qualities, Howells made a pioneering observation which no historian of our culture has yet thoroughly elucidated. "It has been noted," he said, "that our literature has always been distinguished by two tendencies, apparently opposite, but probably parallel: one a tendency toward an elegance refined and polished, both in thought and phrase, almost to tenuity; the other a tendency to grotesqueness, wild and extravagant, to the point of anarchy. The first has resulted in that delicate poetry which is distinctively American, and in that fiction [by those famous Siamese twins—Howells-and-James] which has made itself recognized as ours, wherever it is liked or disliked." The other quality, he thought, came out in "our peculiar species of humor" and in the worst as well as the admirable best of Whitman. "Our literature has these tendencies because the nation has them, and because in some measure each and every American has them. . . .

Our censors may rest assured that in this anomalous fact exists the real nationality of our literature." Therefore the poetries of Whitman and Longfellow are equally American as is also the work of the matched pairs of Mark Twain and Lowell, Artemus Ward and Whittier, Bret Harte and Emerson, G. W. Cable and Henry James, Miss Murfree and Dr. Holmes, James Whitcomb Riley and Thomas Bailey Aldrich.

Unfortunately not pausing to account historically for his anomaly on the plea of lack of time, Howells drove forward to a point from which he could turn the question back from the essentially irrelevant, after all, British to his own countrymen. One of the recent voices from abroad had been that of Arthur Quiller-Couch, complaining that workmen and the life of toil are missing from American writing, which is therefore failing to represent its nation. Why, says the old ironist, how ignorant *this* foreigner is ! Doesn't he know that what American readers want is to escape from the life of toil through fiction about "high life" or through Horatio Algerism? "What we like to read about is the life of noblemen or millionaires, that is our romance; and if our writers were to begin telling us on any extended scale of how mill hands, or miners, or farmers, or iron-puddlers really live, we should very soon let them know that we did not care to meet such vulgar and commonplace people." The well-to-do shut their eyes determinedly and make believe "That the same causes will not produce the same effects here as in Europe." The poor already "know that in a nation which honors toil, the toiler is socially nothing, and that he is going from bad to worse quite as if the body politic had no interest in him." Everybody in America wants to be haughtily patrician in his reverie life if nowhere else. "The life of toil ! It is a little too personal to people who are trying to be ladies and gentlemen of elegant leisure as fast as they can."

Still, Howells concludes, there is great hope for American literature, especially now that international copyright secures the writer against pirated competition. Perhaps some of these immensely superior young English authors, who know "the defects of our literature so well," would like to come over and "show us by example how we ought to write here"?

For all this frequently bruising aggressiveness, "The Editor's Study" succeeded brilliantly. If Howells praised a foreign author like Valdés, he would be translated and published in America.

Joseph W. Harper wrote Howells thoroughly approving the way the Study had caught on with the firm's good readers. He argued that Howells' socioeconomic criticism was an attraction because, queer as it seemed, "imaginative literature is supported by men and women of limited income": parsons, teachers, white-collar workers, Army and Navy officers, and the few professional civil servants. "Does prosperity," Harper wondered, "deaden our sympathies?" Every young writer knew what was eloquently expressed by an obscure Western poet named Eugene Ware—favorable treatment by Mr. Howells, almost no matter how qualified, catapulted a new author into fame. After the Study praised his "Rhymes of Ironquill," Ware wrote, he became a celebrity over night. It "brought me a cloud of letters . . . from England . . . and from the Continent, and from far away referring to your article. . . ." If Alden, who was mainly in sympathy with Howells anyway, wanted as editor of *Harper's Monthly* to change the Study, he was reduced to pleading, cajoling, or asking in advance that he not be embarrassed. He could not command, and he very seldom tried to interfere. For as long as he cared to continue, the "unreal editor" had made his Study a force in international letters.

THE REALISM WAR

N O FORCE CAN BE EXERTED IN THE WORLD OF ART AND INTELLECT
without meeting resistance. The greater the force the
greater the resistance—and the higher its temperature. As
we have seen, Howells was surprised into his first battles by the
entirely unexpected attacks upon his radical but innocent praise of
Henry James in 1882, which were launched by critics who formed
part of what had seemed a friendly London literary world. His
refusal to knuckle under made him, already a prominent author
and editor, a target for envy as well as honest difference. When
he persisted in the logic of his artistic development, romanticists
became increasingly fundamental and personal in attack. And
then, when as the country's most conspicuous critic Howells turned
to the offensive and fought first for realism and then for social
concern, he became the focus of a true literary war. It was only
intensified when Howells engaged in his long, often expert, polemic.

By reaction from that war and from other events which coincided
with it, Howells grew into a stature of far greater significance to
American creative and intellectual life than he might otherwise
have reached. Its repercussions on other minds were such that
Howells' central role in it constitutes one of the several ways in
which he contributed fundamentally to the character of his age and
the age which followed him. The full pattern and meaning of the
Realism War, on both sides of the Atlantic, needs to be studied with
a scope and at a depth of complexity which can only be hinted at
here. It would make an important project for some interested
historian.

I

Though eventually some significant books of criticism came out of the Realism War, it was basically a magazine and newspaper battle which rumbled on clear past the end of the century. Virtually every important general periodical took part in it, often on both sides. An idea of the way things went may be gleaned from the list of articles, including only those indexed under "Realism-Romanticism," which appeared in *Forum* magazine. In July 1888 George Pellew, a young Boston friend of Howells, published an expert account of "The New Battle of the Books." March 1890 brought W. H. Mallock on "The Relation of Art to Truth." But in the middle of the decade there was an upheaval. An English critic, Frederic Harrison, reflected on "The Decline of Romance" in April 1893, which inspired W. R. Thayer to a vicious attack entitled "The New Story-Tellers and the Doom of Realism" in December 1894. That called out H. H. Boyesen in rebuttal with "The Great Realists and the Empty Story-Tellers" in February and H. W. Mabie to act as mediator with "The Two Eternal Types in Fiction" in March 1895. As a trailer, G. R. Carpenter did "The Neo-Romantic Novel" for March 1898.

Forum's case was common. On both sides of the ocean magazines, and apparently their readership, since the flow of articles continued, fought the issues again and again. And Howells was more often than not the hero or villain of the piece. In *A Hazard of New Fortunes* he let Fulkerson, the wiseacre publisher of a new magazine, advise Basil March on ways to pull circulation for their critical columns: "Go for Bevans' novels. The popular gag is to abuse Bevans. People read his books and quarrel over 'em; and a regular flaying with salt and vinegar rubbed in will tell more with people who want good old-fashioned fiction than anything else."

Certainly there was enough of a barrage to draw regular complaint from Howells himself. As early as February 27, 1887, he felt it necessary to reassure his family about the fuss engendered by *The Minister's Charge* and the Study. Please don't worry, he urged his father, about "the things you see about me in the newspapers. . . . I'm now something of a 'shining mark' and because in fiction I've identified myself with truth and humanity, which you know people always hate. It will pass, and pretty soon I shall be accepted. My ideas are right." It was hard, he wrote, to devote the Study to "serene inquiry"—for it was too liable to "have its windows broken by all the little wanton boys of newspaper criticism, who like to throw stones at the light whenever they see it" (November 1889). More plaintively in August 1890, he pointed out that "the Study," despite its "invariable courtesy towards persons, . . . has every month been assailed with personal offense from the whole cry of anonymous criticism." Hailing Henry B. Fuller of Chicago as an ally, he hoped Fuller would not "have to 'suffer in the cause' quite so much as I. . . ." It wasn't so dangerous, he had found, as it was wearing and irritating: "It was like living in a boiler factory, for a while, but when I found the clangor was not going to hurt me, I thought it such an infernal nuisance."

Much of what Howells complained of was the mere professional wisecracking of smart press Paragraphers—youngsters whose ignorant irresponsibility Howells could appreciate, and resent, when he remembered himself as the columnist of "News and Humours of the Mails" on the old *Ohio State Journal*. Typical of that sort of thing was a squib from what was then *Life:* "The London *Standard* . . . goes so far as to assert editorially that America has never produced a writer equal to Shakespeare," the Paragrapher recorded solemnly. And then, "Here is an opportunity for Count Tolstoi to say something pleasant about Mr. Howells."

This sort of thing stung more than it hurt. Much more serious were the well-informed efforts to destroy Howells' hold on the "good readers." Too much of the opposition was either deliberately nasty, as when H. C. Vedder, purporting to write contemporary literary history, asked, "Can it be that Mr. Howells gives us in his books a fair representation of life as he has known it? Has his whole experience been of this stale, flat, unprofitable sort? Has he never known anybody who has a soul above buttons?" And some of it was hardly short of paranoid. William Roscoe Thayer's *Forum* article snarled at "the obscene rites of French realism" and said it should be called "Epidermism," not Realism, because it reduces "literature, art, and morals to anarchy," loves filth, and dehumanizes life through science. *Silas Lapham*, Thayer said, had been "produced by Epidermist methods" by an author who "smacked his lips" over Zola's filth and was disguisedly only "a very clever disciple" of Zola. Thayer raged because Howells had been able to "use as a mouthpiece a magazine with a very large circulation" and "spread the gospel of Realism in a very brief time before multitudes who are usually slow to feel the direction of literary currents."

Worse yet, the war seriously strained Howells' ties with some of his closest friends. His gift for friendship managed to preserve most personal contacts, but the friendships were not intact. Aldrich got to writing snide remarks in letters to mutual friends—as when he questioned why his pet dog Trip should "be dead, and these other creatures exhausting the ozone? If he had written realistic novels and 'poems' I could understand. . . ." Publicly Aldrich mourned the times and Howells' mores in a poem entitled,

REALISM
Romance beside his unstrung lute,
  Lies stricken mute.
The old-time fire, the antique grace,
You will not find them anywhere.
Today we breathe a commonplace,
  Polemic, scientific air:
We strip Illusion of her veil;
We vivisect the nightingale
To probe the secret of his note.
The Muse in alien ways remote
  Goes wandering.

Horace Scudder, Aldrich's successor on the *Atlantic* and Howells' closest friend left in Cambridge, protested repeatedly in print against his heretical practice and opinion. E. C. Stedman, though he later deplored all the puppy-dog yelping after Howells, devoted an article as thoroughly learned as he could make it to refuting Howells' rejection of the idea of genius—and got a warm letter of applause from Edmund Gosse. Charles Dudley Warner tried fence-sitting for a while in his critical articles and then, most embarrassingly, began sniping at Howells from the "Editor's Drawer" directly behind the Study. Tolstoi, he opined, was merely "locoed." The Young Woman, Warner advised, should rise towards Idealism, not sag towards Realism, no matter how flattered she might be because "the novelist of today gets her to sit to him as his model." Art and woman alike are degraded, Warner proclaimed, by "servile imitation of nature." Only transcendent idealization in both could save us from "a realistic vulgarity and commonplace."

And if some old friendships weakened, by no means all the comradeships Howells had generously built with younger writers survived either. He lost the sympathy of Lafcadio Hearn, among others. But as an example of this and of the dangers of Howells' career in the Realism War, there is nothing more interesting or illustrative than the case of Maurice Thompson.

A Confederate soldier who had migrated North after the war to Crawfordsville, Indiana, to seek his fortune as a county courthouse lawyer, Thompson had seemed at first like exactly the sort of Southern and Western young writer Howells delighted all his life to boost along. He had done an early volume of Indiana dialect pieces called *Hoosier Mosaics*, 1875. Howells had encouraged him in reviews, printed his poetry in the *Atlantic,* and acted as go-between with Osgood in getting Thompson's *A Tallahassee Girl* and *Summer Sweethearts* published. He got Thompson a job on *The Independent* magazine.

The result was a friendship so cordial that Howells must have found the gush of Thompson's epistolary gratitude hard to stand. When Howells retired from the *Atlantic,* Thompson mourned his loss and proclaimed that Howells was truly his master. And when Howells proposed to come to Crawfordsville to see the sort of divorce trial which would climax *A Modern Instance,* Thompson was overjoyed. He would be honored and delighted to pick just the right trial and guide Howells through it, entertaining him the meanwhile; but if Howells proved unable to come, he would be glad to write that part of the book for him secretly.

As late as May 9, 1885, Thompson wrote Howells in the old vein of admirer and dependent. And as late as July 1886, Howells penned new praise of Thompson as "one of our most charming and original poets." Before what he wrote in July was printed in October, Howells had reason for chagrin. The July 10 *Critic* had carried an article by Maurice Thompson called "The Analysts Analyzed" which ripped viciously at everything the realist stood for. Not resting on his unfair misrepresentation of Howells' words, position, intentions, and theory, Thompson compounded the bitterness of his dose to an old ironist by stupidly defending Howells against himself and his theory.

All art is imaginative and true to nature, but realism is neither, Thompson began. The realists represent "a literary decadence. They are confessed time-servers, given to unblushing self-praise and to intemperate attacks upon every literary form save their own." They are guilty of stressing "foibles and peccadilloes of character, instead of attempting to imagine noble instances of human self-sacrifice, of lofty aspiration and of soul-stirring passion"; guilty of "aversion to having a fiction end pleasingly"; of "worship of the vulgar, the commonplace, and the insignificant" of praising Thackeray (!) and dispraising Scott, Dickens, and Victor Hugo. "One of the striking tricks common to contemporary realists is that of simulating a cordial good-humor and a perfect sincerity while nagging at the life-cords of the most sacred things," cried this baffled romantic. "For instance if the realist be a critic he will never fail to close up even his most favorable estimate of a book with a jolly sneer which he is sure will go to the very soul of the author. . . ."

If it was some barb of irony buried in his personal soul that so infuriated Thompson, he got his own back with interest better through innocence than he was capable of doing through malice when he turned openly to Howells. For he tried to save something of his relationship by arguing that in creative work Howells was no realist at all. The "most charming" part of Howells' work is "romance disguised as realism," he said, and instanced Bartley Hubbard to prove it. Howells is a genius, he proclaimed, though he denies it. "His literary tissue is healthy, the spirit of his work is even, calm, just, and his purpose is pure. . . ." He *cannot* be a realist.

But Howells' criticism, his part in the War, cannot be endured, Thompson makes plain. His attacks on Dickens and Hugo argue arrogantly that Howells is a better novelist than they. Every effort to criticize technique, Thompson supposes, simply camouflages self-flattery by denigrating others. Howells' fault is that he thinks "his specialty covers the world."

To know whether Thompson was just personally piqued or whether this was a normal stage in his evolution into the author of *Alice of Old Vincennes*—to know whether a brief critical celebrity went to his head or he was angered by counters to his *Critic* article —would require information which appears not to be in print. For whatever reason, he persevered to the point where he found out what it was like to be caught in the Realism War's no man's land. Somehow he could not resist falling into the vein of thought as well as oratory of the old-fashioned, country-vulgar complex of bigotries over sex, status, and religion as familiarly expressed by backwoods preacher and politician. He made a speech to the American Association of Writers at Indianapolis vituperating Tolstoi and Howells—and was called to account by *The Literary World,* which compared Thompson with his adversaries in terms which made him write a letter of explanation. His explanation was bracketed by an editorial and article which made him look still worse. And when he let himself go in full spread-eagle orotundity in a piece in the Chicago *Sunday Times,* he had delivered himself into the hands of his enemies. *The Literary World* could and did prove that he was "grossly unfair," most "ungenerous and untrue."

Poor Thompson, not a tenth so intelligent, so informed on his subject, or so experienced either in the dangers of public controversy or in handling his own thoughts as Howells, was caught dead-to-rights by an ordinary magazine editor. "To Mr. Thompson," commented the editor, "we . . . suggest that truthfulness is the first weapon of the critic, and that until he has learned the art of stating the case with which he is dealing in fair terms he would better leave it alone. It is no honor to American letters that a reputable and sincere author can be spoken to in the public press in a way at once so inaccurate, so intemperate, and so abusive." But it was small consolation to the author in question to have Thompson disciplined. For the sake of realism he had lost a friend—perhaps even been betrayed by a friend. He had been not only attacked but maliciously if ignorantly slandered.

II

The Realism War, as Howells never tired of pointing out, was by no means confined to the United States nor mainly centered on Howells—it only seemed that way much of the time in the American context. Actually, this late nineteenth-century battle of the books was symptomatic of a major convulsion in the life of Western culture. And its true storm center hovered most of the time over the genius whom Howells (and most discriminating critics with him) held not to be a realist at all. Conservative criticism in France, defending the very life of its order, raged against Zola. From England no influential voice was heard against the condemnation of Zola until the fickle Gosse tried in 1890 to defend him in *Forum,* an

American periodical. And in 1888–89 Zola's English publisher was harried, fined, and at length jailed for merely presenting him to the British public. In Scandinavia and Germany the same battles were fought, with figures so central as Brandes and Nietzsche required to justify an audience for Zola.

Consequently, when Howells dared announce publicly his support of Zola, he risked ultimate, automatic condemnation from the whole self-constituted body of respectable and right-thinking citizens. But he dared it, and repeatedly. First in a pair of interviews in 1886 and 1887, he staked out his ground with the reporters who came round regularly to dig up "live" copy from him. "Zola is a great writer," Howells said categorically. Zola made French realism second only to the Russian in the world, though he was too much of a romanticist to suit a thoroughgoing realist. Ultimately Howells developed the penetrating theory that Zola, as a naturalist, was not truly realistic at all but a new and legitimate kind of romancer. Zola was, in "Anglo-Saxon" terms no doubt indecent, abhorrently so to the eyes of Puritanic tradition. But he was not immoral; on the contrary, he was one of the greatest of moralists. Writing in *My Literary Passions,* published serially in *The Ladies' Home Journal* in 1894–95, Howells summed up firmly his view of Zola's "epic greatness." Though "every literary theory of mine was contrary to him when I took up *L'Assomoir* . . . , the book possessed me." He admitted all that could be said against Zola but then awarded him the highest Howellsian palm: ". . . for what he is, there is but one novelist of our time, or of any, that outmasters him, and that is Tolstoi."

The fact that Howells could say such things in *The Ladies' Home Journal* in 1895 proved that he had won a grand victory for realism and the freedom of the critic seven years before. But that victory had come hard. The Study of March 1888, in which Howells dared to recommend one of the most repellent of Zola's books, *La Terre,* was brilliantly designed. Howells began by reviewing a history of the Inquisition and pleading eloquently for toleration. Let no one solace himself "with the delusion that it is a Catholic and Spanish or Italian crime" or a mere custom of the outmoded past to ruin, burn, torture, and murder for opinion. That impulse "flourished up from the profoundest depths of our common human nature, from the roots of greed and hate and fear that take hold on hell in every

Protestant and Anglo-Saxon heart today as firmly as in the dark ages and the Latin races. Whenever one man hates another for his opinions, there the spirit of the Inquisition is as rife as ever."

As Howells no doubt expected, reactions to his defense of Zola confirmed those words. But he went right ahead in the second essay of this Study with *La Terre*. "Filthy and repulsive as it is in its facts," he began, "it is not a book to be avoided by the student of civilization, but rather to be sought and seriously considered." It was not for "young people," weak people or those who read to be amused. On the contrary, "it legitimately addresses itself to scientific curiosity and humane interest," he continued, because it is seriously concerned with important intellectual questions. In brief, why has the old agrarian myth (so fundamental to American thinking) been proved wrong in the France of *La Terre*? Why, when the Revolution gave land to the French peasant, did he become not the Happy Farmer of the Rousseau-Jefferson myth but rather Zola's avaricious "earth-fiend"? "The story is a long riot of satyr-lewdness and satyr-violence, of infernal greed that ends in murder, of sordid jealousies and cruel hates; and since with all its literary power, its wonderful forces of realization, it cannot remain valuable as literature, but must have other interest as a scientific study of a phase of French life under the Second Empire, it seems a great pity it should not have been fully documented. What are the sources, the proofs, of this tremendous charge against humanity, in those simple conditions, long fabled the most friendly to the simple virtues? This is the question which the reader, impatient if not incredulous of all this horror, asks himself when he has passed through it."

He had spoken his honest opinion, and, if he expected the Inquisitor's reaction, he was not to be disappointed. He did not stand entirely alone, and perhaps that fact saved him. The *Critic* must have spoken for a host of Joseph Harper's "good readers" when it noted that, "Mr. Howells's statement that *La Terre* represented a phase of life which had a legitimate place in fiction has aroused almost as much discussion as the book itself," and added, "Mr. Howells is right in saying that the phase of life is one it behooves us not to ignore." The professional Victorians and Howells-haters, who were sometimes the same thing, had no least intention of letting Howells get away with it. They attacked immediately, in full force, and with all their accustomed irresponsibility as to both emotion and fact.

It was only a matter of days before Alden was forced to write on behalf of the firm that, though he had seen "nothing wrong in what you actually said," he was now worried. "When I see how the mat-'ter is treated by the press—how persistently most of the news-papers referring to the matter misunderstand you and insist upon making Harper's Magazine responsible for the admiration and 'approval' of such a book, it really does seem as if we had been tempting Providence."

Among the clippings Alden sent along to show what troubled the Harpers was a representative one from the Troy, New York, *Daily Times* for March 1: "Novelist Howells uses *Harper's Magazine* as a vehicle for expressing his admiration of Zola's late upheaval of filth. It looks as if $10,000 a year is an exceedingly high price for the Harpers to pay for such stuff as some of Howells' contributions to their monthly." It all must have taken Howells back to the disas-trous days of the *Atlantic* catastrophe over Mrs. Stowe and Byron. Except that now Howells had no intention of backing down.

III

Of course Howells had friends and allies in the Realism War. For one thing the Harpers and Alden were strongly behind him. Though there were occasional quaverings from the counting house at Franklin Square, no effort was ever made to discipline Howells, and the only time anything was ever suppressed was when Howells seemed to be using the magazine to counterattack Andrew Lang— who was himself a member of the Harpers' organization. On the few occasions when the firm wished to remonstrate with the "unreal editor" of the Study, Alden as real editor of the magazine had of course to write the letters for the record. But, after years of slow meditation over his *magnum opus*, Alden made it abundantly clear in *Magazine Writing and the New Literature*, 1908, that he had long believed with a fervor almost mystical in the rightness and inevitability of realism and admired Howells as its chief exponent.

Though Warner might nag and titter from behind the Study in the *Monthly*, from the infinitely more influential "Easy Chair" in front Curtis steadfastly defended Howells. "I greatly enjoy watch-

ing your fight with the new form of Philisteria," he wrote Howells
in that most critical of years, 1887, "which without the priggishness
and awful solemnity of Wordsworth reminds me of his." When opportunity offered, Curtis spoke out from the Easy Chair; and when
the grand opportunity offered to review *A Hazard of New Fortunes*
(since the Study could hardly do it), Curtis made the best of it. He
praised Howells' "literary judgements" as "sound and thoughtful
and humane . . . obviously rendered solely in the interest of truth
and candor, of good literature and morality. . . ." The greatest
value of these judgments, Curtis pointed out to a world of letters
which badly needed the information, is that they "proceed upon
conceived fundamental principles. The function of criticism is
something else than the expression of a feeling. It is the estimate
of works of the imagination by the canons of literary art, which are
not arbitrary and whimsical, and the very first and chief of which
is holding the mirror up to nature." Curtis hinted that he by no
means always agreed with Howells, but he did think it clear that
"realism is of the very substance of legitimate fiction."

And there was other substantial support from outside the Harpers' circle, both from those who agreed and those who disagreed.
Howells' relations with Mark Twain, who agreed, increasingly deepened through these years. Lowell, who did not agree, wrote: "I have
seen some of the unworthy flings at you in the papers of late. I
know you will not feel them more than an honest man should. But
I have indignantly felt them. You are one of the chief honors of our
literature and your praises are dear to us all"—a mighty accolade
from the mentor of one's youth, especially when the mentor has
long been outgrown. Gilder, editor of *Century*, who mainly agreed,
wrote that he too had "come under the spell" of Tolstoi and Turgenev and sympathized with Howells' effort to bring "reality and
freedom" to the American mind. Maurice Thompson's attack Gilder
called "shameful as well as ridiculously false," and he added that,
if he sometimes had to quarrel with Howells, nevertheless "you are,
I know, whipping a lazy horse up hill ! . . . I hold out my hand to
you as to a voice crying in the wilderness. . . ." More concretely,
Gilder could use that hand in practical defense by barring Thayer's
attack from the pages of *Century* and so helping to postpone it long
past the time when it would have been most damaging. In the same
way, Whitelaw Reid, who did not agree at all, kept an old Ohio

friendship green by refusing to let Weeping Willie Winter blister Howells in the New York *Tribune.*

Some of the younger critics, like Brander Matthews and W. P. Trent, rallied to Howells' side, and there were admirably philosophic defenses by two effective women critics, Celia Parker Woolley, and Anna Laurens Dawes. But the toughest of Howells' champions was the ardent young Norwegian he had befriended in Cambridge, now grown into a formidable Scandinavian-American professor, critic, and novelist, Hjalmar H. Boyesen. Past the middle way as in youth, Howells and he found their minds falling readily together. "Boyesen, indeed, outrealisted me, in the polemics of our aesthetics," Howells confessed, "and sometimes when an unbeliever was by, I willingly left to my friend the affirmation of our faith, not without some quaking at his unsparing strenuousness in disciplining the heretic." It was Boyesen who volunteered to answer William Roscoe Thayer, the vitriolic anti-Epidermist, and he did so with a series of blunt, Norse affirmations.

The whole point was in his rugged title, "The Great Realists and the Empty Story-Tellers." The opposite of realism, he said, is simply dangerous. "Dwelling too long in the pleasant land of romance" deprives a reader of "sound standards of judgement." In life "Success and survival" depend on "as intimate an acquaintance as possible with one's environment." Thus the realistic novel becomes "a powerful educational agency. . . . It sharpens our observation and enables us to detect the significance of common facts and events." The great realists "reveal" to mankind "the forces that govern the world" and "the logic of life." Whether one could agree with Boyesen or not, his style and approach contrasted effectively with Thayer's shrillness and pruriency.

The essay which that literary historian of the future who writes the definitive history of this literary conflict will probably find most prophetic, at least in the American context, was written by Howells' young poet-philosopher friend in Boston—George Pellew. "The New Battle of the Books" (*Forum,* July 1888) is neutral and inquiring in tone, well balanced, admirably well informed, comprehensive, and accurate. "For a long time a wordy war has raged in the magazines and the newspapers between so-called realists and romanticists," Pellew begins. Howells has been ranged against Saintsbury, Symonds, Lang, Fawcett, and Stevenson. "One critic violently denounces Rider Haggard's 'She,' and another, with equal vehemence, derides Howells's 'April Hopes.' The ground is strewn with dead and dying reputations." But it has descended now to the level of mere logomachy, says Pellew, and it is time to call a truce.

The light of literary history, he shows, illuminates the scene helpfully. If one goes back to the medieval chivalric romances, he starts from a time when fiction was as unrealistic as it could be. Descending from Scudéry to Richardson to Fielding to Walpole to Ann Radcliffe and at length to Jane Austen, one can observe a growth in richness as well as responsibility in the novel. After all, Pellew argues, the cry of the true romantics was to return to nature. Dickens, Thackeray, and George Eliot would have spurned those neoromantics who "seem to think that the impossible, the preposterous, or the non-existent is more interesting than the actual." These are not the true but the "pseudo-romanticists of our day."

If we then distinguish between the true romantics and the false, Pellew argues at last, the entire weight of the intellectual development of the nineteenth century falls to the side of the realist when he is balanced against the neo or pseudoromantic. "In the beginning of the century the influence of heredity and the dependence of the individual character upon the social environment were not understood. An honest return, therefore, to the point of view of the early romanticists is now impossible," Pellew concludes. ". . . Human sympathy has broadened, society has become more democratic; a scientific study of history has shown the interdependence of all men, the comparative unimportance of exceptional men, and the all-importance of those commonplace individuals who form the mass of a people." Pellew spoke not only Howells' fundamental mind but the dominating intellectual conviction based on the condition of human knowledge of his moment. This was the fact which let the realists speak with quiet conviction and forced many of their opponents into misrepresentation and sensationalism.

IV

Significant as their reactions might be to Howells' success or defeat in the Realism War, most of these people were not of major importance in themselves; and most of those who were seem not to have become directly concerned in the conflict. There was one figure of the greatest importance, however, who was deeply engaged in this battle of the books for himself as well as because Howells was the one friend to whom he could all his life bare his artistic soul. It may also at least be guessed that his reactions to the Realism War played a fundamental part in the development of his art through and eventually out beyond the usual confines of the realistic movement. This was Henry James.

In default of thorough studies either of this part of James's career or of the progress of thought in the English literary mind during the Realism War, much of what can be written about the effect of the conflict on James must rest on hypothesis. Yet there can be no question that James was centrally engaged in the melee from the movement when Howells all innocently cast him into the middle with his *Century* article of 1882. Nor can it be doubted that James then turned more directly into considerations of his craft and to writing frequently and profoundly about those considerations. Finally, it is obvious that James's creative and critical thought became significantly redirected during this period. It seems impossible not to suppose that these events were in large part causally linked to James's relationships with the Realism War in general and with Howells' part in it in particular.

Having chosen in his "Middle Years" to live in England and increasingly to write in and for the English context, James was vulnerable. His attitudes, no less than that increasing fineness of artistry which Howells never tired of praising, cut James off more and more from public acceptance in the United States; and he largely failed to compensate by winning a British public. It must have been embarrassing that his reputation became the objective of Howells' first, unpremeditated battle for realism. Yet James was in no small part responsible for the growth of the convictions Howells expressed. And for a time James neither ceased to incite Howells to continue that growth nor flinched from taking his own part in the battle.

James had written, smoothly but from Howells' point of view with a sly effectiveness, on Balzac, George Eliot, Flaubert, Turgenev, and Daudet, among others. After Howells' *Century* article on James and the blistering reaction to it in *Blackwood's* and *The Quarterly Review*, James kept the faith. In the August 1883 *Century* he sketched "Daudet" as "a master" who stood "at the head of his profession," and specialized, with supreme modernity, in the portrayal of "the actual"—and again "the actual," or "the sensible,"

or "the concrete." There could be no question that "the main object
of the novel is to represent life." But Howells, soon to be swept
away by the passions of religious commitment, profound new
ethical insights, and polemical warfare, might have taken warning
from James's way of holding out the hand of critical reconciliation
to the romanticists.

Untroubled by the personal epiphanies of Howells' war, James
kept his eye precisely where the pure literary theorist's eye belongs: on considerations of literary art simply as art. "The success
of a work of art," he concluded, ". . . may be measured by the
degree to which it produces a certain illusion . . . that we have had
a miraculous enlargement of experience." Some readers might find
"that miracle of living at the expense of others" in fiction like that
of Alexander Dumas. "Others revel in them in the pages of Mr.
Howells." Essentially the same points were made in James's piece
on Turgenev in the January 1884 *Atlantic*. And finally, in *Longman's Magazine* for September 1884, James declared the first major
dividend of the Realism War. That war can claim to be more than
a squall in the teapot of minor literary history because it inspired
novelists to think through the theory of their craft for the first
time. That movement had well begun in France but, to the disgust
of James and Howells, been ignored in English and American criticism. James's "The Art of Fiction," triggered by the fight Howells
had precipitated, was the first major Anglo-American contribution.

James begins, indeed, by suggesting ironically that he hardly
dare criticize Dickens and Thackeray (Howells' crime), even
though their theory of the novel was naive. He rejoices in the
return of discussion of the subject, the advent of "a serious, active,
inquiring interest," and proceeds to develop his own wise and
thoughtful insights. First and last the novel shall be "one of the
fine arts," to be taken with the highest seriousness. But no one can
prescribe for the novelist, except to say that he must be faithful to
his experience. And, in marvelously Jamesian phrases, "Humanity
is immense, and reality has a myriad forms. . . . Experience is
never limited, and it is never complete; it is an immense sensibility,
a kind of huge spider-web of the finest silken threads suspended in
the chamber of consciousness, and catching every air-borne particle
in its tissue. It is the very atmosphere of the mind; and when the
mind is imaginative . . . it converts the very pulses of the air into
revelations." This being true, "the air of reality (solidity of speci-

fication)" may become "the supreme virtue of a novel," and no one may "bring it down from its large, free character of an immense and exquisite correspondence with life." These facts exclude all abstract restrictions on the author. Nothing counts but true artistic success. James ridicules Walter Besant for placing neoromantic and Mrs. Grundian manacles on the novelist. But the "unreal editor" in his Study might better not have forgotten how James praised *Treasure Island* as well as George Eliot, and, if he courageously praised Zola, also noted "that talents so dissimilar as those of Alexander Dumas, and Jane Austen, Charles Dickens and Gustave Flaubert have worked in this field with equal glory."

What Howells forgot, in short, was that James, while thoroughly loyal in supporting the struggle of realism for the right to exist, flourish, and prosper, saw no point in denying the equal right of romance—or any other esthetically successful mode. In a position economically more vulnerable than Howells', James fought with courage up to the point where the integrity of his balanced insights seemed threatened. There he withdrew.

When James wrote about Howells himself, in the midst of the War, he was well aware that strategic cautions had to be observed to evade the reverberating international charges of puffery and Mutual Admiration. He had "cultivated (in your own interest) a coldness which I didn't feel," he told Howells. Presumably for the same reason, the firm placed James's essay in *Harper's Weekly* for June 16, 1886, rather than in the *Monthly* alongside the Study. James admired Howells' growth in scope and skill, praised the definiteness of practice reflected from his "vivifying faith," and predicted a still greater future for him. He objected that Howells' good theory threatened to carry him too far from the pictorial, made him too suspicious of style and form, and inclined him to concentrate too exclusively on dialog and "verbal drollery."

As of 1886, James's summary could hardly have been more masterly. Howells, he said,
'is animated by a love of the common, the immediate, the familiar and vulgar elements of life, and holds that in proportion as we move into the rare and strange we become vague and arbitrary; that truth of representation, in a word, can be achieved only so long as it is in our power to test and measure it. He thinks scarcely anything too paltry to be interesting, that the small and the vulgar have been terribly neglected, and would rather see an exact account of a

sentiment or a character he stumbles against every day than a brilliant evocation of a passion or a type he has never seen and does not particularly believe in. He adores the real, the natural, the colloquial, the moderate, the optimistic, the domestic, and the democratic; looking askance at exceptions and perversities and superiorities, at surprising and incongruous phenomena in general. One must have seen a great deal before one concludes; the world is very large, and life is a mixture of many things; she by no means eschews the strange, and often risks combinations and effects that make one rub one's eyes. Nevertheless, Mr. Howells's stand-point is an excellent one for seeing a large part of the truth, and even if it were less advantageous, there would be a great deal to admire in the firmness with which he has planted himself. He hates a "story," and (this private feat is not impossible) has probably made up his mind very definitely as to what the pestilent thing consists of. In this respect he is more logical than M. Émile Zola, who partakes of the same aversion, but has greater lapses as well as greater audacities. Mr. Howells hates an artificial fable and a *denouement* that is pressed into the service; he likes things to occur as they occur in life, where the manner of a great many of them is not to occur at all. He has observed that heroic emotion and brilliant opportunity are not particularly interwoven with our days, and indeed, in the way of omission, he *has* often practiced in his pages a very considerable boldness. It has not, however, made what we find there any less interesting and less human.'

Yet as Howells' warfare came to resemble an Anglophobic feud, the situation became increasingly dangerous for James—he had no Harpers behind him—and his sympathy for the feud lessened sharply. As he wrote his brother William in October 1887, it was nice to be praised in the Study, especially since Howells and Stevenson were the only novelists in English he could stand. "It gives me pleasure, but it doesn't make me cease to deplore the figure that Howells makes every month in his critical department. . . . I wish he would 'quit,' and content himself with writing the novel as he thinks it should be. . . . He talks from too small a point of view, and his examples (barring the bore he makes of Tolstoi) are small still."

Cut off from Stevenson by the ferociously misguided personal attack Stevenson had launched over *A Modern Instance,* Howells avoided mention of him and apparently read nothing more by him.

But Stevenson, whatever their lack of technical literary sympathy, had now become one of James's dearest friends. If symbolically Howells and Stevenson polarized James's feelings, that meant James would, as he did, move toward a center from Howells and toward Stevenson. That movement is reflected in James's work as well as in his critical responses. Two of his masterpieces of realism, *The Bostonians* and *The Princess Casamassima* came out in 1885–86 and failed miserably with the public. James felt stalled and frustrated.

It was "mysterious" and "inexplicable," he wrote to Howells how those two novels, from which he had hoped so much, had collapsed and apparently brought the general "demand for my productions to zero." Then he proceeded, gently but clearly, to tell Howells that he thought him often mistaken in "your monthly polemics in *Harper*." If James thought there was a connection between his unpopularity and Howells' polemics, he may well have been right. The two names were closely linked in public reputation and frequently condemned together, either openly or through intimation, by their opponents. And Howells, with his feud well under way, became involved in a great deal of combative but otherwise irrelevant unpleasantness with English critics which it took many years to get clarified and set aside in the public mind.

Accustomed to that impunity in the exercise of cruel prejudice which jailed Vizetelly and expelled Thomas Hardy from his profession as novelist, English commentators were outraged at a victim who dared hit back. Even some of Howells' English defenders were aghast at his "churlishness." As in this country, most English publications would balance an attack with a defense if a defender could be found. But "the chief offender," never relenting, said Howells' friend Brander Matthews, was the "obstinately conservative, Tory, reactionary" *Saturday Review*. A good sample of its approach, safely anonymous for the critic, was the spluttering cry of astonishment and indignation entitled "Scott's Latest Critics," on May 4, 1889. The Reviewer was incredulous that anyone, anywhere might question the utter greatness of Sir Walter. He could credit this only to American cheek: they always brag that they are superior to everyone else, and of course that is what Howells has done by presuming to criticize Scott, Dickens, and Thackeray. But, then, these half-literate Yankees might do anything. It is beyond the power of a good Englishman even to comprehend their barbarous mangling of the mother tongue. For instance, this Howells has blamed Scott's style because the Wizard "went about half a mile to express a thought 'that could be uttered in ten paces across lots.'" The Reviewer gave up in bewilderment. English isn't *written* this way, and what such gibberish means, he said, "we cannot pretend to know."

Perhaps the most joyous Howells-baiter in England, however, was the collaboration with H. Rider Haggard, the mentor of Stevenson in claymores and derring-do, the folk-lorist and fairy-tale expert, Andrew Lang. Writing as free-lance critic for several magazines and newspapers but settling finally into a column called "At the Sign of the Ship" in *Longman's Magazine,* Lang specialized in inflaming the popular prejudice for lightly entertaining as opposed to serious literature. He delighted in the opportunities the all too serious Howells provided for a gay repartee in which Lang need assume responsibility for nothing but "fun." What such fun did to Howells' reputation, or, perhaps more disastrously, to Henry James's, was no concern of Lang's. One of the few real bitternesses of Howells' relations with his firm over the "Editor's Study" must have come when Alden, for the only time such an omission was made, cut Howells' counterattack on Lang out of the Study in 1891. The reason was that Lang, having become editor of the English edition of *Harper's* in 1884, had continued in a sense a member of the official family and could not be attacked personally in the pages of the firm's own organ.

It could have been no surprise to Howells, who had been better at this sort of thing at the age of twenty-three than Lang was at almost fifty, that he had made himself vulnerable to what Lang called "a little chaff." But it must have been maddening to have the expression of one's deepest convictions treated so boyishly— and it certainly was damaging with a British public already devoted to Haggard and the neoromantics. It was when Howells relinquished the "Editor's Study" in March 1892 that Lang outdid himself. "Is this to be the end of the game?" he mourned. "Are there to be no more snaps and scoffs, no more international tennis of flouts and jeers, with Mr. Howells 'smashing' at the net?" He hoped not: Howells provided so many happy topics.

But just in case it might be the last, Lang bade him farewell in a little poem:

To W.D.H.

And have we heard you, W. D.,
  For this, the latest time, declare
That Intellectuality,
Save in these Islands of the sea,
  Is everywhere?

That all the world, the Muscovites,
  The realists of Sunny Spain
And every Frenchman who delights
To count the smells and name the sights
  Of every drain,

Is greater than clean clumsy Scott,
  Than inartistic Thackeray?
Oh, hast thou fired thy latest shot,
Or is it but a cunning plot
  That thou dost lay?

And shall we hear thee, elsewhere, still
  Repeat the old familiar chatter,
Loud as the hopper of a mill?
Well, as it does not seem to kill,
  It does not matter !

Nay, far from earth, serene and strong,
  The smiling Thackeray forgives;
While 'Yarrow as he rolls along
Bears burden to the minstrel's song'—
  Sir Walter lives !

While Hawthorne holds unshaken place
  Among the children of the pen;
While wit, adventure, joy, and grace,
In every clime, in every place,
  Are dear to men,

You cannot, though you strive and sigh,
  Shake one leaf on the laurel crown.
Write not yourself,—none else will try,
T' were grossly rude,—what Dogberry
  Would be writ down !

Of course Howells survived all this easily enough and lived to read Lang's ever-so-grudging apologies in 1895. But for James it was tougher, and the enemies who would not long after destroy his bid for theatrical success were given aid and comfort. It is no reflection on his courage to suppose that such pressure coincided with a natural tendency of growth in his creative psyche to steer him away from realism. There were to be no more novels like *The Princess Casamassima*. His next writings were concerned more exclusively with the life of art and esthetics as in 1888 he published "The Reverberator," "The Aspern Papers," and "The Lesson of the Master." Utterly loyal to the sacred cause of the literature within him, he was now increasingly to transcend the battle for one kind of fiction. Loyal, as he should have been, to the need of his own imagination to grow into the forms of expression which would give the fullest freedom to his unique creativity, James would move on to the point where, with *The Ambassadors*, he broke through the limits of realism in the novel to something new and great.

Howells too was growing into a new creativity. He and James would never cease to be warm friends, and, as James's letters often testify, Howells would be able to serve James most importantly in the years to come. But their work and criticism would never coincide so meaningfully again as it did in the early stages of the Realism War.

V

To the development of literature, particularly to the evolution of the novel, the significant contribution of the Realism War, in all its international scope, would be that out of the conflict came the first serious, coherent, sophisticated, complete, and useful theory of the novel. Zola and the French contributed to that, and the Russians, of course, and the Spanish realists. In English Besant, Stevenson, Moore, Meredith, and Hardy all wrote important reflections on the neglected problem. And of course James, with his long program of criticism looking forward to the classic prefaces to the New York Edition, capped the work and made such later theorists as Forster, Lubbock, and Beach possible.

Howells had played his part in this development as we have seen and would continue to do so in critical series, special essays, prefaces, and critical volumes for years to come. The first such volume, gathered out of the "Editor's Study" materials as a sort of by-product of the Realism War, was *Criticism and Fiction*.

In his farewell Study of March 1892, Howells indulged himself in a rarely permitted Swiftian figure of speech: "Not content with the passing result of his monthly ministrations of gall and worm-wood, the ill-advised Study-presence thought to bottle a portion of it, and offer it to the public, with the label, 'Criticism and Fiction,' and a guaranty of its worst effects in any climate, which has been everywhere received with wry faces and retchings, and among the inhabitants of the British Isles has produced truly deplorable consequences." Actually, however, the original idea for the book was not Howells' at all, and it seems clear that he never had any large enthusiasm for it. His old agent and publisher Osgood had gone into business in England and thought he saw a fine opportunity to exploit the English notoriety of Howells' critical heresies. Late in 1890 Osgood proposed to the Harpers that a volume be gathered out of the Study pages and be published by the Harpers but handled by Osgood abroad. He was successful in persuading both Howells and the firm. By March 1891 the arrangements were complete, and the book was published on May 9, 1891.

Even if we did not know from the dates of the correspondence how quickly the book was prepared, there is all too much internal evidence to prove it. With a minimum of editorial rearrangement and the addition of a couple of perfunctory transitional passages, Howells threw this book together as if it were an irritating chore. He picked out many of the best things he had said on the major issues of the Realism War, put them in a rudimentary kind of progressive order according to topic, and then, not pausing to build any sort of general intellectual structure out of the mass, stuffed it into his book as if he were putting it away in a drawer for future reference. With the painful battle still raging in the background, with his absorbing creative work surging ahead in the foreground of his energetic mornings, he had given a little grudging time to a project which might help a dear old friend. Most unfortunately, the jumbled result became the volume by which most future readers would judge of the nature and quality of his critical thought.

It ought also to be noted in passing that it makes a difference which edition of *Criticism and Fiction* one reads. When Howells edited the 1891 edition, he was in hot combat. By the time he redid it for his Library Edition of 1910, his warfare was mostly accomplished. He edited out the toughest and earthiest cracks at critics and criticism, all the really provocative comments upon the English, his praise (for no reason I can see) of Juan Valera, and most of the references (presumably because he knew the last thing that old friend wanted buzzing about his ears were recollections of the Realism War) to Henry James. What Howells did in that war is better represented in 1891 than the 1910 edition of his book, though the only right place to find him for that period is in the "Editor's Study" itself.

Criticism and Fiction did concentrate in one place what Howells had been spreading piecemeal in an ephemeral form, however, and the result proved Osgood right in supposing that it would stir up interest. Representative reviews showed how very far Howells had come in the ten years since his resignation from the *Atlantic*. John Burroughs, who had once threatened to send an arrow at him, now wrote with bland contentment about "Mr. Howells's Agreements with Whitman." Burroughs praised Howells' "inductive" and "comparative" criticism, his "revolt against the dogmatic method." The emphasis on a direct relation of literature to ordinary life is the same in Howells as in Whitman, Burroughs said (apparently oblivious to the entire metaphysical disparity between the transcendental context of Whitman's and the agnostic context of Howells' phrases), and proved it by citing parallels between Howells' quotations from Emerson and Whitman's words.

By the same tokens but on the opposite side, Howells' old friend and neighbor Horace Scudder, who had succeeded Aldrich as editor of the *Atlantic,* was as coldly disapproving in that magazine as friendship could permit. Howells, he finds, has grown into a "second period" of which, however politely, he cannot approve. He is struck by Howells' "sincerity" but regrets that this only leads him into the vehement intemperateness and zeal of "a crusader." However "shrill" and "aggressive" he finds the book, Scudder refuses, making it clear that he does so only by effort, to quarrel. He declines "to divert attention from the main question by indignantly declaring that Howells is slandering Scott and Thackeray and setting up a Russian idol in place of our native gods." The main point is that Howells is philosophically mistaken, Scudder concludes. Since human nature never changes, Howells' claim for newness in art must be mistaken. The fault in Howells is that he is too contemporaneous and individual, too much in key with contemporary science and religion.

Perhaps the most interesting fact revealed by the conjunction of those two opposing views is that they both represent, though from opposite poles, the elder romantic attitudes against which Howells and his generation had rebelled. He could respect both, where the neoromanticism of a Thompson or a Lang disgusted him. But he could be sure of being misunderstood from all three points of vantage.

A much more sophisticated, and from a Howellsian point of view more modern and satisfactory, understanding came from the Columbia professor and man of letters, Brander Matthews. Reviewing *Criticism and Fiction* comparatively with John Morley's *Studies in Literature* and Anatole France's *La Vie Litteraire*, Matthews found much in Howells to admire. Like such English defenders of Howells as Archer and Quiller-Couch, Matthews suggested that Howells had often been too "combative, not to say aggressive," and was most effective when most urbane. But he defended him directly against the attacks of the *Atheneum* and *Saturday Review*, among others, and noted what no Englishman would have thought of: that Howells in daring to persist in fighting back had contributed immensely "toward destroying the tradition of deference toward British criticism . . . a survival of colonialism." Howells, he noted quite justly, had been led astray in coming to ignore form in the novel, not form as plot but form "composed as a picture is composed"—which is exactly what James would have said. Whatever lapses in matters of detail or exhaustive scope in scholarship Howells had committed, however, Matthews found him strong in thought and felicitous in expression. As "a coordinated code of criticism," employed in "a sortie against those who are besieging the citadel of literary art," Matthews found this book comparable to Schlegel's *Lectures on Dramatic Literature* or Zola's *Une Campagne*. He praised the author's stand for democracy and Americanism and found him, in the last analysis, "not far wrong in the main question" because his work was "a plea for truth in fiction . . . a request that literature shall be judged by life and not by the library."

Needless to say, Howells was touched. He wrote Matthews a note admiring Matthews' approach in detail, defending his view of

Thackeray against Matthews', and revealing, in his gratitude, the hold on himself the passions of war still exerted: ". . . You have treated me not quite like the Pariah those English and their apes affect to consider one."

For one last point about *Criticism and Fiction,* Matthews had been far from wrong in considering it in the context of comparative literature. Howells' book concentrates also the intensity of that internationalism which made him see his fight for realism as part of a world war—or at least a Western world war. He delighted to list the great realists he was introducing or defending before the reluctant English-speaking audience. He reminded that audience in *Criticism and Fiction* of his part in that great interlocking, international movement, as he praised "the universal impulse which has given us the work, not only of Zola, but of Tourguenief and Tolstoy in Russia, of Björnson and Ibsen in Norway, of Valdés and Galdós in Spain, of Verga in Italy." Elsewhere he added the names of Thomas Hardy, George Eliot, and Juan Valera. It was in the Study that he introduced Dostoevsky to Americans. He not only introduced Giovanni Verga to that public, but talked the Harpers into translating and publishing *I Malavoglia.*

When on the great public celebration of his seventy-fifth birthday in 1912 Howells rose to speak, he would be at special pains to make his point absolutely clear. "I would fain have it remembered," he told the assembled literary world, many of a generation too recent really to know, "that it was with the French masters, the continental masters, we studied to imitate nature, and gave American fiction the bent which it still keeps wherever it is vital. . . . And though a flood of unreality followed us and swept us under," he continued, to set the record straight, "when that deluge went down there all over the land, the seed that we had planted, behold ! it had sprouted and stood. . . . I would have you all, whatever esthetic thinking or feeling of art you are of, look about you and see whether every plant now bearing good and nourishing fruit is not of that growth."

VI

Such was Howells' testimony, even perhaps his boast. But he had suffered for the right to make it. For his realism war was not only painful in itself, it was soon to end in much the sort of swamping, the overwhelming if temporary defeat, the paradoxical victory-in-defeat he described. When in 1894 an ardent young follower named Stephen Crane wrote for the New York *Times* the most perceptive of the many interviews Howells underwent, he ended the story with a dramatic bit which provided the excellent headline for his piece: "Fears Realists Must Wait." Crane had been quoting the great man on the need for unpopular writers to persevere with courage:

" 'Mr. Howells,' said the other man, suddenly, 'have you observed a change in the literary pulse of the country within the last four months? Last Winter, for instance, it seemed that realism was about to capture things, but then recently I have thought that I saw coming a sort of counter wave, a flood of the other—a reaction, in fact. Trivial, temporary, perhaps, but a reaction, certainly.'

"Mr. Howells dropped his hand in a gesture of emphatic assent. 'What you say is true. I have seen it coming. . . . I suppose we shall have to wait.' "

The old realist and his disciple were talking about no mere abstraction. The fight of the realists for American public taste was literally overwhelmed in a flood of favor for the neoromantics at their shoddiest and most sensational. Alden, who had bowdlerized *Jude the Obscure* and went home nightly to meditate on the glories of serious literature in the new age, was as responsible for breaking the realistic dike as anyone. Du Maurier's *Trilby*, featuring the arch-hypnotist Svengali and all kinds of weird suggestions of wild Bohemian life, rape, and lustful domination via hypnotism, and art as the product of evil, was submitted to the Harpers. Alden tumbled head over heels for this perfect vulgarization of neoromanticism and the decadence blended, overruled the scruples of his staff, published *Trilby*, and scored "the greatest serial success of the decade."

The same year Anthony Hope published *The Prisoner of Zenda*, and the deluge was at hand. It did not fully arrive, however, until the end of the decade. Then the schools of irresponsible, neoromantic best-sellerdom came truly into their own to rule American popular taste—and often corrupt even the "good reader"—until pushed out in turn by the movies, the radio, and now television. *Zenda* was capped in 1901 by George Barr McCutcheon's *Graustark*. There arose the vast school of the new historical romance: *The Choir Invisible, When Knighthood Was in Flower, Hugh Wynne,*

Richard Carvel, Janice Meredith, Alice of Old Vincennes (Thompson's triumph), *The Crisis.* Dickens and Bret Harte rode again in the huge-selling volumes of local-color sentimentalized and local folk caricatured into "characters" in *David Harum, Eben Holden, The Virginian,* and *The Little Shepherd of Kingdom Come.* When that approach was combined with the old-fashioned sentimentality of *Mrs. Wiggs of the Cabbage Patch* or *Rebecca of Sunnybrook Farm,* there came Gene Stratton-Porter. The ghost of Cooper was conjured up and maligned again by Jack London and, in descending order, Stewart Edward White, Zane Grey, and Edgar Rice Burroughs.

When a literary tradition has exhausted its normal possibilities, writes Professor William Tindall in a wise definition, three possibilities remain: imitation, which is death; striking out on new lines, which requires the help of social change; or wringing the last drops of the fantastic and *outré* out of the tradition. The writer who does this last is decadent. In that sense the Yellow Book crowd and their tiny group of American followers were decadent but knew it. The overwhelmingly best-selling neoromanticists were also decadent and didn't know it. Howells, aware of social change and striking out in a newness to meet it, had to know that he had lost the American public for the time being. "I told you that we realists should some day drive our go-cart over the hill, and so hang down the other-side," he wrote Thomas Wentworth Higginson in noting the reaction against realism: " 'God fulfills himself in many ways,' but I think we must find the neo-romanticists a little difficult. He made them, however, and he knew they must sometime have their bray."

But even at the lowest point, Howells saw no reason to "bate my hope for the time to come or the time that then was." No doubt he would have been appalled to see what electric and electronic media of mass communication would bring the American public—and bring it to. Yet like every believer in the true possibility of a viable mass democratic culture, he would still have continued to believe that this too must pass. And that great battalion among the army of serious American writers who owe Howells a debt of paternity would be concretely visible to his eyes which in faith looked forward to them.

Howells' fight for realism went on, of course, for the rest of his life. For obvious reasons, it was never so fresh or intense either for him or his audience after the Realism War slackened in the nineties. For Howells personally, in fact, it began to slacken as soon as he gave up the "Editor's Study." As journalism his warfare was often magnificent. As occasional criticism and book reviewing it was ordinarily sparkling and in flashes deeply penetrative. As a literary crusade it was of true importance in calling American readers and writers to become intellectually and emotionally mature and responsible and to look beyond the exhausted conventions of the old romanticism. As formal literary criticism, however, this writing suffers from its journalistic and polemical aims. It is not nearly so sustained, coherent, or searching as Howells' best work when his goal was formally critical.

Howells meant to speak to the literary condition of his country with force and relevance. The importance of what he said and the way he said it is clear to any careful student of the emergence of modernity in American cultural history. There is bound to be yet a great deal more to be written in elucidation of Carl Van Doren's testimony that "any serious study in the intellectual and spiritual history of America discovers more and more lines converging to the controversies of the decade from 1880 to 1890 when Howells's was the most eloquent voice."

THE BLACK TIME

HOWELLS THE GAY, HOWELLS THE AIRY PLAYFELLOW OF ALL THE Cambridge, Boston, and Nook Farm wits, the Howells whose life had seemed such a serene and roseate idyll to Boyesen in 1871, the Howells of the "good great time," disappeared in the latter eighties. "Black care has not left so much laugh in me as there used to be," he wrote the Gosse who had so loved to giggle and make giggle with him. It was not enough that he fought and suffered for his critical principles. Or more fundamentally that his whole pattern of ethical ideals was redirected and his moral sensibility etched deeper and much darker. Or that his creative impulses shaped themselves to increasingly tragic conclusions relieved only by the realist's deprecating pity for human littleness. His life was also harrowed to its psychic depths by slow, tantalizing, psychologically crushing personal tragedy.

The black time started in October 1885 when it became clear that Winifred Howells' stubborn illness had reached another climax. The Beacon Street house had been acquired and refurbished as a base of operations for Winifred's debut in Boston, and 1885–86 was to have been her year. But the summer vacation had somehow failed, and her always mysterious malady struck hard. Mrs. Howells, also frail, could no doubt have summoned up strength to see her lovely, gifted daughter through a winter of health and social triumph. A year of strenuous social obligation with Winifred defeated and languishing was too much. "I have let the pretty house in Beacon Street because poor Winny is too poorly to do any society in it, and without that her mother and I have no heart for it," Howells reported to Gosse. He sat in the perfect study which was to have housed him all the rest of his life and recorded a last, loving impression of the view across the Charles from its windows, and left for a winter at Lee's Hotel in Auburndale.

Though of course Howells could not know it, his brief period as truly a Bostonian ended with this withdrawal. For the rest of his long life, almost thirty-five years, he would be a nomad. February and March of 1886 he spent in Washington, seeing much of John Hay and Henry Adams, lionized at big parties, which seemed "more like London than anything else," because almost everybody was official. He was entertained by Cleveland at the White House and showered with "blobs of compliments." Though Howells was shy of his "public" and enjoyed the confusion more than the assertiveness of the people who crowded on him, he liked Washington and proposed to Twain that they both move there. But of course nothing more came of that than did of the effort to move him to New York when he signed the Harpers' contract.

In the same October when he retired to Auburndale, he resisted the Harpers' pressure through Osgood to move him to New York and begged that they not "Barnumize" him. Returning from Washington in the spring, however, he was Barnumized a bit with a gay reception at the Author's Club, with all his old New York friends as well as S. Weir Mitchell and Mark Twain imported for the occasion. There was much chaff about his refusal to be transplanted to Gotham (this was when Aldrich wrote "come back to Boston and all will be forgiven"), and *The Literary World* reported "the intense disappointment in many New York circles over the decision of Mr. Howells to remain in Boston." Presumably that marked the beginning of the familiar clichés about Howells' moving from Boston to New York and taking the center of American literature with him. Howells, who emphatically and on democratic principles did not believe in a literary center for America, would have enjoyed the sober fact that the instability of his residence makes it difficult to date the time of his move before 1891. And, as we shall see, even that date is somewhat shaky.

What is quite clear is the pressure of anxiety and pain upon Howells' life in this period. In December 1886 he was called to the last, terrible scenes of his favorite sister Victoria's death from malaria in Jefferson. Yet far more excruciating was the drama of Winifred's descending levels of invalidism, rally, and relapse. Reminiscing to E. C. Stedman's granddaughter in 1909, Howells summed up the period perfectly: "It was a rather distracted time with us, for our daughter was dying, although we didn't know it then; and we had no heart for anything. She was gradually wasting away with nervous prostration, and in a short time she died. . . . It was a black time."

I

In the long run these personal facts become significant mainly because they affected the creative work Howells persisted, in the teeth of all troubles, in pouring out. With his work habits solidified, his command of his own technique both practically and theoretically mature, his imagination teeming with character and theme, Howells simply came to his desk and produced manuscript—every day. In this period he did it without the least forcing or strain, the thoroughly arrived master of his craft. Indeed his ease and joy in work were such that, far from becoming blocked or frustrated in his writing by the black cares of life, he found in work a refuge. His productivity was enormous through the years of his greatest trouble. It was as if the suffering he had once feared might destroy him instead unlocked new powers to create within him. His warfare and his tragedy sensitized him to suffering and drove his moral imagination to search out remedies for the pain of humanity. The black time did not leave his literature untouched. He was never "escapist" in that sense: quite the opposite. His creativity was freed and deepened.

The creative first fruits of the early years of that time was a neglected little masterpiece called *April Hopes*. This was, he told a friend, the first novel done "with the distinct consciousness that he was writing as a realist." That is, the first done as a conscious testimony by the fighting champion of the movement. The hopes of the book are those of the romantic Hero and Heroine whose fictionized passions the critic had so caustically condemned. They are April hopes because, of necessity, the course of their passion must not run smooth. It must oscillate like the weather of spring: "You know how it is with an April day," says Robert Frost.

With scalding irony Howells proposed to take up the formal conventions of romantic fiction about love and engagement and, without scanting any of the conventions, show through the realist's eyes what the ordinary progress of passion from love to engagement to marriage meant. He will recognize that in our culture people's experience actually is determined by their adherence to the expectations of the conventions of popular romantic sentimentality about love and marriage. He will accept the proposal that young people do convert the effects of proximity and natural susceptibility into the clichés of passionate fatality, inflate their emotions toward supreme and absolute expectations, and insist on committing matrimony in spite of every consideration of common sense and long-range probability.

Very well, said Howells, let us accept this and see what really happens. The result is a fascinating but painful little book in which savagery and pity struggle within the irony until, somewhat wearily, pity wins out. It is done with the utmost artistry. The scenes, especially the lovers' dialogues alternating (April's weather) the intoxicating bliss of courtship's unfolding discoveries with stupid quarrels motivated by the girl's disappointment at the human impossibility of sustaining the always more supernal mood, are often perfect. Pictorially, with impressions of a Harvard Class Day, a picnic at Campobello, a New England industrial village dominated by the owner's mansion, and Washington in the spring standing out brilliantly yet organically integrated with the onward progress of theme and action, the book was all Henry James could have hoped for—tight, swift and clean in development, and dense-packed with suggestion.

Since to the realist the characters were ultimately everything, there is little point in discussing them separately except to say that Howells had never before succeeded in making them all, perhaps especially the minor ones who surrounded the pair of lovers, so definite and so vivid, with such economy. He was writing consciously, even demonstratively as a realist, and for that reason it is perhaps worth while to take note of one matter of technique he preserved from the past. He was determined to be "objective." He scolded Hamlin Garland for suggesting that more of his own warm personality should be allowed to show through the cold irony. "To infuse, or declare more of my personality in a story, would be a mistake, to my thinking: it should rather be the novelist's business to keep out of the way. My work must take its chance with readers. It is written from a sincere sense of the equality of men, and a real trust in them. I can't do more."

To pick up some of Howells' critical phrases, there was to be no "confidential manner," no "intrusive author," the work must be "dramatic." The narrative point of view was definite. It varied purely scenic representation with narration by a neutral, third-person storyteller's voice which was permitted to "go inside" only the mind and emotion of the hero, Dan Mavering. And yet, Howells permitted that voice to editorialize and deliver small asides on psychological and moral aspects of his story. The quality of these asides may be seen in the narrator's comment on the heroine's scheming mother, Mrs. Pasmer: "she was morally all a bundle of finesses." Apparently Howells had decided that the intrusive or confidential author sinned only when he appeared *in propria persona* as the creator who exposed the machinery of his art and shattered its illusionary integrity. If the narrative voice kept neutral enough in tone and directly relevant enough to the immediate concerns of the fiction, it might intrude editorially. Interestingly enough, Henry James shows in many of his mature fictions the effects of a like decision.

Ethically, *April Hopes* contained the first new thing fiction had had to say to the young engaged since *Jane Eyre*. Howells presented a dramatic analysis of the education of two ordinary egotists. Dan Mavering is a simple romantic egoist anxious to float and lave his vanity in the sublimities of premarital emotion. An easygoing temperament, anxious to please and be pleased, a sensitive, arty, spoiled boy, he takes no thought for the future problems of establishing a maturely successful marriage, and there are no conventions in his society to guide him into taking responsibility. His best advisers are silenced by the romantic tradition of unique, eternal, overmastering love.

His fiancée, Alice Pasmer, is a more complex and, in a sense, inverted egotist. She is another Howells feminine quixotic, a romantic dutiolatrist whose yearnings for sublimities of self-sacrifice are complicated by a muddled Anglo-Catholicism and fantasies of self-immolation in a Sisterhood. If Dan is slippery and irresponsible, Alice is little short of vicious. Where Dan will offer anything and hope everything for the sake of peace and pleasure, Alice must torment and be tormented to indulge her idiotic and unconsciously hypocritical yen for melodrama. Alternately cold and wild, she completely fails to understand Dan and almost never makes any ordinary human contact with him or anyone else. He finds her psychologically absurd but terrifying. She is almost sure either to tear him apart or force him into a defensive alienation if they marry. Yet both persist in their passion.

Howells' handling of the passion, of the lovers' scenes and action, is fascinating. Since these are by definition the normal, well-reared young people of the time, Howells must by his own theory concentrate on the sublimated intoxications of a chaste courtship. Yet since he is out to show the long-run futility, even the irrelevancy of young love's passion, he sketches in what is for him an extraordinary amount of hand and waist holding, of embracing and caressing, even at one point a "wild kiss."

The reason for these unusual Howellsian concessions is reductive. He aims to deflate the ideal of passion. Naturally, his technique is that of bathos. Whenever the protagonists build up a particularly high head of romantic steam, some more mature or worldly character trips the safety valve. For Mavering the agent of the author's reductionism is Dan's old Harvard friend Boardman. Perhaps the very best of Howells' newspapermen—humane, tough, humorous, and pragmatic—Boardman is perfect as the clear-eyed confidant. At one point Mavering comes to Boardman direct from a session with Alice in which he has soared to undreamed-of heights of romantic ideality. He needs Boardman as an audience for his ecstasies. But Boardman is busy; he has just been called out to cover the story of a "suicidal Chinaman." If Dan wants to spill over on Boardman, he must walk along with him on Boardman's business. He does so, not noticing how deep they are penetrating into a dismal slum until they stop before the door. Boardman invites the raving lover to come in and see the poor suicide and Dan, suddenly aware, draws back and exclaims,

> " 'What have I got to do with him?'
> " 'Both mortal,' suggested the reporter."

It is Boardman who, when Alice has "forever" dismissed Mavering, suggests that stage and novel have failed to represent the impact of "tragedy" upon people truly because they show catastrophe and our response to it as sudden and unitary. Actually both are blunted and diffused—so that we bear them and do not instantaneously die of broken hearts—by the real necessity of taking and responding to life in "little steps." Full of what he supposes ought to be utter, tragic woe, Dan can return Alice's gifts and keepsakes not in a grand, operatic gesture but only in an absurd little scene made comic by the question of how to wrap them—will a collar box do? what sort of paper? what sort of string? He is distracted and saved by the vulgar but iron need of "the little steps." Life just won't be melodrama.

Nevertheless, a broken engagement and torn love hurt, both Dan and Alice discover. There is a mystery of human pain here as in other parts of life. Dan goes back home, where his helpless family rejoice to see him free while they mourn for his pain. Eventually he goes to Washington on business for his father, and Howells prepares the way for a happy ending which is at once utterly cynical and profoundly moral. He has demonstrated the absolute temperamental incompatibility of the young people. "Marriage is a perpetual pardon, concession, surrender; it's an everlasting giving up; that's the divine thing about it; and that's just what Miss Pasmer could never conceive of," says Howells' chorus figure, Mrs. Brinkley, "because she is self-righteous and conceited and unyielding. She would make him miserable." The realist refuses to believe in absolute character. He knows that "we all have twenty different characters . . . and we put them on and take them off . . . for different occasions." He insists on the variable growth and development of personality. Yet the likelihoods for Alice Pasmer are all too disastrous. "It's what she's going to finally harden into—what's going to be her prevailing character." Mavering ought to get and stay away.

On the other hand, great forces conspired together to persuade Howells to compose a "happy ending." The conventions he mocked in observing them demanded it—as did the expectations of the army of shallow readers, with the critics who pandered to them, who could never see the real point anyway. But ultimately compelling was the fact that faithfulness to the normal possibilities—the realities, as Howells saw things—within romantic American culture dictated that two such ego-crossed lovers come together again, become reconciled and married. Once again Howells paid his respects to the cliché. Sketching swiftly, he showed how normal sexual susceptibilities could start Mavering on the road to a love much better for him because the girl was level-headed and complemental instead of opposing him in temperament. As soon as the point was made, however, he snatched that girl away and reunited Dan with a remorse-ravaged Alice and closed out the book abruptly with a glimpse of their marriage.

As they drive away from the church in the last snatch of a scene, neither can refrain from being himself. Alice says, "Oh dearest ! let us be good ! . . . I will try not to be exacting and unreasonable, and I know I can. I won't even make any conditions, if you will always be frank and open with me, and tell me everything !" Immediately the theatrical Dan promises, "I won't keep anything from you after this," seals it with a kiss, and begins making mental reservations about that girl in Washington. Says the narrator's voice, wearily, "If he had been different she would not have asked him to be frank and open; if she had been different he might have been frank and open. This was the beginning of their married life." Like most marriages, in other words, having begun in a whirl of irresponsible emotion sanctified by romantic delusions, this will be painfully difficult and probably unsuccessful.

Mainly *April Hopes* stands as a chapter in Howells' gospel to the married, or the marrying, with a basic morality more Swedenborgian than Tolstoian. Incidentally it functions as an indictment of the heartlessness, materialism, futility, and snobbery of Society —an unsparing critical analysis of the Respectability which everywhere ruled the Victorian world. Portraying the social system at Harvard, or an "evening" at the James Bellinghams' (complete with an aging Bromfield Corey), following the maneuvers of the mother of an eligible daughter with fading funds but excellent family connections in Boston, imagining a wealthy but provincial New England family, Howells is bitterly brilliant. He notes the tendency of these gay young people to treat servants or workers as if they were personally nonexistent—either machines or, at best, picturesque fauna.

He wrote so much about, though not for, the "upper class" because he knew how desperately the decent, hard-working middleclass mass of Americans yearned to be like them. He was determined to show up the vanity, the moral dreadfulness of what that upper class had become and to redirect, if he could, the national ambition. In that context *April Hopes* becomes paired with his next novel, *Annie Kilburn*. In both, sighting along the edges of the upper crust, the realist's eye finds shocking moral deviations. *April Hopes* indicts the actual social aspirations of the nation. *Annie Kilburn* condemns the nation's betrayal of the American Dream— the dreams of democracy and the American Way as they had been understood, for example, by the editor of the Hamilton, Ohio, *Intelligencer* during the Log Cabin and Hard Cider campaign.

II

The Critic magazine, which liked to keep close track of literary gossip, noted on February 26, 1887, that Mr. Howells had been in Lowell, Massachusetts, inspecting factories. So unusual an activity that it merited reporting, that trip marked the first maturation of a growth which had started in Howells when as editor of the *Atlantic* he had explored the meaning of the depression of 1873. Ever since *A Modern Instance* his imagination had been probing the widening fissures in the face of American civilization. Now it was ready for a major illumination. Howells the realist and social critic was planning the first of his economic novels. Its working title would read, *The Upper and the Nether Millstones*, but it would be published as *Annie Kilburn*. It would be the first of his works intimately engaged during its composition with Howells' black time and his heroic responses to it.

Most significantly, Howells reported to his father on February 20 that Elinor had accompanied him on the trip, and that they were agreed in their reactions. His own marriage was precisely the opposite of an *April Hopes* affair; and when the keen-minded wife who often seemed his other and better self agreed with him, Howells felt confident. They came away from Lowell shocked, he wrote. The "slavery" of "the labor that suffers" in those mills demonstrated that "civilization is all wrong." And yet, in the words of the Tolstoi tract Howells was reading, *Que Faire?, What Shall We Do?* They came away feeling "helpless . . . realizing the misery it must cause to undo such a mistake in the structure of society."

Here we cross one of the most frequently noted frontiers in Howells' development. He became fifty on March 1, 1887, still growing significantly. As Percy H. Boynton remarked in 1923, Howells now entered upon a "new consciousness of the institutions of which the individual was always the creator, sometimes the beneficiary, and all too often the victim." He attained a new "maturity" affording him a finer "human and artistic balance." This humanitarian passion and critical indignation were not to be entertained without risk, of course. Most of the people of America were emotionally and intellectually possessed by the attitudes explicit in one children's story after another in, for example, *McGuffey's Readers*. In many families destitution, class degradation, and economic desperation must be taken for granted. The poor ye have always with you, and their troubles are the wages of sin or the deeds of Providence. Only good fortune or the sentimental-miraculous rewards of suffering virtue were admissible remedies.

Howells had been reared not on *McGuffey's Readers* but in the radical-talking print shop of a Utopian socialist, Swedenborgian, and abolitionist. He had by no means always followed his father's teachings. Indeed, during the sixties and most of the seventies his social ideas had been mainly conservative. Even in the early eighties he had so much admired John Hay's antilabor *The Bread-winners,* aiding its publication and encouraging its author, that the book was almost dedicated to him. The curve of departure from his father which had become noticeable about 1860 and reached its furthest point in the early seventies had begun to bend back during the latter *Atlantic* years, however. In the middle eighties it came back around full circle to cordial concurrence again.

After "the bottom dropped out" midway through the writing of *Silas Lapham;* after the doctrine of complicity was established in *The Minister's Charge;* after Tolstoi was discovered—then Howells could be at one with his childhood training. Other influences played upon him from his reading. The logic of events in American life focused his attention in 1886 upon the more than 10,000 strikes that set the nation to seething with labor troubles. Howells could well believe that Roswell Smith, publisher of *Century,* had been right in urging him to turn to "the relations of capital and labor. There is room for a half dozen authors to write on the subject," Smith urged, "and if you ever think of taking it up I should like to talk with you about it. Perhaps there is no country in the world where the abuses of capital are so great as in this country and where the strife for wealth is so eager. . . . On the other hand, there is no country where what we call Socialism is likely to take so deep a root and flourish and grow strong as here."

Factual articles on these questions, Smith concluded, worked out badly. The public was not yet ready for what would soon become Muckraking: such pieces "bristle all over with libel suits, and seem mere personal attacks on individuals, and, what is worse, prove ineffective and uninteresting. Now we are waiting for the coming man to treat them through the medium of fiction." Writing months before the consummation of the Harpers' contract, Smith was playing the publisher's role of honest intellectual broker brilliantly.

Though fate thwarted his desire to have this work done for *Century*, he understood his author perfectly. When Howells launched out as economic novelist, it was with exactly the goal Smith pointed out to him: "Some writer of fiction may do a great service in this country, and help to postpone if not prevent the great impending struggle between labor and capital."

As Marxian class war that great struggle was long postponed, and it now seems safe to say that the evolution of American labor and capital has proceeded to the point where that war no longer threatens. As Smith supposed, Howells could be enlisted in the effort to prevent it. His whole aim as economic novelist was toward reform and reconciliation.

Having finished *April Hopes*, Howells took his family off to Lake George for the summer. There a reporter cornered him, looking tanned and ruggedly healthy, sitting with the family, "upon the front piazza of his cottage, in a soft felt hat, a white flannel shirt, and a large easy pair of corduroy trousers." Howells was feeling fine, full of energy and mentally aggressive. He had moved into his furnished cottage, picked a study, put pictures of Lincoln, "of Tolstoi, Björnson, Hawthorne, and others" on the walls to make himself at home, and was writing a steady four hours every morning. He preached Tolstoi to the reporter, razzed Rider Haggard and the neoromanticists, praised the Russians for leading the world in fiction, and mocked the English for not appreciating Thomas Hardy. He could not know that he was basking in the last days of an Indian Summer before the black time descended on him in full earnest.

"I have just written the first pages of a new novel not yet announced," he told the reporter, meaning *The Upper and the Nether Millstones*. "I began it, in fact, only the day before yesterday. It will be a purely American story, its chief events centered in a New England country town, though it will relate to both city and country life. I have not thought of a name for it yet, nor, though I have its plot pretty well sketched out in my mind, should I feel at liberty to detail it to you just now. The nature of my arrangements with the Harpers, who have contracted with me for all I write, is such that my entire good faith requires me to leave with them the time and form of any extended announcement. We shall not leave Lake George before October, and by that time I hope to have the book in fairly good shape." It was kind mercy he could not know that it would be an entire year before he finished that novel, know that he would find it to that date "the most difficult of all my stories," nor foretell what desperate interruptions would occur.

The first problem was that Winifred's health went suddenly down again—decisively, this time, as the future was to prove. In a family circle where warm and gay affection had been the rule, it hurt, of course, to have the oldest daughter failing. Winny "is a burden on my heart," Howells wrote his father only the day after *The Critic* published the reporter's account of his idyllic life. She lives in a "sort of dull painful dream," he confided. He did not object to caring for her or supporting her psychologically. Americans in that twilight dawn of medical science were used to dealing with more or less desperate invalidism, and Howells was famous for the cheerfulness and devotion with which he did his duty as husband and father to his invalids. But the doctors, unable to diagnose, talked a particularly painful sort of gobbledygook.

There wasn't really anything wrong with their daughter, the Howellses were told. Her pains were illusory, her troubles basically moral. She must be forced to eat, to exercise, to make herself healthy again, to acquire enough moral fiber to avoid lifelong invalidism. It was really a matter of character-building, and truly loving parents would see to it that her character was built—no matter how it seemed to hurt. And so they tried to force themselves, and their well-loved child, storing up dreadful potentialities of guilt for the future, and failed. Defeated, they decided abruptly in September to place Winifred in a sanatorium at Dansville, New York, and went along to keep her company. The new book was far from done.

III

In Dansville, Ferris Greenslet, then a shy but ardently reading twelve-year-old whose type Howells must have recognized instantly, found himself welcome in the little sanctum where the author quietly worked. To that hut on a hillside, with a crude table, some old chairs, and a Franklin stove for heat, Howells could escape from the hospital and write. No doubt he enjoyed befriending a lonely boy and even conspiring to feed him more of the blood-and-thunder literature a boy's imagination delighted in. For on that hillside, as if the slow heartbreak to which he must return down the slope as each day's work was done were not enough, Howells was swiftly to pass through one of the major crises of his life. It is one thing to be a theorist and a moralist on principle, to be an unreal editor and write passionately from the confines of an imaginary study—or even to present in art one's earnest visions of life as formed by the moral imagination. It is something else to face the practical test where one must, in the face of whatever penalty, act on principle. When the moral option becomes live and choice may really alter the pattern of a man's fate and future, then he discovers what his faith really is, whether he actually has any morals, and, if so, what they are. The choice came to Howells in his cabin at Dansville in the case of the Chicago Anarchists.

The rise of labor troubles throughout the Western world which, especially in their American aspect, had suggested to Roswell Smith of *Century* that labor against capital would make a great field for the novelist and which had set Howells to speculating about the upper and the nether millstones, had provided conservative (that is to say, most) Americans with a chilling new bugaboo in the 1880's. Suppose the poor began to refuse to live according to *McGuffey's Readers*? Suppose they began to act like Europeans? What was that line about a specter stalking Europe? Johann Most arrived in New York in 1882 and preached his anarchism—the smashing by violence of the forms and power of capitalism—to a cheering crowd in Cooper Union. In Chicago in 1883 the International Working People's Association was formed on Most's principles. Nearly all its members were recent immigrants. The anarchist press was almost entirely foreign-language. To the soaring incidence of strikes and the outrageous sound of this hectic alien propaganda was added the fear of Mr. Nobel's new explosive compound that would make war too horrible to contemplate yet was readily available to any farmer and to many workers.

The mood of the country was interpreted to Howells dramatically by the reaction to that one word in the original script of *The Rise of Silas Lapham*. When Bromfield Corey rallies the ladies about their long, cool vacations from summer Boston, he indulges in a moment of wondering, as Howells had, how the poor of Boston tolerated suffocating in their slums while airy Beacon Street homes stood empty and inviting, row on row. Why didn't they just break in and take over? Why, Howells originally had playful Bromfield suggest, didn't the poor indignantly dynamite them? When Richard Watson Gilder saw that awful word, he rushed with his proofs to his publisher, and both wrote Howells to plead and cajole that he suppress that dreadful term. Our circulation is up to 210,000, please don't knock us down, Gilder pleaded. Roswell Smith, who thought Howells should write about labor troubles, argued disaster if he said "Dynamite." That word "suggests nihilism, destructiveness, revenge, etc.," Smith said. With labor troubles rife in London and New York, "the Law might stop the magazine or make the Publishers trouble in England." He wished to add his plea to Gilder's to get that word suppressed.

Of course Howells toned down Corey's joke. But he could feel that he had been supplied authoritative, inside information on the national mood as he considered a few days after reaching Dansville what his reaction should be to the conviction of the Chicago Anarchists.

Gestating a novel about current economic conditions, Howells naturally followed with care the events which came after the fairly concerted wave of strikes beginning May 1, 1886, for an eight-hour day. The worst trouble came from the reaction to the strike at the McCormick Reaper Works in Chicago. On May 3 the "scabs" who had taken McCormick jobs were mobbed as they left the plant, and the police shot down strikers and were otherwise rough in restoring order. The next night, May 4, an Anarchist meeting was called in Haymarket Square to exploit the brutality of the police. As long as the mayor of Chicago attended, the meeting was orderly, though the speeches were inflammatory. When the mayor left, the police moved in to break up the meeting. As their formation swung toward the crowd, somebody threw a grenade which burst among their ranks, killing one man outright and mortally wounding seven more. The response of the newspapers and most of the influential people of the country was instant and bitter. That phase of the collective temperament which then often expressed itself in Lynch Law prevailed. The Anarchists acted like mad dogs. If that was their religion, hanging was too good, but it would have to do.

All the known Anarchists the police could bag were picked up and grilled. When it was found that no real bomb-throwing suspect could be established, eight men were picked out, regardless of alibis, of whom it could be proved that they were Anarchists. In an atmosphere of hatred, with a prejudicial judge and packed jury, these men were tried on the theory that, regardless of the ordinary legal principles of particular personal responsibility, Anarchism had done the murders, these men were Anarchists, and these men were guilty. On August 20, seven of the accused were found guilty of murder in the first degree and sentenced to hang. The eighth, about whom nothing very much at all had been proved, was sentenced to fifteen years in jail. Judge Roger A. Pryor, the Anarchists' chief counsel, immediately began the process of appeal and came before the Supreme Court in September.

Very soon after Howells came to Dansville (September 19 or 20), he wrote to Judge Pryor, whom he had once met in Washington, expressing his hope that Pryor's appeal would save the Anarchists, "for I have never believed them guilty of murder, or of anything but their opinions, and I do not think they were justly convicted." In answer Pryor urged further reasons for believing that his clients had been railroaded and asked permission to print Howells' letter. On the ground that publication would harm himself without affecting the Court, Howells declined. But apparently he did take the trouble to travel to New York to confer with Pryor and his sympathizers. And when, despairing of the Court's conclusion, Pryor urged that an appeal by Howells might really help influence the Governor of Illinois to commute the sentences, Howells got ready for action.

On November 2 the Supreme Court denied Pryor's appeal. Howells conferred with his wife, and they agreed that, whatever the penalty, they must take their stand. On November 4 he wrote a letter in Dansville and sent it to the only publisher of a nationally influential newspaper who was his old, trustworthy, and therefore exploitable friend. Whitelaw Reid was reluctant but faithful. On November 6 his New York *Tribune* carried the headline "CLEMENCY FOR THE ANARCHISTS. A Letter From Mr. W. D. Howells," and the text of the letter. There Howells urged readers to join him in petitioning and writing the Governor of Illinois in favor of commuting the Anarchists' sentence. The Supreme Court, he said, had only "affirmed the legality of the forms under which the Chicago court proceeded; it . . . by no means approved the principle of punishing [the men] because of their frantic opinions, for a crime which they were not shown to have committed." The court had protected the legal letter, not justice, he said; and he predicted, accurately, that "the decision of history" would be that injustice had been done. Yet "the worst" could still be avoided by the Governor's clemency. "I conjure," Howells wrote, "all to join in urging him by petition, by letter, through the press, and from the pulpit and the platform, to use his power, in the only direction where power can never be misused, for the mitigation of their punishment."

In the East, where reason might be heard, that was a good approach. In Chicago, where blood-lust had taken over, the leverage of Howells' name might better be applied more emotionally. On the same day, November 4, he wrote a "personal" note, almost surely knowing it would be published, to a Chicago poet, Francis F. Browne, who had sent him some impassioned verses defending the Anarchists. To Browne he wrote that the "impending tragedy" had not "for many weeks, for months . . . been for one hour out of my waking thoughts; it is the last thing when I lie down, and the first thing when I rise up; it blackens my life. . . . I feel the horror and the shame of the crime which the law is about to commit against justice." With the help of Henry Demarest Lloyd's influence, that somewhat atypical bit of rhetoric proved newsworthy enough to be printed in the Chicago *Tribune* on November 8. It did not matter to Howells that the paper framed him in sarcasm. If his appeal could help the still-living men, only that counted.

He could know that he was taking chances because he stood so alone in his protest. Even the great liberal reputations of the nation had stepped aside from appeals to join him. George William Curtis, for all his cordiality from the "Easy Chair," gently declined to be drawn in to the question when Howells tried him as early as August. And John Greenleaf Whittier, who had lately requested Howells to become his biographer, made it clear that the fires of social indignation were now banked very low in his mind indeed. To Howells' plea for aid to the Anarchists in September, Whittier replied blandly that he was against capital punishment but (absurdly in the old professional defier of the ante bellum Supreme Court) had "never interfered with the law" and could "see no reason for making the case of the anarchists an exception." Though Whittier signed himself "always thy admirer and friend," he seems to have felt that Tolstoi had rather unhinged Howells. During the next year Whittier confided this opinion to a friend who was indiscreet enough to slip it to a Boston reporter. Then Whittier had to swallow one of the iciest rebukes Howells ever wrote.

When the storming reaction to his appeal broke, therefore, Howells stood alone. No doubt it was lucky for him that, if the

Anarchists were to hang, execution day was November 11. The issue was live for less than a week. So long as it remained live, however, the mood of the country was that of a peculiarly cold, vengeful frenzy. The pages of the New York *Tribune* and representative journals round the country reeked of hysteria. It was reported repeatedly that Anarchists were trying to scare the country out of wreaking justice by threats of retaliation: they would take 100 lives for every hanged Anarchist; they would assassinate "every newspaper editor and reporter who has written anything against the condemned. . . ." Avoid "THE MISTAKE OF COWARDICE," shrieked the *Tribune*. "Are we to confess that we dare not hang men (not for 'frantic opinions,' as Mr. Howells has it, but for conspiracy to murder and for carrying out that conspiracy to its frightful ending)," the *Tribune* demanded "—because we are afraid their sympathizers will, some day, throw more bombs?"

In the clipping file Howells kept on the case there is an unidentified editorial he must have recognized as coming from the hand of an old friend, for he wrapped a bit of cardboard round its edge on which he wrote: " 'Et tu, Brute?' " The writer was joining Howells in calling for commutation—but on the grounds of opposition to capital punishment; and he went out of his way to slap an old friend across the face. "Mr. Howells, the novelist, has set himself up in opposition to the Supreme Courts of the United States and of Illinois, and says he doesn't believe the anarchists had a fair trial," ran the lead sentence. "Happily it doesn't much matter what Mr. Howells believes on this point. . . . It is high time for mere sentimentalists, the friends of the condemned and others, to stop prating about the unfairness of the trial. . . . It was fair, and its result was just."

Lesser journalists, and most of them were lesser, registered mere astonished anger at Howells' plea. Small-town papers are representable by the Cedar Grove, Maine, editor who could "hardly believe these words embody the sentiments of the greatest of American novelists. What—after they have been judged guilty of murder: after the Supreme Court has affirmed the legality of the lower court proceedings which convicted them, and dynamite bombs are found concealed in the cells where they are now confined? They are murderers, bomb throwers, enemies of our civilization, destroyers of homes, villains and cut-throats. Why should they not suffer for their wrong doing like other convicted murderers? The position which you have taken, Mr. Howells, must sever you from the loyal friendship of thousands of your readers and admirers."

The simple country editor spoke out what more dangerous adversaries had in mind. Howells could be disciplined, for this as for other crimes, by separating him from his audience. H. C. Bunner took his crack at Howells in *Puck*. But it was the genteel jokesters of *Life*, the elegant spokesmen of the smart set, who hit him most shrewdly. "They say that Mr. Howells headed a petition to the Governor of Illinois in behalf of the Anarchists," *Life* observed. "Has our Boston friend followed Tolstoi so far as to have become a non-resistant? If so, how long may we expect him to keep personally clean and wear boiled shirts?" Just below that quip it ran another merry jest. From a crude black gallows dangled seven bound and hooded figures. The caption read: "Seven Up. A Game that will be Played in Chicago Next Month." Reproved by the *Boston Transcript* for this brutality, *Life* angrily refused to apologize. "Would the *Transcript* have moralized and characterized us as brutal if *Life* had jested on the approaching destruction of seven rattlesnakes? We believe not, and, with our apologies to the rattlesnake for saying so, we venture the assertion that it does not require a very large stretch of the imagination to find a parallel between the two cases."

This brief chrestomathy of lyncherism by no means exhausts the possibilities, of course. Fortunately for Howells, the full effect of that barrage had hardly begun to hit him before, after one suicide and two commutations had reduced their number, the remaining four anarchists were hanged on November 11. Yet the anguish of that defeat stung the brooding thinker on his hillside almost to desperation—and to a most definitive statement of the truth about the Chicago Anarchists and what their case revealed (and still reveals) about civilization in the United States. Howells sat at his battered kitchen table and penned an extraordinary countereditorial for the New York *Tribune:*

A WORD FOR THE DEAD

To the Editor of the Tribune:

　　　　　　　　　　　. . . It seems of course almost a pity to mix a note of regret with the hymn of thanksgiving for blood going up from thousands of newspapers all over the land this morning; but I reflect that though I write amidst this joyful noise, my letter cannot

reach the public before Monday at the earliest, and cannot therefore be regarded as an indecent interruption of the Te Deum.

By that time journalism will not have ceased, but history will have at least begun. All over the world where civilized men can think and feel, they are even now asking themselves, For what, really, did those four men die so bravely? Why did one other die so miserably? Next week the journalistic theory that they died so because they were desperate murderers will have grown even more insufficient than it is now for the minds and hearts of dispassionate inquirers, and history will make the answer to which she must adhere for all time, They died, in the prime of the first Republic the world has ever known, for their opinions' sake.

It is useless to deny this truth, to cover it up, to turn your backs upon it, to frown it down, or sneer it down. We have committed an atrocious and irreparable wrong. We have been undergoing one of those spasms of paroxysmal righteousness to which our Anglo-Saxon race is peculiarly subject, and in which, let us hope, we are not more responsible for our actions than the victim of petit mal. *Otherwise, we could not forgive ourselves; and I say we, because this deed has apparently been done with the approval of the whole nation. The dead men who now accuse us of the suicidal violence in which they perished, would be alive today, if one thousandth part of the means employed to compass their death had been used by the people to inquire into the question of their guilt; for, under the forms of law, their trial has not been a trial by justice, but a trial by passion, by terror, by prejudice, by hate, by newspaper.*

To the minority who asked mercy for them because they had made this inquiry (but who were hooted at in your columns as ignorant sentimentalists and cowards) the whole business of their conviction, except for the hideous end attained, might seem a colossal piece of that American humor, so much admired by the English for its grotesque surprises in material and proportion. But perhaps the wildest of our humorists could not have conceived of a joke so monstrous as the conviction of seven men for a murderous conspiracy which they carried into effect while one was at home playing cards with his family, another was addressing a meeting five miles away, another was present with his wife and little children, two others had made pacific speeches, and not one, except on the testimony of a single, notoriously untruthful witness, was proven to have had anything to do with throwing the Haymarket bomb, or to have even remotely instigated the act. It remained for a poetic brain to imagine this, and bring its dream yesterday to homicidal realization.

I mean the brain of Mr. States Attorney Grinnell, who has shown gifts of imagination that would perhaps fit him better for the functions of a romantic novelist than for the duties of official advocate in a free commonwealth. It was apparently inconceivable to him that it was the civic duty as well as the sacred privilege of such an officer to seek the truth concerning the accused rather than to seek their destruction. He brought into court the blood-curdling banners of the Anarchists, and unfurled them before the eyes of a jury on which eight or nine men had owned themselves prejudicial against Anarchists before the law delivered the lives of these Anarchists into their hands. He appealed to the already heated passions of the jury; he said the seven were no more guilty than a thousand other men in Chicago, but he told them that if they would hang the seven men before them the other nine hundred and ninety-three equally guilty contrivers of bombs would not explode them in the bosom of the impartial jurymen's families and Society would be saved.

If he proved absolutely nothing against the anarchists worthy of death, it cannot be denied that he at least posed successfully as a Savior of Society—the role once filled by the late Emperor of the French (on the famous 2nd December) with great effect against the Socialists of his day. He was, throughout, the expression of the worst passions of the better classes, their fear, their hate, their resentment, which I do not find so much better than the worst passions of the worst classes that I can altogether respect them. He did not show that any of the accused threw the bomb, or had anything to do with throwing it; but he got them convicted of murder all the same. Spies was convicted of murder partly because he conspired against Society with men some of whom he was not on speaking terms with. Among the crimes for which Parsons was convicted of murder was quoting in his paper General Sheridan's belief that a dynamite bomb might kill a regiment of soldiers; and the Supreme Court of Illinois, reviewing the testimony, located him at two points, a block apart, when the bomb was thrown, and found him doubly privy to the act upon this bold topographical conceit.

But Mr. Grinnell does not deserve all the honor—if it is an honor—of bringing the Anarchists to their death. He was ably seconded by Judge Gary, whose interpretation of the law against murder, to make it do the work of the law against conspiracy, is a masterpiece of its kind; though perhaps even this is surpassed by his recommendation of Fielden and Schwab to the Governor's mercy because (it is like the logic of a "Bab Ballad") they were pretty-behaved when brought up for sentence. It has indeed been proved, as proof went in that amusingly credulous court, that Fielden was the very man who gave the signal for throwing the bomb; but Judge Gary contributes to the science of jurisprudence the novel principle that if you are pretty-behaved when asked to say why you should not be hung for a crime of which you know your innocence, you ought afterwards to have your sentence commuted. He himself was not always pretty-behaved. When he asked Parsons that comical question, and Parsons entered upon his reasons, he refused to let him pause for a moment's refreshment while delivering his long protest, and thought it good taste and good feeling to sneer at him for reading extracts from the newspapers. Perhaps it was so, or perhaps the judge was tired—the prosecution had been reading whole files of newspapers.

When he said that the seven were no more guilty than a thousand other Anarchists, Mr. Grinnell was counting for Chicago alone; but he could doubtless have figured up ten thousand men equally guilty, upon the same medieval principle, if he took in the whole country. Seven is rather a small percentage, though seven is a mystical number, and he may have thought it had peculiar properties for that reason; but it always struck me as much too few, or wholly too many, according as the men accused did or did not do murder. With his love of poetic justice (I will call it melodramatic justice if the word poetic seems too strong) I rather wonder that Mr. Grinnell did not at least want the men's families hanged; but since he did not ask this, I do not see why he could not have satisfied himself with having the seven Anarchists hanged in effigy. Possibly if Parsons, believing that he could suffer no wrong in an American court, had not come back and voluntarily given himself up after having made good his escape, Mr. Grinnell could have demanded [that].

But this is more conjecture, and I have wished to deal with facts. One of these is that we had a political execution in Chicago yesterday. The sooner we realize this, the better for us. By such perversion of law as brought the Anarchists to their doom, William Lloyd Garrison, who published a paper denouncing the Constitution as a compact with hell and a covenant with death, and every week stirred up the blacks and their friends throughout the country to abhor the social system of the South, could have been sent to the gallows if a slave had killed his master. Emerson, Parker, Howe, Giddings and Wade, Sumner and Greeley, all who encouraged the fight against slavery in Kansas and the New England philanthropists who supplied the Free State men with Sharp's Rifles could have been held morally responsible, and made to pay with their persons, when John Brown took seven Missourians out of their beds and shot them. Wendell Phillips, and Thoreau, and the other literary men

whose sympathies influenced Brown to homicidal insurrection at Har-
per's Ferry could have been put to death with the same justice that
consigned the Anarchists to the gallows in Chicago. The American law
yesterday was made to do a deed beside which the treatment of William
O'Brien by British law for the like offense is caressing tenderness.

But the men are dead. They are with God, as the simple, devout old
phrase goes; or if the scientific spirit of the age does not consent to the
idea, I will say that they are at least not with the newspapers. They
are where, as men your words cannot hurt, nor mine help them more.
But as memories, they are not beyond the reach of either, and I protest
against any further attempt to defame them. They were no vulgar or
selfish murderers. However they came by their craze against society it
was not through hate of the rich so much as love of the poor. Let both
rich and poor remember this, and do them this piece of justice at least.

I dread the Anarchy of the Courts, but I have never been afraid of the
prevalence of the dead Anarchists' doctrine, because that must always
remain, to plain common sense, unthinkable; and I am not afraid of any
acts of revenge from their fellow conspirators because I believe they
were never part of any conspiracy. I have no doubt that Judge Gary
will live long to enjoy the reward upon which he has already entered in
his re-election. I have no question either as to the safety of Mr. States'
Attorney Grinnell, and I hope he has not suffered too keenly from the
failure to realize his poetical ideal in the number of Anarchists hanged.
He himself helped to reduce it to four; perhaps he will yet wish that
none had died.

W. D. Howells
Dansville, Nov. 12, 1887

Placed in an envelope and firmly addressed to Whitelaw Reid or
his managing editor, this manuscript was never sent, though Howells had at least thrice revised it. Perhaps he mailed a clean copy to
Reid and Reid refused to print it. But the likelihood is that it was
never sent. Some of the reasons for not sending it are obvious. It
was at least potentially libelous of Grinnell and Gary, and Reid
could have justified not publishing it on that ground even if, improbably, he would have been otherwise so inclined. Howells' document mingled human appeal, logic, moral protest, political idealism,
and withering irony with great effect. Yet in the long run, since
the Anarchists were dead, he laid himself open to unfair but even
more withering attack from a press and public opinion already

passionately decided. It had destroyed the Anarchists and it might destroy him. The men were dead. Protest could not restore them but it could, and almost surely would, have left Howells open to crushing proofs that he was engaged in self-justification (which in a sense he was) and in unendurable assertions of self-righteousness (even though he was not).

Howells hesitated, and finally withdrew from further combat. His hesitation might have been confirmed, though of course it could not (as a matter of timing) have been caused by a note Alden wrote him on November 13—probably not deliverable in Dansville until the fifteenth. You survived the Zola episode, Alden told him in effect, and your plea for clemency for the Anarchists has been understood; it will be all right. But stop there—don't, whatever you do, get publicly identified as what you are not, an Anarchist yourself.

For all these reasons, practical, strategic, and principled, Howells' editorial remained unpublished. That fact diminishes, though it does not destroy, the historical stature of this document in the context of the Anarchists' case. Once the journalistic instant was lost, all normal reason for publishing the piece in the author's own time was lost with it. What Howells had wished to say to the American people in that instant they needed, and still need, very badly to be told. He did not communicate it then, perhaps there really proved to be no way to do it; but he did not lose either his sense of what needed to be said or his determination to say it. As we have seen, his critical attitude toward American society began long before his concern for the Anarchists. Naturally, of course, that concern was a product of the critical attitude. But this experience thoroughly confirmed him in alienation from the dominant political, economic, and social ideas of his age.

Six days after dating "A Word for the Dead," Howells wrote his sister Annie, recording his "heartache and horror" over the whole "atrocious piece of frenzy and cruelty." It would be hard for anyone to believe how changed the Howellses were, he warned. "Elinor and I both no longer care for the world's life, and would like to be settled somewhere very humbly and simply, where we could be socially identified with the principles of progress and sympathy for the struggling mass." He was always to be too complex—and too honest—to achieve that simplistic dream. Its existence, and the emotions behind it, however, reveal the profundities of the changes time, suffering, and thought had brought to Howells.

He had always been critical of upper or "conventional" Society, but he had once loved its glitter, too. Now he was in open disdain of it—as he knew it would be of him if it dared. Without the glamor of Howells' fame, Henry Demarest Lloyd was snubbed in Society for years on account of the Anarchists. Even devoted friends like Thomas Sargent Perry and William James were out of sympathy with Howells about the Anarchists. Fearing the retaliation Victorian society wreaked on the maverick, one poor soul named William Hoopes Howells had written to the *Tribune* immediately on publication of the plea for the Anarchists, begging to "exempt" himself from anybody's "mistaken impression" the *he* had done that. If a major novelist's fame shielded him, Howells knew it would only send suspicion underground. As late as 1901, Theodore Roosevelt blamed Howells, among others, for the shooting of President McKinley.

On the other hand, of course, Howells' stand for justice won him some sympathy. Among the few open defenders of the Anarchists he became a hero. Some who did not agree could honor his moral courage. Private, but very few public, messages of sympathy came in. Late in November he went to New York and found among the authors and publishers at a Copyright Convention "many interesting men who thought as I do about the murdered anarchists"— though apparently they had been afraid to say so. Early in December Joseph W. Harper let him know that the worst was over by writing a most friendly note glossing over the event by reporting conversation at his club. There men "spoke of you warmly and with almost affectionate appreciation of your frank and earnest devotion to the truth," Harper said, "—yet they deprecated what seemed to them the almost profanity of criticizing publicly the decision, any decision, of the highest tribunal, state and national."

No doubt Harper would have been shocked to know how little Howells cared at the moment what the clubmen thought. Yet, for all his yearnings toward simplicity and the common life, Howells had, for his wife and children's sakes, if nothing else, to be glad that his calculated risk for the truth had brought him only suffering, not destruction. He was right about the verdict of history. As Miss Mildred Howells noted thirty years ago, when Governor of

Illinois John P. Altgeld pardoned the three surviving Anarchists in 1893, his official message vindicated Howells' view of the trial, and it has rested unchallenged by historians. Howells stood alone among American writers, virtually alone among Americans of major national reputation, in his protest. It is of course significant that he was not penalized severely for his courage. Had his Harper contract been canceled, his enemies might have been able to drive and hound him into complete disaster. Or they might not.

In the moment of doubt, with the real possibility before his face, Howells did, however, take the real chance for the truth's sake. Lloyd stood by him, and Colonel Robert Ingersoll, the compassionate atheist, and from England William Morris and Walter Besant. But no one of larger stature—at the time even such future great reformers as Eugene Debs, Washington Gladden, and Altgeld himself were silent. Howells' heroism in this moment—and indeed throughout this whole period of his life—has almost never been adequately recognized. "Gentle and gracious he assuredly was," wrote Joseph Henry Harper at Howells' death, "but if occasion required it, he was forcible and as uncompromising as the most upright judge."

IV

For a few months after the Anarchists, there came one of those breaks of lightening and warmth in the midst of the black time which deluded Howells into hopeful security. The Dansville doctors, anxious for a free hand in the "moral" aspect of their case, urged the family to get away from Dansville and leave Winifred to them. To obey yet not desert her, they moved to a hotel in Buffalo. There, in pleased surprise, they found society not only agreeably cultivated and anxious to lionize Howells, but also anxious to talk Tolstoi and reform. The sanatorium sent on falsely optimistic reports about Winifred's progress, the hotel was pleasant, young Mildred found congenial company. The family settled in happily for the winter.

In these extraordinary circumstances, with his Tolstoian novel occupying his mornings, with all the effects of the Anarchist experience to digest, and with a favorable environment at hand, Howells grew swiftly into new ways of thought. He approached as close in this Buffalo winter to becoming a convinced, party Socialist as he ever would. As Howells told Hamlin Garland in January, he felt his horizons widen indefinitely—and was now "reading and thinking about questions that carry me beyond myself and my miserable literary idolatries of the past. . . ." He hinted that these questions would appear in his work but proved that Tolstoi and Swedenborg still ruled his mind by adding, "I am still the slave of selfishness, but I am no longer content to be so. That's as far as I can honestly say I've got."

In 1898 he summed up that earlier winter in an interview for the *American Fabian,* laying down the lines of his advance toward Socialism very clearly: "It was ten years ago . . . that I first became interested in the creed of Socialism. I was in Buffalo when Laurence Gronlund lectured there before the Fortnightly Club. Through this address I was led to read his book, 'The Cooperative Commonwealth,' and Kirkup's article in the Encyclopedia Britannica. Afterward I read the 'Fabian Essays'; I was greatly influenced also by a number of William Morris's tracts. The greatest influence, however, came to me through reading Tolstoi." As almost always, it is important here to attend exactly to Howells' words. He says that he was much interested in Socialism and influenced by its writings. He mentions its creed, and the use of the word is significant, because Howells constitutionally resisted creedal formulations. He is careful *not* to say that he adhered to the creed or accepted the forms or disciplines of the party. He did not do so then. In April he told Perry that he felt alienated from political parties. "Sometimes I think that if there were a labor party, embodying any practical ideas I would vote with it." He was never to find any of the several Socialist parties quite practical or be nearly so impressed by their creeds as by their critical analyses of society.

By the end of February it was apparent that the Dansville experiment had failed after all, and it was decided to establish a base in New York to see what its doctors could do. The city now hit Howells hard, with its "bigger life . . . immensely interesting" and "lordly free with foreign touches of all kinds all through its abounding Americanism." One of the effects of the black time on Howells' nerves was to redouble his sensitivity to life. "Every inch of this America is interesting," he had exclaimed from Buffalo. But this time they camped in the city for only about three months before taking a big, secluded estate at Little Nahant, on the sea outside Boston, to try that environment on Winifred. And in the midst of all this expense of purse as well as soul, the work continued on the overdue Tolstoian novel.

By the time Howells had finished enough of his novel to let Alden start publication in June 1888 (Alden got the last installment in August, a timing not unusual for Howells), it had lost its portentous working title and been christened with the name of its main character, *Annie Kilburn.* In proposing to explore the "audacity" of his new ideas in a story which must be shaped and controlled from the point of view of a nearsighted, thirty-one-year-old spinster of the international set, Howells gave himself problems which would have made a much later "proletarian" novelist shudder. Yet he had his reasons, and they were justified by solid success. His own audience was used to the people of his world, and to certain expectations about their backgrounds, habits, interests, and levels of perception. The neoromantics already clamored against the vulgarity of his people, but Howells knew his audience would accept insights downward into the common folk if he let them enjoy his easy command of Society figures too. He knew his women were, if controversial, intensely interesting. He therefore set out deliberately, for the sake of reaching his audience with the radical concerns which now possessed him, "to sugar-coat my medicinal properties" as he confessed to E. C. Stedman, and the sugar was mainly Miss Annie Kilburn.

When Annie Kilburn's aged father died in Rome after years of empty "social" life abroad, he left her rich, lonely, and determined to go back home and try to discover her soul in being of use in the world, in doing good. Typically, Howells offers various reasons for her concern. She has a New England conscience. She has rather Swedenborgian notions of morality. Social life leaves her hungry for reality. The motive shown truly significant by the development of the whole novel, however, is that she feels urged to realize herself as an American. She responds, the narrator says, to her sense of "the opportunity which America supremely affords for the race to help itself, and for each member to help all the rest." To fulfill the American Dream—our democracy is the last, best hope of earth—Annie Kilburn comes home. This is to be an American Dream novel, and many of the central characters will register their views of that ideal.

At home in Hatboro, Massachusetts, Annie finds it immensely more difficult to go good than she had supposed. Reared on her father's views, the fiercely competitive and snobbish notions appropriate to the Whiggish view of a simpler American society of forty or fifty years earlier, Annie finds her values irrelevant to

contemporary Hatboro. The old village—and its people—are gone.
Annie's prevision of herself as Lady Bountiful distributing largesse
to simple and grateful inhabitants tantalizes her. It is so difficult
to find anywhere to begin. The great trouble is that Hatboro is now
an industrializing provincial town. It is incomprehensible from the
old village points of view. And, to her dismay, Annie finds that not
even the most intelligent, most sensitive, and best educated people
around seem to have any better way of grasping and solving its
problems.

The education of an idealistic lady in the puzzle of how to make
the American Dream real in modern times thus becomes the problem in *Annie Kilburn*. To the solution Howells brings his fictional
skills now at the peak level they would keep for the next fifteen
years. Pictorially, scenically, atmospherically, dramatically, symbolically, this novel proceeds with a magnificent power to command
the reader's imagination to see, hear, and reflect. Stylistically there
is a new maturity: the old Heinesque virtuoso disappears behind
the solid fabric of the fiction. Formally there is a new economy of
movement and directness of development lent by the new concern
for ideas.

Much of that fine economy results from the fact that Howells
developed his theme by attaching all the elements of his novel organically to one major action. A Social Union Plan is proposed for
the healing of all the divisions in Hatboro's life. Ingeniously am-
biguous, the Social Union is to be all things to all classes. The gay
Society summer people are to unite with the best of the surviving
Old Hatboro families and the wealthiest of the commercial powers
of New Hatboro, and together they are to raise money for a social
center for Over the Tracks Hatboro, the factory workers and common people. This will be Social Union for the divided upper classes
and provide them a chance to "do good" for the lower classes without risking social contamination. The means of raising the money
will be amateur theatricals put on by united Society. Miss Kilburn,
who has contacts by caste with the New York and Boston summer
folks and by inheritance and childhood acquaintance with Hatboro
folks, is to act as promoter and coordinator.

With the Social Union Plan as vehicle, Annie is provided with a
series of guides, almost Dantean guides, to sadly complex and
warring Hatboro. Geographically she finds the area divided into
three parts. South Hatboro is occupied by summer folk and rich

invalids. It is Society, and her guide to it is the leathery Mrs. Munger, expert conniver and social strategist whose life is given to colonizing the place with rich people and to reaping the ego-rewards of the social game for herself. Though South Hatboro pretends to esthetic and ethical concern—the Social Union Plan is Mrs. Munger's—Annie quickly sees that its life is just as "idle and vapid" as that she left behind in Rome. Hatboro proper is divided by the railroad into the respectable town and "Over the Tracks"—was Howells the first novelist to use that significant folk-notation? In Hatboro proper there are the old families, like her own, fading out and breaking up, and an aggressive new commercial set. Over the Tracks is ugly but at first unimaginable to Annie.

As she renews contacts, Annie finds keys to the mysteries of modern Hatboro. And they reveal that its people are locked in dark but bitter conflict. Three old girl friends and their husbands come forward as guides. First are the Gerrishes. A self-made man who adores his Creator, William B. Gerrish has come swiftly up the Horatio Alger trail. Shrewd and ruthless application of big-city department store techniques to Hatboro commerce has brought him commercial status and prosperity. These marks of the divine favor are almost more than this two-bit disciple of the Gospel of Wealth can bear. He browbeats his employees, and advocates the same for all labor. He grasps at the place of leading citizen by donating to good causes and loudly advertising his beneficence. He mouths the old phrase "Christian gentleman": the first term he would attain by ostentatious piety as a church deacon, emphasizing other worldly evangelism, and "the *promises* of Christ." The second term to Gerrish has no relation to the first. Gentility is snobbery to him: climbing up oneself and stamping down those below; excluding and snubbing and, if necessary, using economic power to discipline the unruly.

Herself securely Social, Annie, like Mrs. Munger, finds Gerrish "an odious little creature." Yet Annie also knows how worthless even that superiority is. And she is supplied with important new insights by the representatives of Old Hatboro, the Putneys. Brilliant and sensitive, Ralph Putney has been held from following the rest of the able members of the old families (like Annie's father) to major success in the centers of national power by alcoholism. His intelligence, good taste, and traditions make Putney the natural enemy of Gerrish. His disgrace, indulged as eccentricity because he is Old Hatboro, has made him sympathetic to the hidden third, to Over the Tracks.

Putney's ironic keenness sees through Gerrish, the Gospel of Wealth, and Manchester economics. Life is ideal, Putney tells Annie, in Hatboro, "a community where there is neither poverty nor richness, and where political economy can show by the figures that the profligate shop hands get nine-tenths of the profits, and starve on 'em, while the good little company rolls in luxury on the other tenth." More seriously, the kindliness of people to his own affliction because of his tradition, he says at another meeting, made him resolve to "give all my help to the man that hadn't a tradition. That's what I've done, Annie. There isn't any low, friendless rapscallion in this town that hasn't got me for his friend—and Ellen. We've been in all the strikes with the men, and all their fool boycottings and kicking over the traces generally. Anybody else would have been turned out of respectable society for one-half that I've done, but it tolerates me because I'm one of the old Hatboro Putneys."

Reality and the real issues come, then, to seem to lie Over the Tracks. There is the real point, if any, to the Social Union Plan. Many influences conspire to turn Annie's yen to do good in that direction, and she finds two good guides. One is Lyra Wilmington, a girlhood friend whom family misfortunes had forced to work as a hand in the stocking factory until she could marry the dried-up old boss for his money. Life as an old man's darling has made Lyra comfortable, secure, and respectable—but neither happy nor dishonest. She plays the social game indolently and for fun and is either having an affair with her husband's nephew and heir or is at least playing with fire. But she keeps her friendships and contacts with the working people of the town, and she can guide Annie to them.

As Lyra guides Annie through the stocking mill, Howells exploits his visit to the mills of Lowell. Annie sees that "the tireless machines marched back and forth across the floor, and the men who watched them with suicidal intensity ran after them barefooted when they made off with a broken thread, spliced it, and then escaped from them to their stations again. In other rooms, where there was a stunning whir of spindles, girls and women were at work. . . . She tried to understand the machinery that wrought and seemed to live before her eyes. But her mind wandered to the men and women who were operating it, and who seemed no more a voluntary part of it than all the rest. . . ." The whole wrong-headed procedure is capped with falsehood at the end where they see girls "counting and stamping the stockings with different numbers. 'Here's where *I* used to work,' said Lyra, 'and here's where I first met Mr. Wilmington. The place is *full* of romantic associations. The stockings are all one size, Annie; but people like to wear different numbers, and so we try to gratify them. Which number do *you* wear?' "

Annie Kilburn's last guide is Putney's friend, Dr. Morrell. And of all her guides he is the only one not warped, not somehow what Sherwood Anderson would later call a "grotesque." Well-balanced and attractive, though not at all what Annie is used to admire as a man of the world, Morrell does his healing work intelligently, objectively, and humbly. It is he who can teach Annie how to do some limited good with her money. She can send certain sick children to the shore for convalescence and save their lives. Puffed up by a success or two, Annie fancies herself again as the fairy godmother and, not waiting to consult Morrell, sends a couple of families off on her own. Then she learns how truly to make contact with the poor. One of those babies dies, and Annie must share some of the grief and guilt. Carefully constructing their shared scenes to hint at what he will not consummate, Howells shows that Annie and Morrell are falling in love. But he will not let the reader drift off from the point into familiar romantic satisfactions. Annie must complete her education, not her "fate," in this novel.

That education, and of course the reader's in Howells' new perceptions, requires a commentator. And the commentator, the suffering prophet, even, of *Annie Kilburn* is the fascinating figure of the Rev. Mr. Peck. This minister might be said to be out of Tolstoi by Hawthorne. Mr. Peck is, though the Russian's name does not appear in the book, the most Tolstoian in origin of all Howells' characters. As Tolstoian, he sits in rigorous, prophetic judgment on Hatboro and its social tensions. From the beginning Peck shatters Annie's complacency by pointing out that no good can come from patronizing, Lady Bountiful, impersonal, superior-to-inferior charity. Only where common suffering, shared experiences—"like hopes, like fears"—unite rich and poor in a bond of equal humanity are love and the accomplishment of real good possible. Peck's ideas destroy Annie's inherited Federalism. The Social Union is social disunion in practice. Social equality and the abolition of classes are the only solution to Hatboro's problems, the only way of realizing the American Dream in the present, Peck argues. The essence of Annie Kilburn's education consists of her coming to see and accept Peck's point. "Brother Peck," says Putney, is pretty shocking to women used to the usual minister. "He doesn't flatter you up worth a cent. There was Annie expecting him to . . . tell her what a noble woman she was . . . but instead of that he simply showed her that she was a moral Cave-Dweller, and that she was living in a Stone-Age of social brutalities. . . ."

Such a prophet, especially when William B. Gerrish is one of his deacons, was bound to have trouble in a Hatboro pulpit. Peck preaches that the American achievement of political liberty will rot if it is not used as an evolutionary step on the way to equality, that universal fraternity is higher than nationalism, that justice is better than charity, that "in the truly Christian state, there will be no more asking and no more giving, no more gratitude and no more merit, no more charity, but only and evermore justice; all shall share alike, and want and luxury and killing toil and heartless indolence shall all cease together." The modern age is one "of seeming preparation for indefinite war," he observes. Little business is swallowed up by bigger until the great monopolies stand unchallenged by all but the growing power of the labor organizations. But in these growths Peck (like Edward Bellamy) sees hope: "They prophesy the end of competition; *they eliminate* one element of strife, of rivalry, of warfare." Not the "godlessness of science" but "the doubt of [Christ] that the sins of Christendom inspire" should be the concern of the church, says Peck.

All this is more than fundamentalist, petty monopolist, and social climber Gerrish can stand. He stalks out in the middle of the sermon. In another of the scenes which must have given Harold Frederic rich suggestions for *The Damnation of Theron Ware*, Gerrish impeaches Peck at the next Congregational meeting. Although the meeting vindicates Peck overwhelmingly, the real issues having been skillfully avoided by local politicians, the minister resigns anyhow. And here the author's Hawthornian skepticisms about his prophet come out strongly.

Howells, who often inserted a literary reference into his texts where he thought honesty demanded it, had Annie think of *The Blithedale Romance* when she first met Peck. It is through quite

Hawthornian devices that Howells registers, in Peck, his reservations about the problems of the reformer, the deficiencies of programmatic Socialism, indeed, about Tolstoi. Devastating in prophetic judgment, Peck vacillates confusedly about positive remedies for the ills he condemns. He cannot bridge the practical middle gap between present evils and the ideal future he imagines. Worse yet, he is cold and passive in human relations; the price for his intellectual clarity and high, abstract moral perception has been isolation from ordinary human warmth. He is lost in speculation. His orphaned little girl, Idella (in much reminiscent of Hawthorne's Pearl), he keeps dressed in rags, squabbling with the slum children for petty satisfactions, and just as deprived of normal love and guidance as they. Accordingly, Idella is a greedy gamin, a selfish, love-starved little savage. It is Peck's sense of failure, his own hunger for reidentification with the working poor from whom he sprang, that make him resign his pulpit. When in a fit of abstraction he steps from his train into the path of a thundering express, he is destroyed by the monster of modernity he could not master. Idella is left to Annie, who can and does really love her. Both are left, by implication, to Morrell, whose struggling but humane, gradualistic but this-worldly approach to life can implement Peck's vision far better than the prophet himself.

It is worth noting that, in the struggle to get *Annie Kilburn* reduced to its forceful economy of form, Howells had recourse to unusually effective symbolism. Annie's nearsightedness—of which much is made early in the book and less, dwindling to nothing, as her education proceeds—is an obvious case. More subtle is the repeated association of Mrs. Munger with leather gloves, belts, hats, accessories—fine leather, expensive leather, but always leather. Then suddenly the point dawns. There is no space to let Mrs. Munger, the social strategist and ego-serving Society Woman act out her hatefulness. That would spoil Howells' form and blur his concentration on the right, necessary themes. She gets just enough scenic rope to hang herself, acts and talks just enough to let us register the point: her conscience is made of that same fine, expensive leather.

Still profounder is Howells' use of architecture to reveal basic truths about Hatboro. Indeed, some student of this age might profit from a careful study of Howells' use of architecture throughout his works. Not only have the economic and social arrangements of the old village gone, and its intellectual life disappeared as the "learned professions yielded in distinction to the growing wealth and plutocratic influence of the prosperous manufacturers," the objective face of the town has changed its look also—and much for the worse. Presumably Howells was helped in these observations by his knowledge of Brattleboro, Vermont, deepened through the insights of the artistic and architectural Meads, perhaps confirmed by the observations of the architectural genius who was Howells' son. The old unconscious, organically grown beauty of the New England village has been ruined in Hatboro. The dirty, negligent ugliness of the factories is bad. The meretricious commercial building of the new downtown center is worse—Gerrish's "large, handsomely ugly brick dry-goods store" standing out. But worst of all is the theatrical, conspicuously consuming, self-consciously esthetic architecture of the rich in South Hatboro: "a strange world . . . of colonial and Queen Anne architecture, where conscious lines and insistent colors contributed to an effect of posing which [Annie] had never seen off the stage. . . . The whole was a violent effect of porches, gables, chimneys, galleries, loggias, balconies, and jalousies, which nature had not yet had time to palliate." When Annie went to visit Putney's home, she found it a place of old-American "humility" and "unimagined simplicity." Not touched by the "aesthetic craze . . . the parlor was in the tastelessness of fifteen years before." But after South Hatboro, "she found a delicious repose in it." The date was 1888.

The point, finally, of Putney's alcoholism was functionally symbolic. The brilliant survivor of Old Hatboro, the scion of the New England Brahmins—always essentially a village race—is helpless. The old intellectual aristocracy, great and good in its day, can never cope with the new problems. Only fresh principles democratically expressed offer hope. And so Putney suffers from what Howells, far in advance of popular opinion, called on his readers, through Mrs. Putney's speech, to recognize as "a disease." It suited his purpose that it was a psychic disease, perhaps a disease of the will. Through it Putney could be at once a sparkling critic of Gerrish, a Hawthornian sympathetic fellow sinner with the poor and misguided, but out of the question as an aristocratic savior.

Howells painted alcoholism here, in *The Lady of the Aroostook*, and in *The Landlord at Lion's Head* as horrifying. His drunk scenes with Silas Lapham and with Bartley Hubbard in *A Modern*

Instance are accurately observed and, especially Bartley's, funny. But they drip disapproval. Was Howells a teetotaler? Certainly, except perhaps for his latest years, not. He learned as a young journalist to go out with the boys and joyfully consume Ohio "Rhine wine and Swiss cheese with mustard" at midnight. In *The Nation* in 1866 he wrote that "the beauty of lager is that a little makes a man comfortable, and a great deal won't make him drunk." In the early nineties he kept his aged father well supplied with port and champagne by the case. In his Cambridge years he learned to conform to the local custom of wine at table. But Howells was not, on the other hand, really a drinking man. For one thing, alcohol made him sleepy. He tended therefore to avoid it when he wished to be alert and to use it pretty regularly for many years as a soporific— a favorite being hot Scotch at bedtime. His fictional uses of drink and drunkenness were strategic, organic to his creative intention, not covert propaganda for Prohibition.

The critical reception of *Annie Kilburn* was, of course, mixed. When the volume was published in 1889, critics got their chance to report their disagreements with its realism, or even what one saw as its socialism. But even if Hamlin Garland had to have it explained to him in one-syllable words, the over-all response to his novel must have been much as Howells wished. Alden, acknowledging the last pages of the manuscript, glowed that it was perfect— "has the heavenly light running through it all." Edward Everett Hale, one of the already converted, received Howells into the fellowship with wide-opened arms. "Thank you, from the bottom of my heart, for Annie Kilburn," he wrote after reading the first half of the novel: "first, that you are willing to attack such problems—and second that the attack is so wise—so kind—so direct . . . so successful. . . . It is a pulpit indeed—to write such a book for a million readers."

But the effect Howells aimed for was far more intelligently grasped by Elinor Howells' cousin, Republican ex-President Rutherford B. Hayes. *Annie Kilburn* fascinated Hayes, as he wrote in his diary, "It opens the democratic side of the coming questions. I do not find a ready word for the doctrine of true equality of rights. Its foes call it nihilism, communism, socialism, and the like. Howells would perhaps call it justice. It is the doctrine of the Declaration of Independence, and of the Sermon on the Mount. But what is a proper and *favorable* word or phrase to designate it?" Howells would have liked to know, too. He would have liked even better to know just what he was going to do with the new insights which had come as a total response to his freshened sensibilities in this black time. His intimate correspondence was loaded with his problem. "I should hardly like to trust pen and ink with all the audacity of my social ideas," he announced to Henry James in the autumn just after he had searched out a place to live in New York for the winter; "but after fifty years of optimistic content with 'civilization' and its ability to come out all right in the end, I now abhor it, and feel that it is coming out all wrong in the end, unless it bases itself anew on a real equality. Meantime, I wear a fur-lined overcoat, and live in all the luxury my money can buy."

It had been hard for Howells to discover what the problems were. He had little light as to what the answers were. Neither, as it has turned out, did most of the other thinkers of his day, including the prophets and visionaries who preached their simple solutions. That Howells pretended neither in his art nor his other writings to have the light gives him a relevance and a vitality which most of the prophets have lost. That was a compensation, to him unguessable, for his black time.

HOWELLS AND TRAGEDY

THE SUMMER AT LITTLE NAHANT SEEMED AT FIRST TO HELP Winifred. Howells issued cautious bulletins on her improvement to cheering friends. He concealed from all but his father how slow and tough the process was for her parents. Winifred suffered excruciating pains after eating, naturally resisted food, and tended toward increasing debilitation. It was the task, heartbreaking and guilt-making, of her parents not only to force her to eat but, as prescribed mental discipline, to convince her that it was all in her mind, that her pain was imaginary. "At last she seems better, but O what a heaviness of the heart still at times !" Howells confided to T. W. Higginson.

Meanwhile the novelist's great spurt of creative energy continued ever fresher. His new ethical sensibilities had fused with his new concern for the meaning of America and then with the exciting sensations from his previous spring's residence in New York. He visualized still another kind of novel. It would be laid on new ground—New York, a setting far richer in implication than Hatboro. There all American and, if useful, some foreign points of view could realistically be brought to bear on the riddle of the industrializing world.

Howells began this novel at Little Nahant. But there was no question of staying there past the summer. With a New York novel on foot, a profitable New York experience behind him, and freedom to live where he would, with the ever-present hope that some new doctor might cure Winifred, the Howellses decided to return to New York for the winter. Early in September they went down, and, as Howells told his father, "Elinor and I were six days in New York, and looked at nearly a hundred flats and houses." Finally they found what they wanted in the Folsom House on Stuyvesant Square, and on November 1 they moved in. The location was attractive, friends like Stedman, the Stoddards, Brander Matthews, Gilder, and Joseph Jefferson, the actor, were readily available. Howells could hope for a pleasant winter and smooth sailing with his novel.

As things turned out, however, not even this was to be Howells' definitive "move to New York." In his very announcement of arrival in the city to his father on November 4, he also announced that the next winter—it turned out to be the next two—would be spent in Boston for the children's—John and Mildred's—sakes. He longed, Howells said, to live in the country all year. Perhaps he was recalling the mood in which he had seriously dickered the winter before with James Parton over the possibility of buying a house in Newburyport. The simple fact was that Howells felt, like many people, a strong ambivalence toward New York. In one phase he thrilled to the vigor, immensity, and color of Gotham. In the other he was wearied and annoyed. In the latter mood he put off deciding to attach himself to the metropolis, as when his February 19, 1888, letter to his father had complained that "the stress of the great city is in many ways very troublesome to me." Then he dreamed again the vision which would always elude him, of "settling for life"; but not in New York.

I

In New York that winter of 1888–89, nevertheless, the most exhilarating experience an artist can have was coming to Howells about as richly as he was ever to know it. His imagination was working at the height of its powers. *A Hazard of New Fortunes* was taking form. Throughout most of Howells' creative life, his fictionizing impulses had confined their operations to fairly narrow regions of his large experience. Beginning with the sense of international difference, his imagination had moved on to consider social difference manifested in tensions between representatives of the normal American middle classes and prestigious, usually Bostonian, "High Society." He had begun by contrasting Midwestern "unconventional," or Jeffersonian, natural ladies and gentlemen with "conventional," artificially aristocratic counterparts. His games, though scored against the Proper Bostonians, were played on Bostonian ground, either in the city, or, if in the country, at summer vacation spots. As Howells' maturing concern for ideas and for the meanings of American and modern life had deepened, he had also increasingly mastered New England life until, in both city and country, he became the greatest of New England local colorists. For the maturing artist, however, that had become only the medium he worked in, the stuff through which he expressed his perceptions of themes which transcended the parochial. With his social "audacity" begun and at length fully achieved, he had in *The Minister's Charge, April Hopes*, and *Annie Kilburn* successively reworked and, at least for the present, exhausted his New England ores. It was time to unlock the stores of all-American experience he had been amassing since childhood.

Apparently the idea of a New York novel crystallized into structure a great deal of this experience which had been floating in solution within Howells' mind. In *Annie Kilburn* he had wrestled with the meaning of a changed New England. But he was aware that his native Midwest had lost its agrarian simplicity too. Visiting Findlay, Ohio, in the midst of its wealth-squandering natural gas boom in 1887, Howells saw what he promised Mark Twain he would think "a No. 11 astonishment." They "blew off" gas wells all around —and then hardly knew what to do with the gas. Huge flares burned day and night in the town for street-lamps. It was exuberant nature-wasting, and it turned a quiet farming area into an industrial hell. What to make of it? How to understand it?

The key to understanding perhaps lay in the place where the process suggested in Findlay as in Hatboro had gone furthest. During his home-hunting trip to New York in September 1888, Howells had proposed to the Harpers that he do what Alden, in accepting the idea for the firm, called "a series of sketches about New York . . . one based on the social meaning of such sketches." They were to be dramatic reporting and show strong " 'democratic' "—Howells must have emphasized the word—implications. Evidently when Howells went back to finish out his season at Little Nahant, characters and themes swam vividly into his consciousness, and a novel replaced the never-written sketches for *Harper's Weekly*.

Not long before he had imagined a Pennsylvania Dutch frontiersman, like his mother's forebears. He was playing, as he did unfruitfully all his life until just before the end, with the creative possibilities of the frontier. This time he got little further than naming his pioneer "Coonrod Dryfoos" before it became imperative to bring a Midwesterner—let him be a tough old farmer-speculator from Findlay, with a family bewildered by the change in their lives —to New York. Howells called the old man Jacob Dryfoos, and named his son Conrad ("Coonrod" to the family). Naive but no longer innocent, let these and like provincials from all sections and every variation of outlook be concentrated in New York.

How concentrate them meaningfully? Well, there is good old Basil March, of *Their Wedding Journey*. He has been living in Boston all these years, is middle-aged and full of literary frustrations. Why not give him a magazine like the one Howells would have left Boston in 1885 to edit if he'd found any takers and the Harpers' contract hadn't come along? A mild but sensitive and honorable man, a frustrated poet, Basil would do excellently as the sort of pivotal figure in a big novel which Henry James liked to call the "center of revelation." No, it's not going to be a sequel to *Their Wedding Journey*, Howells explained to his father in December, it just brings March to New York (actually he's an importantly different March) "in charge of a literary enterprise, and the fortunes of this periodical form the plot, such as there is. . . ."

Tender-minded Basil obviously needed (as the full development of the novel did) a buoyant, tough, audience-wise and experienced journalist to team up with. Howells knew lots of journalists and had enjoyed creating his own. There was a perfect model in Ralph Keeler, the long-mourned and unique playfellow of the *Atlantic* years. If old Dryfoos became the new-millionaire owner of the magazine and Fulkerson became Basil's teammate, someone was needed to oppose Dryfoos utterly. Someone foreign and inspired like a Tolstoian—or an Anarchist—yet someone more acceptable to the American audience because, for instance, he had roots in the native American radical traditions like Howells' father. "You askt me once if the old German revolutionist who dyed your watch yellow in Columbus, were not the origin of Lindau," Howells replied to his father when the characters of *A Hazard of New Fortunes* had become national celebrities in 1890. "Yes, he suggested him, but Limbeck and others helped materialize him.—I don't really know where Dryfoos came from, but I suppose I could think him back to somebody."

The last comment in that preceding sentence ought to serve as sufficient warning to anyone who would pin Howells' fiction, in

action or character—or that of any other author, for that matter—
to some simple, objective source. It all had to be created and re-
created repeatedly between his eyes and the tip of his pen. And it
all had to be seen in the mighty framework of New York which
Howells prowled and explored with his heart as well as senses. His
notebook records, among others, the sensations of going "Thro'
Christopher St. to Hoboken Ferry. . . . Foreign faces and tongues
everywhere. Filth . . . in heaps . . . ash barrels and kitchen of-
fal. . . . Manure heaps; such stinks. No bad faces. . . . The poor
have to stand all wrong finally." This was the atmosphere, not so
much the physical as the moral atmosphere in which his New York
novel was written. It was going well into the winter of 1889. Then,
as the story drove toward the special brand of tragedy to which
the necessities of realism must limit the realist, tragedy which was
real in an entirely other way struck down the man. Winifred
Howells died.

II

Born in 1863, the child of the Howellses' Venetian honeymoon,
Winifred had grown up in Cambridge. Charming and outgoing as
a little girl, she had been the playmate of her family's great friends.
When, like all the Howellses' children, she proved to be gifted, and
when the gifts of this first child seemed to be literary, family and
friends were delighted. The best in any child reared amid the
loving warmth, the playfulness, and yet the stimulation of activities
and visitors in that home, with the family travel to boot, would
have been drawn out. The abilities of the Howells children got free
play. And the response of Winifred's personality was that of the
well-loved gifted child. A serious ingenuousness, a single-minded
integrity of devotion to ideals and to the leadings of her mind
emerged which a loving father found awe-strikingly beautiful.

Before her malady, whatever it really was, first struck, apparently
in her seventeenth summer (1880), Winifred promised to become
a magnificent woman—and perhaps a significant writer. From that
time forward the story of her life was that of a long, descending
agony for herself and her parents. She had her plateaus, and she
had her rallies. Occasionally she was able to write again, though
the best of her poems may well have preceded her illness.

A MOOD

I

The wind exultant swept
Through the new leaves overhead
Till at once my pulses leapt
With a life I thought long dead,
And I woke as one who has slept
To my childhood—that had not fled.

II

On the wind my spirit flew;
Its freedom was mine as well;
For a moment the world was new;
What came there to break the spell?
The wind still freshly blew;
My spirit it was that fell.

III

Ah ! fancy so sweet and strange,
On whom shall I lay the blame
That a moment you made me change,
Then left me as when you came,
With my spirit's narrow range
And life before me the same?

To say nothing of their love for her, all this background of Winifred's sensitivity, integrity, and charm made it almost impossible for her mother and father to enforce the doctors' regimen on her while denying, on the doctors' insistence, that her suffering was anything but delusion. In November 1888 they simply broke down. Howells overruled his wife in deciding that the only hope of saving her life was to put her in the hands of the leading alienist of the country, Howells' old friend and correspondent, himself a novelist, Dr. S. Weir Mitchell of Philadelphia. Mitchell agreed that Winifred's case was psycho-neurotic; he proposed to disregard her delusions of pain and force-feed her from her shocking state of starvation back to the place where he could safely treat her for hysteria.

Howells, no doubt wondering despairingly about heredity, found himself using the old word of terror—hypochondria—when he wrote his family about "Winnie."

Gradually, though Mitchell found it a tough case, Winifred's weight began to rise. Through January into February she gained, and Mitchell sent her to a country rest home. There, on March 3, she suddenly died. The long battle ended in defeat. She died isolated from family love and care. But even that was not the worst. Mitchell apparently ran an autopsy and discovered that nothing could really have saved Winifred. That her disease was organic, not merely psychic, and that her pain had been all too physiologically real. With this he tried to comfort the Howellses. But of course what he did was to shatter the dikes and flood them with utter, desperate guilt for what they had done to their child.

It is essential to an understanding of Howells' life and work from this point forward to see that Winifred's death was altogether a turning point. Otherwise there would be no warranty for discussing the event so closely. Never again would the old, bubbling Howells sparkle among carefree, playful wits. The buoyant confidence with which he had been advancing intellectually would be sapped. The castle of his heart was breached—and from quarters which he could not defend. Nothing could have prevented his trying to do his duty by his daughter. Yet his reward was not merely the grief from which he might have recovered but the real and inevitable, though undeserved, guilt which time would overlay but not heal. Most disastrous of all, the blow crushed his wife.

Winifred's death came just the second day after the fifty-second anniversary of Howells' birth. He never liked to celebrate his birthday thereafter. To his father, the only one to whom he could tell it, he confessed how he felt "anguish, anguish that rends the heart and brain" over Winifred. And later, the hopeless reflection: "If I could live my life over, it would be to love more, to be gentler and kinder with all. Nothing else is worth while." His power to intellectualize the facts seemed paralyzed. The "law" of death he could accept, he told one friend, but not this specific case. "Whenever I think of her we have lost," he wrote Mitchell after a month, "I fall lame within, as it were, and do not know what to do or say."

For a time he lost the one main escape and consolation he might have had—and, more frighteningly of course, had his whole way of life and future threatened—because he could not write. It was a "most desperate experience," he told an interviewer five years later. "I thought I was never going to be able to get anything done. For weeks I made start after start, and tore up everything I wrote. I was in perfect despair about it." And of course what he was trying to get on with was *A Hazard of New Fortunes*. He knew perfectly well that the long home-hunting chapters at the beginning were out of proportion, he admitted to Higginson in 1891," . . . you are quite right in your criticism of the opening passages; long stretches of carpentry where I arrived at little or nothing of the real edifice. I may tell you that they were done when we were losing, when we lost, our Winny, and that I was writing in the stress because *I must*. Afterwards I could not change them. *Cosa fatta capo ha.*" *

Elinor Mead Howells was two months younger than her husband, and her own health had been precarious for more than a decade. Now, at fifty-two, her woman's nerves and constitution simply gave way under the total impact of Winifred's death. She was swept into an invalidism which lasted, with brief and minor releases, for the rest of her life. The fine-strung keenness of insight and inspiration which she had brought to their marriage as a joint enterprise in life and literature was, if not dulled, at least usually not available. She no longer had the energy to maintain it. Of course that left a gap in Howells' life which nothing could fill. It also affected his work directly.

A scathingly funny critic of sentimentality and pretense, Mrs. Howells must have been her husband's mentor in feminine psychology and made him the almost professional critic of women's quixotism. For years much of their joint life had been lived with the purpose of inspiring his imagination. Every literary idea had been discussed with her, every manuscript read to her, and every proof read by her. Howells reverenced her "wonderful electrically critical nerves," her "insight for truth of character and fidelity to nature." She "had 'absolute pitch' in matters of that sort . . . and loved me too well to spare me," he said. But now very much of that was withdrawn into suffering and despair which Howells could only feel as a second disaster on top of Winifred's tragedy. It would take Howells years to reap the full aftermath—for evil and, in a particular way, for good—of this fate's visitation.

---

* Broadly, "What is done is done."

III

Actually, Howells was much more apologetic to Higginson about the opening of *A Hazard of New Fortunes* than he need have been. He used about 200 pages before he really got into the main action of his novel. But the sharp economy which had brought *Annie Kilburn* nearly to its climax in the same space was not entirely fitted to this novel. He needed leisure in which to introduce a complex panel of characters and to weave the necessary web of their personal interconnections. More important still, he needed space to introduce New York. And the extended device of sending his old Bostonians—March and Mrs. March, he found he had to call them before their middle-aged personages would come alive for his imagination: "Basil" and "Isabel" just took him back to *Their Wedding Journey* —shuttling back and forth through the town and up and down through its social strata succeeded beautifully.

It was essential to the novel that Howells give life to his vision of New York. For the first time in his mature artistic life he had to create a world wholly new to himself and the audience of his faithful readers. It must be a world new regionally, geographically, visually. But it must also be a new social and ethical world, a monstrous but fascinating world of the new American conditions which Howells had set himself to explore. Swarming, immense, contradictory, beautiful in power and promise, hideous and fearful in its brutality and inhumanity—New York.

The Marches looked at palatial apartments, sordid little flats, and everything in between before they settled on Mrs. Grosvenor Green's place with its plethora of bric-a-brac—so pretentious Basil solemnly called it "James-crackery." They drifted through tenement areas and slums on their way from one listing to another. Shockingly, they saw, as Howells himself had done in 1887, a well-dressed man hunting down the filthy gutters for food. The man pounced on a bit of dirty biscuit in the street, crammed it into his mouth, and went on to scavenge in nearby garbage cans. When March (like Howells) spoke to him, the man turned out to be a foreigner, and when he was given a coin he burst into tears of incoherent gratitude and kissed the benefacting hand: New York—modern America.

At the same time, Howells took pains to present the marvelous spectacle of New York, with all its half-realized energy. He became a prophet crying aloud for the "Ash-can" painters of a decade thence. He had the esthetic and well-traveled Marches register "the superb spectacle" of the Elevated railroad, then steam powered, "which in a city full of painters nightly works its unrecorded miracles," and tried to paint the scenes himself:

'The track that found and lost itself a thousand times in the flare and tremor of the innumerable lights; the moony sheen of the electrics mixing with the reddish points and blots of gas far and near; the architectural shapes of houses and churches and towers, rescued by the obscurity from all that was ignoble in them, and the coming and going of the trains marking the stations with vivider or fainter plumes of flame-shot steam—formed an incomparable perspective.'

And they were perspectives with a meaning which the nature-scape and Society-obsessed painters of the time were missing. The Marches went to:

'the gallery that leads from the Elevated station to the waiting-rooms in the Central Depot and looked down upon the great night trains lying on the tracks dim under the rain of gaslights that starred without dispersing the vast darkness of the place. What forces, what fates, slept in these bulks which would soon be hurling themselves north and south and west through the night ! Now they waited there like fabled monsters of Arab story ready for the magician's touch, tractable, reckless, will-less—organized lifelessness full of a strange semblance of life.'

Painters and their art, like writers and theirs, figure largely in *A Hazard of New Fortunes*. But as the art of both is impotent to deal with these mysteries of science in tension with humanity, of man's heart helpless to master the creatures of his brain whether in technology or its social results, that art and its practitioners are null and futile.

As the spring of 1889 wore on, Howells gradually recovered his poise and found, beneath his sorrow, his wells of creativity running stronger than ever. Back in "a country house on the Belmont border of Cambridge," he found the story growing and ramifying under his hand far past his original design. It poured out of him with a speed which let him finish it during the summer. It came so fast, in sharp contrast with *Annie Kilburn,* that he wondered whether it would be any good. But as it turned out, he said in significant though veiled reminiscence, "It became, to my thinking, the most vital of my fictions, through my quickened interest in the life about me, at a moment of great psychological import."

The heart of *A Hazard of New Fortunes* is clearly a tragedy. A realistic tragedy—that is to say a realist's tragedy—it can neither be total, unitary, and immense like a romantic tragedy (say, *Moby Dick*) nor "elevated" in the classic sense because it deals with royal heroes who carry in themselves the fate and meaning of all mankind like Oedipus or Lear. For the realist, tragic events must be embedded in relatively nontragic events. That is the way his vision sees life. For him the tragic characters and their story must be contingent, particular, and yet common. The tragic story must connect intimately with other stories. In short, the tragedy may never seem absolute but always conditional. That is the reason why the tragedy in this novel is so massively framed in the multiple actions centering on the fate of the new magazine *Every Other Week*. That is why the controlling point of view of the novel is that of Basil March, a "center of revelation," a register and informant to the reader who is himself relatively disengaged from the tragedy.

Yet to be tragic, the events must be capable of interpretation. They must imply meanings of importance to every normal reader. Probably for every realist, and certainly for Howells, the possibility of tragic (or any other general) significance in his work proceeded from a fruitful ambiguity in that key realist's word, "common." The common life and common people, who seemed so stale, flat, and unprofitable to the feverish neoromantic, delighted the exploring eye of the realist: because they seemed to him so tangibly and comfortably near at hand and knowable; because he kept making fresh, surprising discoveries as he studied them; because nobody had ever quite dealt with this life in literature before. He loved the common because it was average and normal. But if it were so general, he soon perceived, then it was also extraordinarily meaningful. Who solved any riddle of the common, however incompletely, spoke to the heart of Everyman. The realist's problem was to represent his materials as particular in themselves, as his vision saw them, and yet capture behind that common particularity the blessed commonality which gave them, though paradoxically, general significance.

The tragic core of *A Hazard of New Fortunes,* then, is the story of the fall of Jacob Dryfoos of Moffitt, Indiana. The House of Dryfoos is by no means the House of Atreus, and yet its fall is tragic.

The difference in the Houses and what they signify measures the difference between realistic and classic tragedy we have been discussing. Dryfoos is Silas Lapham turned upside down. The rise to power Silas declined to his soul's salvation Jacob Dryfoos has embraced—and paid his soul for success. Old Scratch keeps his bargain with Dryfoos well. He rockets from million to million. There's no end to the luck; the money just pours in. But the devil's bargain is notoriously empty. Dryfoos' life shrivels. His mind occupies itself wholly with Wall Street speculation, respectable but socially vicious gambling. He becomes arrogant and self-absorbed. He is ripe for destruction.

The right way to see Dryfoos' fall, Howells felt, was in the total context of New York. The best way to create that context, given the possibilities of the creator's own knowledge, was to weave it out of revealing points of view. The basic medium of his art would be the pictures and the dialogue-packed scenes he had become so expert in presenting. But at the next upward level of meaning in his novels, the all-important points of view must inhere in characters. Each person must reveal something and see something. Insofar as possible, the lines of resulting revelation and understanding should lead back to Basil March as a center. But as there seemed to be too much for March to know or carry, additional knowledge could be given the reader by the narrator's voice, or, much better, through direct, dramatic action in scenes, or through a thoroughly interesting secondary center of revelation, the romantic, young artistic-Jack-of-all-trades, Angus Beaton.

The vehicle to carry all this was, of course, the magazine Howells had long dreamed of and now projected as *Every Other Week*. On the base of Ralph Keeler, he imagined a wonderfully breezy promoter, who should meet Basil March on a trip, get the idea of the magazine from him, and have the buoyant push to see it through to realization. Technically in the novel Fulkerson is almost purely a "business" creation. He exists to make connections, to keep the action flowing smoothly, to lubricate the flow of narrative illusions which join to constitute the primary fictional form of the work. Nothing bespeaks the mature power of Howells' imagination at this moment more than his sparkling success in quickening Fulkerson into life and gifting him with so lively and solid a personality, such accurately funny speech. If there is any mark of full artistic command more absolute than a writer's ability to advertise a character as humorous and then make him so, it can only be his breathing full, round life into a "business" character.

For Howells, New York was the focus of the new America. And around *Every Other Week*, Fulkerson gathered characters with most definite regional points of view. The Marches were Boston in Isabel and Midwest-Boston-plated in Basil; and the Leightons were rural New England. Jacob Dryfoos becomes Fulkerson's "angel" (another Howells vocabulary first?) in the hope that a job on so genteel a project will reconcile his son Conrad to business—and so what was then in general the West comes in. The Leightons take in Colonel Woodburn and his daughter, and there are both the New and the Old South. Whether art editor Angus Beaton's coming from Syracuse has much regional significance is not clear.

That Beaton comes from Syracuse (as symbol of the American provincial town) by way of the art-schools of Paris is obviously significant, however. Apparently, one of the exciting things to Howells about New York was its position as a center of the arts. Where he had known mostly literary and scholarly people around Boston, New York was full of painters, illustrators, etchers, sculptors, and their allies. There was no lack of artistic activity. But what did the arts and the new America have to say to one another? For the moment, it seemed, nothing. Anxious to discover the reasons why—and explore their meaning—Howells devoted much of his novel to a pioneering study of this long-vexed question.

With their sensitivity and power to create, artists ought to begin to grasp the human meaning of New York. What kept them back? Well, a good many, like Alma Leighton or young Kendricks, the would-be novelist, were honest but immature. All that could be hoped from them for the present was schoolwork and beginnings. Perhaps they never would be talented enough. Others, like Basil March, were mature and honest, and had at least talent enough to start. What they needed was precisely the education March got from the Dryfoos tragedy.

Still others, and one suspects that Howells feared most of the young talent fell in the class, were like Beaton. Out of the people, his father being a Scotch immigrant tombstone cutter in Syracuse from whom he still borrows money, Beaton is only contemptuous of the vulgarity of his origins. The romantic tradition of the artist has confirmed him in every variety of personal, social, financial, emotional, and professional irresponsibility. Handsome, highly intelligent, talented in half a dozen ways, he poses, plays, sulks, flatters, lies, and dreams his way through life. Only Fulkerson, who cannot be insulted and pays no attention to anything Beaton says or pretends, who can predict that Beaton will in the long run do good work if pushed regularly and will mind the main chance if given long enough to see it, can handle him. To Fulkerson he is "that seven-shooting self-cocking donkey of a Beaton," or, "the most inspired ass since Balaam's." Fulkerson can whip him into shape and use his talents profitably. But what can be expected from Beaton in the way of art which will speak to the condition of New York? His work, like his life or his studio, will be a muddle of tattered fantasies, false, irrelevant, and self-indulgent. Beyond that, he too will make a good "business" character for the novelist.

To Howells at that moment, however, the most interesting points of view were the sociological. They had hitherto found small room in the novel generally. He had made a start at handling them fictionally in *Annie Kilburn*. In the far richer context of this novel, he could do it much more dramatically. And the most colorful, the most violent character he would ever create could be used for that purpose. To complete the regional scrutiny of New York, that increasingly numerous, provincial inhabitant of a nongeographical region of America, the foreigner, had to be included. To fix the last, polar position of social criticism—and to discharge into art the tensions of the fight for the Anarchists—Howells could and did create an Anarchist, the tortured immigrant, poet, scholar, crippled veteran, idealist crazed with disillusion, Lindau.

Lindau's fanaticism Howells will not condone. The idealist's absolutism, his condemnatory judgment of all the rich and all America, the simplicism of his solution (always left implied in the discussions the author quotes for his readers), are rejected by the movement of the novel as well as through specific comment by the Marches. It is Lindau who is the immediate, precipitating agent of Conrad Dryfoos' death; and he dies too, victim also of his irrational philosophy of violence. Yet the force of Lindau's criticism of the state of civilization in his New York, his America, strikes powerfully on the mind of Basil March. As Annie Kilburn ended essentially converted by Mr. Peck, so Basil, like, significantly, his son Tom, finds that his experience of the Dryfoos tragedy has been an education of his thought as well as his sympathies. He ends a far more serious critic, speaking his own versions of Lindau, of American society than he began.

The two other socially theoretical points of view are at least as defective as Lindau's. It should be carefully noted that Howells, with the same powerful effect of negative capability in his moral realm as Hawthorne's in his, preached no answers, urged a diagnostic, not a therapeutic, theme in *A Hazard of New Fortunes*. The possessors of solutions are, in fact, treated with no little irony in this novel. Lindau's burning humanitarian passion leads him to a way of death; the irony is tragic. Colonel Woodburn and Lindau agree in much of their critique of modern society. But the Colonel rides an intellectual hobby horse. He condemns the commercialism, the cash-nexus immorality of the world. As a neo-Carlylean (and therefore proto-Fascist) critic, he has also found an apology for the Old South. The South which lost the War was wrong, he argues, but not because it stood for slavery. It was wrong because it had let the evil of commercialism corrupt the social blessing of slavery. The way of the just society, in which every man shall possess his human rights to peace, security, and well-being is through the restoration of an ideally pure system of slavery in which every laborer, white or black, shall have his place and only the nobly disinterested, self-sacrificial few shall be fit to be free, masters, and governors.

That Howells, deliberately playing on the general American conviction that the abolition of slavery at the end of the Civil War had purged the nation of all civic evil, meant irony through Colonel Woodburn is unmistakable. Repeatedly the Colonel acts out the part of the lovable old shell-back with an eccentric *idée fixe,* and other people unhesitatingly so characterize him in their commentary. The function of his sociology was to startle the reader with the quick, ironic shock of recognition: even under unthinkably evil slavery life might be better for the Bowery folk among whom Lindau sacrificially lived than it was under their conditions of mad life-in-death. Howells would no doubt have been astonished to see in how many forms Colonel Woodburn's ideas were to be taken seriously in the century toward which his New York's hazard of new fortunes was pointing.

A more hopeful, though still unsatisfactory, approach to a solution is that of Margaret Vance and Conrad Dryfoos. They were on the road toward Christian Socialism. It was not quite "the

Social Gospel"—Mr. Peck's way in *Annie Kilburn* was closer to that. It was the way of those High Church Episcopalians, usually regarded as Very Social, who were going down into the slums and giving themselves personally to achieve whatever they could for the poor. Margaret Vance, beautiful, highly cultivated and intelligent, revolts against the hypocritical emptiness of the social position to which she was born. She follows the Anglican priests into the slums. She even helps a group of sweated seamstresses to plan and wage a strike. She finds much more meaning and reality in the slum missions than she can in the "high" society activities which form the other half of her double life.

Through Beaton, Margaret Vance learns of the Dryfoos family and their inability to make any social contact in New York in spite of their millions. Out of a charity like that which sends her to the poor, she calls on them and has them invited to a musical *soirée*. But of course this ends in nothing—except that she discovers that the blond, spiritual-looking young man she has sometimes seen in the missions is Conrad Dryfoos. And, given a chance to know her, saintly Conrad falls all worshipfully and purely in love with her. Conrad's one desire in life has been to become a minister. His father had been determined to make a predatory replica of himself out of Conrad and has succeeded only in thwarting the son and frustrating both Conrad and himself. Conrad has been able to be himself only in his after-hours mission work, but there his spirit has grown.

Howells had long been intrigued by Anglo-Catholicism. From the time of *The Lady of the Aroostook* forward it had fascinated him that thoroughly civilized people could turn away from his own agnostic Church of Doubt toward anything so utterly opposite. Even so recently as *April Hopes,* however, he had drawn that faith as neurotically romantic. In their phase of social concern, on the other hand, church people were more attractive. Howells would himself soon symbolize his sympathy with them at that point by lending his name to the informal Church of the Carpenter inconclusively formed by the Christian Socialist and Episcopal clergyman W. D. P. Bliss in Boston.

This approach fulfilled Mr. Peck's Tolstoian requirement: the rich must give of themselves even more than their money to the poor. And yet there was too much lacking. Margaret Vance and Conrad in the slums were alleviating symptoms, not curing causes.

They were shoveling out darkness, not introducing light. Where Lindau and Woodburn had too much—and too wrong-headed—theory, these Christians had perhaps too little. They had no program for connecting their gospel and the need of New York. They might achieve personal salvation by throwing themselves away, by one form of martyrdom or another: but what had they to say to the nonmartyrs?

The tragedy of the House of Dryfoos proceeded, of course, in stages. It began when natural gas was discovered in great quantities beneath the soil in the area of Moffitt, Indiana, and Jacob Dryfoos' ambitious daughters prevailed on him to sell his farm at a huge profit. Shorn of his occupation, Jacob was at first brokenhearted. Then he plunged into business; the luck poured in on him; he gave his heart to speculation and moved to New York, the national center of the Game. The second victim of this process was Mrs. Dryfoos. Uprooted, lonely, deprived of work and meaning in her round of life, she began to disintegrate mentally, to live in the past, to yearn for the home scenes and associations, the fields and barns, the house, the graves of her children. She could not believe in her heart that they were gone forever, swallowed up by the gasfield, that she could never go home again. New York was her doom of exile.

Quickly, the children also became casualties. Conrad's ministerial "call" was blocked. The daughters, innocent of the world and personal cultivation alike, were delivered over to the ravages of their ignorance and their pride. Christine, the dark, fiery one, became an arrogant, smoldering black panther, ready to lash out with her claws to punish the world for not caring. Mela, the dumb blonde, slopped and giggled her way along, amiably disappointed in New York but unable to know how little she really existed. Jacob Dryfoos took his daily narcotic of luck on Wall Street and worried as little as he could about anything else.

Yet his family was the only possible justification for all the money, and he had to worry particularly about Conrad. Conrad worked efficiently and submissively enough in *Every Other Week*'s business office. But he wouldn't *be* a businessman. The current of his real life ran unimaginably away from his father, his father's money, and his father's proud dog-eat-dog values. The boy took after his mother's simple Dunkard people. It infuriated Jacob. He found a radical, an agitator, this Lindau, working for his magazine and got him run out. But it was irritating that these two-bit literary people like March and with him Conrad seemed sympathetic to Lindau. Jacob had to apologize for ordering March to fire Lindau. Who did these people think they were?

And then suddenly the whole atmosphere of life in New York (and of course the atmosphere and movement of Howells' novel) darkened and tightened. There was a big Traction strike. Transportation all over town was snarled. The newspapers were full of the private war between labor and capital. The streets swarmed with strikers, strikebreakers and their protecting police, and curious, expectant onlookers. As the pressure mounted and the forces of legal government intervened more and more against the strikers, the whole city began to reflect the tension. Antilabor sentiment prepared bitterly for repression. Prolabor sentiment prepared desparingly for defeat—or for the last, hopeless violence.

In this atmosphere Jacob Dryfoos visits Conrad in his office. All the personal frustration and social bitterness seething in the wickedly proud old man expresses itself in cross-examination of Conrad. At length the son is forced to say that, while he thinks strikes wrong on principle (a consistent Howells position) and knows the men will lose, " 'I shall feel sorry they didn't succeed, for I believe they have a righteous cause, though they go the wrong way to help themselves.'

"His father came close to him, his eyes blazing, his teeth set. 'Do you *dare* to say that to me?'

" 'Yes, I can't help it. I pity them; my whole heart is with those poor men.'

" 'You impudent puppy !' shouted the old man. He lifted his hand and struck his son in the face. Conrad caught his hand with his own left, and, while the blood began to trickle from a wound that Christine's intaglio ring had made in his temple, he looked at him with a kind of grieving wonder, and said, 'Father !' "

Dryfoos plunges out of the office, leaving Conrad to wonder and consider. Conrad drifts out into the street and, wandering through the tense traffic, is picked up by Margaret Vance, also wandering in her carriage and grieving for the strikers and her fear of what the police would do. If only a peacemaker could be found, she mourns. Conrad is transported. He will be the peacemaker, and he jumps out, looking for trouble to pacify. Coming down the street-car tracks, he finds, as he was almost sure to find that day, a horsecar driven by a scab surrounded by a mob of stone-throwing strikers.

The mob swarms on the car. A squad of policemen begins to club the mob. An old man, it is Lindau, screams provocative taunts at the policemen. One lifts his club to strike Lindau down. Conrad offers to intervene and is shot dead by a policeman from inside the horsecar.

In the aftermath Jacob Dryfoos learns the measure of his own emptiness and his money's futility. His family moves off to the garish sterility of the American millionaire's progress through Europe. Margaret Vance takes the veil of an Anglican sisterhood. Fulkerson and March are allowed to buy out *Every Other Week*, and Fulkerson can marry Colonel Woodburn's daughter. Basil March is left to talk out with his wife the meaning of his New York education.

That education had its major, negative aspect in an expansion of *Annie Kilburn's* analysis of the state of the American Dream. Its much more limited positive aspect dated from Sewell's sermon, *The Minister's Charge* doctrine of "complicity." To take the positive first, Basil March as a mature student of the life of New York cannot escape becoming seriously concerned with it. He "could not release himself from a sense of complicity with it, no matter what whimsical, or alien, or critical attitude he took. A sense of the striving and the suffering deeply possessed him; and this grew the more intense as he gained some knowledge of the forces at work—forces of pity, of destruction, of perdition, of salvation."

One opposite of complicity is forgetting. And one of the most forcefully presented themes of *A Hazard of New Fortunes* is that of not forgetting, especially, the tragic realms where we all intimately share our humanity in our common fate. Mrs. March is early appalled by the clangor, the mad, screeching gaiety of New York and its noises. The mechanical marvel of the El ignores and shoulders aside the importunate life around it. But it will not do: "They forget death," Mrs. March shudders to Basil. Lindau lives painfully in the heart of the Bowery. "You must see it all the dtime —see it, hear it, smell it, dtaste it—or you forget it," he tells March. "That is what I gome here for. I was begoming a ploated aristograt. I thought I was nodt like these beople down here, when I gome down once to look around; I thought I must be somethings else, and zo I zaid I better take myself in time, and I gome here among my brothers—the beccars and the thiefs !" March looks at New York. The poor forget in their wild gayety. The middle classes forget in their dullness, the rich in their arrogance. But the first essential, the seed and root of hope, is not to forget but to remember our complicity.

A Hazard of New Fortunes' investigation of the state of the American Dream is conducted by Basil March in the center with Lindau and Jacob Dryfoos as the polar opposites. March begins relatively unimpressed by either. Fulkerson is sure that the rise of Dryfoos is a proof of the superiority of American institutions, but that fact troubles March. Dryfoos "must have undergone a moral deterioration, an atrophy of the generous instincts," March tells his wife. "He has sharpened, but he has narrowed; his sagacity has turned into suspicion, his caution to meanness, his courage to ferocity . . . and I am not very proud when I realize that such a man and his experience are the ideal and ambition of most Americans." Therefore the nation has been delivered into the hands of "the plutocracy that now owns the country."

On the other hand, Lindau seems too absolute, too violent. It troubles Mrs. March to have her children hear him. She has nurtured them "in the faith of Bunker Hill and Appomattox, as the beginning and the end of all possible progress in human rights." It upsets her "to hear American democracy denounced as a shuffling evasion," to hear the United States Senate "railed at as a rich man's club . . . to be told that the rich and poor were not equal before the law in a country where justice must be paid for at every step in fees and costs . . . that there was not equality of opportunity in America, and that fully one-half the people were debarred their right to the pursuit of happiness by the hopeless conditions of their lives. . . ."

Lindau has passed the point of entire disillusion. "What iss Amerigan?" he cries. "Dere iss no Ameriga any more !" He has renounced the war pension for his hand lost in battle "begause I would sgorn to dake money from a gofernment that I ton't peliefe in any more. . . . I would *sdarfe* before I dake a bension now from a republic dat iss bought oap by monobolies, and ron by drusts and gombines, and railroads andt oil gompanies."

Unconvinced but troubled in his conscience by Lindau, March is forced to take a conscientious stand when Lindau's opinions are overheard by Dryfoos and the "angel" decrees that Lindau must be

fired from *Every Other Week*. Dryfoos can fire him, too, he tells
Fulkerson, but he will not permit Lindau to be punished for his
opinions. Like Howells with the Chicago Anarchists, March finds
this experience somewhat inconclusive as to heroism. Dryfoos will
apologize through Fulkerson for being peremptory with March, but
he insists that *Every Other Week* shall hire Lindau no more. To
Fulkerson's astonishment, March feels he must stick by the principle: no punishment of Lindau for opinion's sake. The issue is
practically but less than heroically settled when it turns out that
Lindau will not work for the likes of Dryfoos. They can't fire him;
he resigns.

But, like Howells, March gets a sobering education from Lindau
and from the Dryfoos tragedy. The present condition of American
life will not do, he concludes. "Some one always has you by the
throat, unless you have someone in *your* grip. I wonder if that's
the attitude the Almighty intended His respectable creatures to take
toward one another ! I wonder if He meant our civilization, the
battle we fight in, the game we trick in !" It's all too sordid, too
inhuman: ". . . and so we go on," March muses, "pushing and pulling, climbing and crawling, thrusting aside and trampling under-
foot; lying, cheating, and stealing; and when we get to the end,
covered with blood and dirt and sin and shame, and look back over
the way we've come to a palace of our own, or the poorhouse, which
is about the only possession we can claim in common with our
brother-man, I don't think the prospect can be pleasing."

There are mysteries, not just agnostic ignorances, recognized by
the realist for almost the first time in this the first of his tragedies.
They are the mysteries of death and of suffering. Lindau died,
young Tom March points out, in "a bad cause"—appealing to violence when the democratic process offers the ballot as the redress
for wrong. Yes, March answers, "men like Lindau, who renounce
the American means as hopeless and let their love of justice hurry
them into sympathy with violence—yes, they are wrong. . . ." And
Jacob Dryfoos has earned his tragic suffering. Nothing he can ever
do can really make amends. " 'Children,' said March, turning to
them, 'death is an exile that no remorse and no love can reach. Remember that, and be good to every one here on earth, for your
longing to retrieve any harshness or unkindness to the dead will
be the very ecstasy of anguish to you. I wonder. . . . Perhaps, if

we ever come to obey the law of love on earth, the mystery of death will be taken away.' "

But how about poor, saintly Conrad? Why should he suffer and die? What business did he have getting mixed into the tragic folly of the strike? But ". . . Conrad—yes, he had some business there: it was his business to suffer there for the sins of others," March answers. "Isabel, we can't throw aside that old doctrine of the Atonement yet. The life of Christ, it wasn't only in healing the sick and going about to do good; it was suffering for the sins of others. That's as great a mystery as the mystery of death. Why should there be such a principle in the world? But it's been felt, and more or less dumbly, blindly recognized ever since Calvary. If we love mankind, pity them, then we *wish* to suffer for them."

In the face of tragedy—his own personal and his imagination's created tragedy, both—Howells came face to face with mysteries the real relevance of which he would not long before have been disposed to deny. Perhaps he never again came so close to Christianity as in those weeks in Belmont when he finished *A Hazard of New Fortunes*. Certainly he dived deeper into the recesses of his own creative powers than he had ever gone before.

IV

With his own "ecstasy of anguish" hot upon him and Mrs. Howells crushed into invalidism beside him, Howells found that even on the wide canvas of *A Hazard of New Fortunes* he had not exhausted what he had to say about tragedy. Suffering with Winifred and seeing the best medical knowledge of the moment baffled to help her had stirred up all the lees of his own psychic life. Was reality, then, so exclusively a matter of outward facts, of social and economic conditions? Did the good life consist so simply in a clear-eyed understanding, modified by good will, of what the world outwardly was in itself? Or did Winifred's experience—and even more the dreadful intensity of her parents' reaction to it—show that the ancient lore of humanity concerning the shadowy, elusive life within the depths of the heart and soul contained wisdom not dreamt of in the realist's philosophy?

Creative impulse still welling up like a fountain, Howells must have found himself even in the latter stages of *A Hazard* contemplating a psychological tragedy. Basil March, newly sensitive and responsive to life, was in the foreground of Howells' consideration. Let this tale be Basil's, entirely controlled through Basil's eyes, told, in fact, as Howells had never permitted a story to be told before, by Basil as a first-person narrator. Howells must have started almost as soon as he mailed the last of *A Hazard* off to Alden, for Alden was praising the "more dramatic intention" revealed in the first part by October. And apparently the writing swung smoothly along. Howells was at work on still another book, *A Boy's Town*, in December.

For all the swiftness of this creative flow, Howells wrote an extraordinarily balanced and structured little book in *The Shadow of a Dream*. There are three parts, each a unity organized around one main character seen through March's eyes, and each short enough to be published as one unit of a three-part serial in *Harper's*. Each part consists of eight chapters, each of these a scene played in the frame either of a picture, a setting, or of Basil March's reflections. The parts are of roughly equal length, though chapters vary considerably, and the whole volume contains only about 40,000 words. There is even something like unity of place. In the character of March, Howells could hark back to Columbus, named vaguely by March only as "my city" in the West. After an introductory chapter from March's youth there, the rest of the action in Part One takes place at the Little Nahant "cottage" where Winifred's last tortured summer was spent. Part Two opens in March's club at Boston, but the rest is set in the Marches' home. Part Three occurs in the Western city, and most of it in one house. Obviously, Howells' every creative instinct was to concentrate and intensify this story into one probing focus. Thus it could hardly have been more opposite in effect to *A Hazard of New Fortunes*. The author who wrote the second for all practical purposes continuously after the first obviously had a complete stock of technical resources as a novelist completely at the command of his creative requirements.

The fable of *The Shadow of a Dream* is also very simple. In vacation time Basil March meets his friend Dr. Wingate on a train, and Wingate tells him that a new patient says he is an old friend of March's and would like to see him. The old friend turns out to be Douglas Faulkner—an old-fashioned Western romantic who has made a lot of money but is slowly dying of a hopeless disease under

Wingate's care. The Marches compassionately go to visit Faulkner at his summer place (the run-down Little Nahant estate) and find him living in the American *ménage à trois*—the innocent (?) three-cornered household—with his stunningly beautiful wife Hermia and his brilliantly handsome lifelong friend, James Nevil, an Episcopal clergyman. Part One belongs to Faulkner. He confesses to March that he is haunted by a horrible, obsessively recurrent dream. It is obvious to March that this dream is at least one of the things killing him and that it makes Faulkner hate his wife. That afternoon Faulkner has an "attack." He seems to come out of it: '. . . Faulkner opened his eyes. He remained looking a moment, as if he did not see us. Then his gaze seemed to grow and centre upon Nevil. He flung his wife's hand away, and started suddenly to his feet and made a pace toward us.

She rose, too, and "Ah, Douglas !" she cried out.

He put his hand on her breast and pushed her away with a look of fierce rejection.'

Then he dropped dead, and Part One ended.

Part Two belongs to Hermia. In it the Marches, of course intrigued beyond measure by what they have seen, gather information and try to talk it out together, to penetrate to its meaning. From Wingate they learn that, in his opinion, Faulkner's dream (the Marches guess it was a dream that Nevil and Hermia were in love) was a sheer delusion more or less mechanically caused by Faulkner's organic disease. Wingate tells that Hermia has decided not to be told the dream, because it might make her hate Faulkner's memory. He thinks her courage magnificent: she is "superhuman . . . superwoman." But Mrs. March, who has become her good friend and correspondent, says, ominously, "that is the first thing I've ever heard of Mrs. Faulkner that I didn't like." That's the act of "the kind of woman that overtasks her strength, and breaks down with what she's undertaken, and makes us all ridiculous, and discourages us from trying to bear what we really could bear."

Through Hermia's letters the Marches learn that Nevil has left his church and gone to a mission in Kansas, that he has at last fallen in love and is engaged. Then that that engagement has been capriciously broken by the girl or her family; Nevil is shattered; he has come back to live with Hermia and Faulkner's aged mother, to whom he has long been another son. Time, at least two years, is expertly telescoped here. Nevil recovers, goes to Europe, comes back. Then comes the news that Nevil and Hermia are engaged, and right on the heels of the letter comes Hermia. Now the folly of superwomanism is exposed. Now she *must* know the content of Faulkner's dream. And when Wingate tells her, she is, regardless of anything he can say, crushed. Basil must escort her, sleepless and refusing food in a trance of introspective pain, back home. There they must face Part Three—which is Nevil's.

March delivers Hermia and stays over a day to see old friends. He refuses old Mrs. Faulkner's request that he bear the news to Nevil, and in the conversation we learn the specific content of Faulkner's relentless dream:

'He dreamed that she [Hermia] and James were—attached, and were waiting for him to die, so that they could get married. Then he would see them getting married in church, and at the same time it would be his funeral, and he would try to scream out that he was not dead; but Hermia would smile, and say to the people that she had known James before she knew Douglas; and then *both* ceremonies would go on, and he would wake.'

The church, of course, was Nevil's own—the implication being that Nevil was, in the dream, conducting both services.

As March is leaving the house that night on his way to the station, he witnesses from the top of the stairs what is probably the most emotional scene Howells ever wrote. As we learn later, this is the last of a series of alternating scenes of defiance and renunciation which have been going on for hours between Nevil and Hermia in Faulkner's old study:

'. . . I heard a door close in the corridor, which led to Faulkner's den. Steps uneven and irregular advanced toward the square hall at the foot of the stairs, and in a moment I saw a man stagger into the light, and stay himself by a clutch at the newel post. He looked round as if dazed. . . . I have no belief he saw me; but at any rate, Nevil turned at the cry of "James! James!" which came in Hermia's voice from the corridor, and caught her in his arms as she flew upon him. She locked her arms around his neck, and wildly kissed him again and again, with sobs such as break from the ruin of life and love; with gasps like dying, and with a fond, passionate moaning broken by the sound of those fierce, swift kisses. . . . I perceived that this was the end . . . and that he had decided against this love. It maddened me against him. . . . But I was sensible, through my compassion and indignation, that whatever he had done, she was admiring, adoring him for it.

I saw that in a flash of her upturned face, as I stood, with my heart in my mouth, before the tragedy of their renunciation. The play suddenly ended. With one last, long kiss she pushed him from her, and fled back into the corridor.'

March spent the next hours trying, successfully he thought, to convince Nevil that he ought to defy Faulkner's dream "in the interest of human enlightenment, from the duty every educated man has to resist the powers of darkness that work on our nerves through the superstitions of the childhood of the world." By the time he had talked Nevil into what seemed agreement, it was train time. Nevil followed him aboard, talking gratefully, and then stepped off as the train moved and began to gather speed:

'Clinging to my hand, he pressed it hard, and stepped back from the car to the ground. I saw him look up at me and then he gave a wild cry, and I could feel the car grinding him up against the stone jamb of the archway through which the train was passing. There was a hideous crashing sound from his body, and I jumped at the bell rope. . . . When the train slowly backed and set him free, he dropped forward a crushed and lifeless lump.'

Howells himself had once missed the same death by inches.

The tragedy of the book was not, of course, Nevil's accident or even Hermia's subsequent death, "as we say, of a broken heart." Those were devices for snapping the action off, for preserving the economy of the book, and, most of all, for centering attention not on the lovers and their fable of fate but on the problem of the book. Clearly three lives have been destroyed, so tragically destroyed psychologically and spiritually that the physical deaths are relatively insignificant. We are back again at the mysteries. The mystery of suffering is there, but now there are new mysteries. Are there dark truths which come from a wild, unconscious side of the mind? Or is this all nonsense? The real problem of the book is expressed in a running debate among the characters which can be established in one question. Is there any reality, any weight, any substance to the shadow of a dream, or is the world of dream only agonizing delusion which the civilized mind ought to ignore and deny?

As one would expect, *The Shadow of a Dream* is most Hawthornian. Unlike *A Hazard of New Fortunes*, the title of which comes from the rich tapestry of a Shakespeare history play, *The*

Shadow of a Dream comes most fittingly from Keats's *Endymion*. Keats's hero has been dreaming of spiritual love, "that which becks/ Our ready minds to fellowship divine,/ A fellowship with essence; till we shine,/ Full alchemize'd and free of space." This, the highest imaginable reach of man's spirit, will raise him above self and fame to immortality. Nothing less will do:

> . . . No, no, I'm sure,
> My restless spirit never could endure
> To brood so long upon one luxury,
> Unless it did, though fearfully, espy
> A hope beyond the shadow of a dream.

This was the grand romantic, the transcendental affirmation of the supremacy, the secure and lovely supremacy of unconscious— superconscious—mind. Hawthorne, checked by temperamental skepticism and the vision of evil, had his cogent doubts. Howells, the agnostic realist, would long have carried Hawthorne's doubts over into antiromantic conclusions: there was no evidence to prove that the transcendent mind existed. But now, also afflicted by a tragic vision, he was finding it necessary to ask whether there might not be sinister subconscious realities in the mind of which his philosophy had taken no account.

Like Hawthorne he found it useful to convey essential parts of his meaning through symbols and the manipulation of atmospheres. The symbols—the sadly rotting old garden at Little Nahant as the symbol for Faulkner's wasting mind, the tide as death, Nevil's study as a black Protestant confessional where evil must overcome good— Howells had often shown his power to employ. The atmospheres, so Hawthornian, a realist had perhaps necessarily been chary of using. But now they came effectively to hand. Faulkner, host of the dream and caster of the shadow, is dark. Night and moonlight are his atmospheres, and his light, when he has it, is thin, misty, and tenuous. Nevil, on whom the shadow falls, glows with life and color. His hair is golden, his eyes shine, his complexion is almost "peachy" like a girl's. Where Faulkner has faded and dimmed through the years, Nevil has "gathered brilliancy." But on his brightness falls the shadow.

When Faulkner and March first begin to debate whether the shadow of a dream may be substantial or not, they, like Howells, have only pre-Freudian words and concepts to employ. Yet Faulkner, the amateur romantic, has a fairly ordinarily post-Freudian proposition to put. He says to March, the narrator,

'"There's a whole region of experience—half the map of our life—that they tell us must always remain a wilderness, with all its extraordinary phenomena irredeemably savage and senseless. For my part, I don't believe it. I will put the wisdom of the ancients before the science of the moderns, and I will say with Elihu, 'In a dream, in a vision of the night, when deep sleep falleth upon men, in slumberings upon the bed; then He openeth the ears of men, and sealeth their instruction.' "

"It's noble poetry," I said.

"It's more than that," said Faulkner, "It's truth."'

March's eventual reply, framed in agnostic amiability, sets the other side of the debate to run through the book. Let's not, he urges, "return to the bondage of the superstitions that cursed the childhood of the race . . . , there may be something in dreams; if there is, our thoughts, not our fears, will find it out. I am a coward, like everybody else. . . . But if I had a dream that contained a forecast or a warning of evil, I should feel it my duty in the interest of civilization to defy it. . . ." Dr. Wingate, representing science and civilization, goes further than March. Dreams, he says, are only the products of organic conditions. The mind is, by implication, simply a reflexive organism. But you can't get Faulkner, or the women of the book, to accept this. And even March has his doubts. Wingate cannot cure Faulkner or reassure Hermia—as the doctors of the country had failed with Winifred.

Back and forth the question is debated until, at last, the Marches, chorus-like, get the last word. Nevil and Hermia, they decide, could never have emerged from under the shadow: "We saw that it was impossible Faulkner's dream should not always have had power upon them; and the time came when we could regard their death without regret." "Real" and true in itself or not, the dream exerted, through the weight of its shadow, all too real a psychological effect on its victims. Good Victorians, the Marches "always denied, in the interest of common-sense and common justice, any controlling effect to the dream itself, except through their own morbid conscientiousness, their exaggerated sensibility." And they are sure that "the hapless pair" were "wholly guiltless of the evil imported to them." Civilization wins out.

That is what March agrees to with his wife, in response to her necessities. But March has one last disturbing thought of his own which he reserves for the last paragraph of the book:

'Of course there is always the human possibility that the dream was a divination of facts; that Hermia and Nevil were really in love while Faulkner lived, and were untrue to him in their hearts, which are the fountains of potential good and evil. . . .'

Either way we take it—or if we take it both ways as the author's Hawthornian procedures perhaps invite us to do—we come face to face with tragedy. And much of March's reflection is given to the problem of the meaning of tragic destruction and the loss of human good and goodness. The power of the shadow of Faulkner's dream was uncanny. "Something impersonally sinister was in it all, and the group involved was severally as blameless as the victims of fate in a Greek trilogy," says March. "Neither I nor any other witness of the fact considered for a moment that Faulkner had cause for the dark suspicion. . . ."

If there was fault, Mrs. March argues, it was Faulkner's for maneuvering Nevil and Hermia into the *ménage à trois*. Hermia is left "like some innocent thing caught in a trap; and she can't escape and no one can set her free. I shall begin to believe that there is such a thing as Fate, in that old Greek sense; something that punishes you for your sorrows and for the errors of others." March prefers to believe, with Nevil, that there is, however veiled from man's understanding, a real providential purpose in human suffering. As before, he comes to see one graspable solution in human complicity—we realize our connectedness with the rest of mankind in suffering and death if nowhere else. But now March is supplied with a word new to Howells which marks a step forward in philosophy. Man's this-worldly answer to the mystery of suffering and loss is "the mystery of our human solidarity." In both we are not merely interconnected, we are one throughout the world. "Poor mortality !" March sighs, "Between the two worlds, how its difficulties are multiplied." But the living must live, if not for themselves, for the other living. One world at a time; "the dead must not master us through an immortal grief."

In July 1891 the lead item in the "Editor's Study" was an enthusiastic and perceptive review of William James's *Principles of Psychology* in which Howells commented that psychology seemed a vast, obscure field "not yet explored or mapped except at a few points." After two generations since of exploring and some mapping, it still largely remains true as he said then that "the talk is not only about, but round about the human mind, which it penetrates here and there and wins a glimpse of unsayable things." His pre-depth-psychology problem of lack of vocabulary has been mainly helped in our post-depth-psychology era by the possibility of faith in certain intellectual structures and their terminology. So that we can say, if we wish, that Howells' intimations through Basil March that more lay in the shadow of Faulkner's dream than the Victorian eye would see was quite correct.

Freud found that the artists, especially the writers, could help him clarify his insights because they had often preceded him in them. Howells is by no means one of the major examples of this. Yet a careful study of his writings for that sort of content would be revealing. Physical details of sexual practice are, of course, almost completely absent from Howells' work. But that does not mean that he wholly failed to understand sexuality or to use it effectively in his work. His understandings were not, could not have been ours. And there were restrictions on his expression which no longer affect many writers. We may assume, perhaps, as a necessity of faith, that our knowledge and practices reflect final truth. Many men equally time-bound have made fools of themselves that way in the past, however. And perhaps there may turn out to be value in taking Howells and his work on its own terms in this realm.

Take Faulkner and his "very romantic," lifelong friendship for golden Nevil, have Nevil introduce goddess-lovely Hermia to Faulkner with Faulkner's resultant love at first sight, let Faulkner use his illness as a lever to force Nevil into the *ménage à trois* and then give him his agonizing dream. The readings back and forth and round the triangle in every direction a Freudian method would yield are obvious. They could not have been read in those terms by Howells—to whom the terms were unknown. And yet it is clear from his text that he *saw* all the possibilities a Freudian could name. He wrote, in other words, a tragedy with profound psychosexual and moral implications. And since there has been a great deal of misunderstanding—and no little downright nonsense, usually based on some sort of fantastic extrapolation—about Howells' attitudes toward sex and sex in literature, this may be the best context in which to examine the main facts.

The question of Howells and sex has already been considerably clarified by Mr. Everett Carter, but there may be a few points worth adding to his analysis. The dominant official position in Howells' time held, of course, that sexuality ought to be suppressed. There were three general sources for this attitude. A long-standing tradition of the Christian churches urged that men and women should subdue the lusts of the flesh in the interests of spirituality. The nineteenth-century romantic-chivalric ideal supposed women to be the vessels of a unique, fragile spirituality which had to be guarded from degradation by brute male lust—guarded if necessary by a double standard which kept prostitution flourishing on the theory that naturally brutal or morally weak women were well sacrificed for the benefits conferred upon the race by the pure and *spirituelle*. The third source was the one which had most appeal for Howells. It was the "soft" Darwinian conviction that Man had climbed from bestiality to civilization by rising above the strong natural lusts—for battle and prey-making as well as sensual indulgence—which had armed him for victory over nature. The next ascent, *vide* John Fiske, was to be of new spiritual heights. The old lusts were atavisms; they must be checked if not eradicated or man sinned against progress, and the Beast-man came again.

All three convictions admitted that copulation was necessary to the procreation of the race, but they would have limited it severely to that purpose. But one trouble with all was that they proved immediately and totally unable to suppress sex. Prostitution flourished. In 1882 Howells visited the Harlot's Market in London to watch it open, and calmly noted the gaiety of the girls arriving "as if going to a ball." The Marches leave a *soirée* in *A Hazard of New Fortunes* commenting on the exquisite perfection of Margaret Vance as the flower of civilization—and immediately see and hear a policeman chase a prostitute screaming down an alley. Equally dismaying, sexuality kept popping up to dominate the life of the imagination of the time. The popular literature, especially, was obsessed with courtship, engagement, and marriage, with abduction, seduction, adultery, and rape, with (perhaps most damning of all) every possible variation of the technically innocent and well-clad "compromising situation." In disguises which even the dullest sincere observer could never fail to penetrate, the age just couldn't let sexuality alone. And because the split between conviction and practice was so painful in so many directions, the convention was to pretend that the problem did not really exist. To pretend that nothing was disguised or, if it was, the disguises were perfect. Opponents who would tear away the disguise were hateful.

And of course such opponents arose, even out of the times which had spawned the chivalric ideal. The Utopian communalists and Perfectionists of the romantic era were much concerned with sex. Some of them developed principles and practices of "free love," and almost all were accused of it. In the house in which Howells was reared, they seem to have developed a healthy compromise out of the ideas of Swedenborg, from whom the household religion was taken. Much attracted by Utopians, William Cooper Howells appears to have held fast to a good citizen's interpretation of Swedenborg's *Conjugial Love*. True love, which seeks the joy and fulfillment of the loved one without fear for its own gratification, is the type and figure of the heavenly love which saves. It is, in fact, the nearest human road to that salvation. It must be profound and enduring—monogamous.

Howells may well have had the Swedenborgian ideal in view when he chose the title of *The Shadow of a Dream* from Keats's meditation on heavenly love. He reinforces one's suspicion that he did by letting Faulkner's mother cite Swedenborg to Basil March as she tries to guess the import of Nevil and Hermia's tragic dilemma. Howells is careful, however, not to wander past hinting into the wilderness of Swedenborg. It was too esoteric for any imaginable public.

For Swedenborg, on the other hand, promiscuous sexuality, self-seeking sensuality, were types of, and very direct doors to, the stinking smog of Hell as he imagined it. Howells' vision of women was extraordinarily clear. And he sympathized cordially with their femininity, neither fearing nor hating it, as his dozens of effective literary portraits prove. His own marriage worked out beautifully. In both instances that was because he was prepared to live normally and cordially with sexual human nature, his own included. But Swedenborgian images of unbearable disgust blackened Howells' view and choked off his expression at any image of illicit, promiscuous, or violent sexuality. He was not immune to the humor of bawdry, and yet it bothered him.

When Edmund Gosse sent him the "scabrous treasure" of a "report on the night-side of Hong-Kong, full of details," evidently thinking Howells might like to use it as a realist's literary document or at the least would enjoy it, Howells burned it. He had to endure the just mockery of Mark Twain and the indignant protests of his Civil Service Reform friends and allies, but he could not support Grover Cleveland for the Presidency. Not with "that harlot and her bastard in the background !" In these negative attitudes, though not in his positive ones, Howells agreed with the overwhelmingly dominant conventions of his age.

The result was an interesting kind of compromise. As realist both in art and thought, he had no least use for the Rider Haggard school of sexuality inverted into sadistic superhumanism. Nor could he care for the chivalric illusionists. Much of his work, both critical and creative, he devoted to a skillful reduction of chivalric passions. "It is not to be supposed that primitive man altogether idolized primitive woman," the Editor observed in the November 1890 Study, "or if he did he made his divinity pay for any failure to come up to his expectations, as primitive man does yet." Just so, in March 1887, he paid off the author of *The Idylls of the King,* once the poetic ideal of Howells' youth, for the asperities of "Locksley Hall Sixty Years After." If the hero of Tennyson's poem, "were living in the possible future of this hopeful evolutionist, he would probably not scream at 'author, atheist, essayist, novelist, realist' for being true to their knowledge of human nature, and would regard 'the maiden fancies wallowing in the troughs of Zolaism' as perhaps no more dangerously employed than in conjecturing the precise character and experience of such ladies as Vivien and Guinevere, Ettarre and Isolde."

Having cut the romanticists down to size, Howells then had to deal with the difference between European life as reported by their realists and American as reported by ours. The European "tragedy of love," Howells maintained, is only a "sensation" in America. When instances do happen, they are "puzzling departures from the normal, without deeper significance." The reason for this difference, Howells told the interviewer who drew out these generalizations from him in 1904, is that there are important social differences from one side of the Atlantic to the other. As the "Study" had said in June 1890, "the pursuit of wives by villains is so very uncommon in our society as to be scarcely representative or typical; where there is any pursuit of the kind, the energy and initiative of our women would rather imply that it is the pursuit of villains by wives."

Howells like Henry James had long praised the innocence of American society as contrasted with European. But to the 1904 interviewer he had less pleasant things to say. Warning that this did not apply to artistic marriages (like his own), Howells analyzed the general national condition caustically. "Honestly speaking, the average American—the rushing, moneymaking, preoccupied man of business—is a stick. He is chivalric, devoted, true as steel, he means generously well, but the graces of the higher intellectual and emotional life are strange to him." Discovering this the hard way, women as a group conclude "that it is the inferiority of the sex: their very isolation forces our women to flock together. The semiconsciousness of a void is transmuted into activity, the boundless energy of the American woman, perhaps not always wisely expended, but beneficial as the safety-valve none the less."

Finally, it was Howells' conviction, presumably based on his own experience, that love is really only for young people anyway. The romantic convention has been that one's youthful love experience dominates all of life—winning means eternal happiness, losing a life "spent in gentle melancholy" like a character out of Thackeray. But it isn't really so for real people. "Life drives them on" from youth, win or lose, Howells said, usually to marriage and eventually to "placid contentment, or internecine war ending in armed neutrality," or, at best, "into a beautiful friendship." But love is for the young.

It was from this basis of compromise and reduction that Howells constructed his theories of the place of sex in literature. "How many times," he demanded from the Editor's Study, "has not this apartment rung with entreaties to be simple, to be rational, to be cleanly, to be decent, to be natural, addressed to the prodigious forces which too often revel in blood and tears, filth and crime, shame and vice, in order to enable the average novel-reader to pass an agreeable half-hour?" That expressed one half of his thesis. The other came in his statement to interviewer Van Westrum that, for all the American regard for "our young girls" as novel readers, "our fiction reflects, in its treatment of the love *motif*, the real state of affairs among us."

Until Howells became a full-fledged realist, until the time of *A Modern Instance*, it was easy enough to go with the age and his own taste. The early experiences on the *Atlantic* with Holmes and Mrs. Stowe and Charles Reade taught Howells what the public would not stand. He probably never knew that S. Weir Mitchell threw his first copy of the writings of Freud into the fire. But he knew very well what Mitchell meant in writing to thank him "for the wholesomeness of all your work." He understood perfectly the dangers involved in associating his name with the defense of Zola, or of Tolstoi's *Kreuzer Sonata,* or of Herne's *Margaret Fleming.* It is worth remembering that Howells profoundly admired Herne's play and Mrs. Herne's playing of the heroine and was a prime mover in getting it staged and in recruiting an audience for it in Boston. The Howells whom Henry James, on the basis of early 1870's experiences, always thought so timid (James never apparently sensed the fullness of Howells' growth) was also the Howells who could promote Herne's play in full expectation of the Boston response recorded in the journal of Thomas Russell Sullivan: "Henry Rogers and I . . . came away after the great situation of the third act, when the heroine, in sight of the audience, prepares to suckle her husband's illegitimate child." The audience, Sullivan noted, "received this strong [scene] with depressing coldness. To me it seemed false in sentiment, and my gorge rose at it."

Howells paid the price to learn that "it is hard for people to understand that realism excludes nothing that is true." Yet he was repeatedly caught in the paradox of saying that, nevertheless, American fiction should contain nothing corrupting to the morals of the young girl reader and that therefore all bawdry, scatology, or direct reference either to sexual immorality or licit sexuality were out of bounds. What could he do with his paradox, with the ambivalence which underlay it? About all he could do was to mitigate it, to dull its edges with rationalization.

He could plead that the audience wouldn't permit anything else. He could defend Zola, Verga, and Tolstoi by arguing on the one side that they were very moral. As Boyesen, who thoroughly agreed, argued in defending Howells, some people think any "book which touches upon the question of sex *ipso facto* immoral. Nothing can . . . be sillier." To "deal with sin . . . untruthfully" is what is "immoral." Howells really made his whole argument swing on the pivot of "truth." Latin fiction, and Russian too, were free to deal directly in sex. They sprang from societies where conditions gave honest license for that. But Anglo-Saxon "strait decorum" was right for American conditions. It was especially so for (soft Darwinian argument) *civilized* Anglo-Saxon conditions. Progress was leaving "the beast-man" behind, and literature should recognize the fact.

It was on this basis that he read Owen Wister's first "long, rebellious novel" in manuscript and urged him not to publish: "There are too much hard drinking and hard swearing in it and too much knowledge of good and evil. Were it a translation from the Russian, I shouldn't object." Yet this same man loved Stephen Crane's *Maggie* and arranged its first true publication. The ambivalence was real. Sometimes Howells rebelled against himself. In 1902, for instance, he discussed "What Shall Girls Read?" for *Harper's Bazar*. And there he argued that they should read *anything*—almost. He began with challenges: what can be any tougher than the Bible? And further, "the things which defile are from within"; "innocence only gathers honey in the fields where experience sucks poison from the same flowers." Therefore, he concludes, "I would almost say, but not quite say, Let a girl read anything she finds in her father's library."

But these are really the worst things one can truthfully say on this subject against Howells. His mind was not "morbid" or in any way diseased about sexual matters. He had at least as much right to be pre-Freudian in his way as his critics of the 1920's had to be post-Freudian in their fearlessly half-informed way. A cultural historian might find a useful gauge in noting, in fact, the breathtaking speed with which critics accusing Howells of mental morbidity shifted from one pole to the other. It might even prove true that, somewhere toward the middle of the shift, the historian could find an old romantic chivalrist accusing Howells of morbidity for rejecting the sex-chivalry ideal in the same year in which an early Freudian blackened his character for not being "frank" enough.

Fundamentally, what interested Howells as artist and critic was his ideal of "the American novel." In it, he proclaimed ironically, "Nothing happens; that is, nobody murders, or debauches anybody else; there is no arson or pillage . . . not a ghost, or a ravening beast, or a hair-breadth escape, or a shipwreck, or a monster of self-sacrifice, or a lady five thousand years old . . . yet it is alive with the keenest interest for those who enjoy the study of individual traits and general conditions as they make themselves known to American experience." For Howells, in other words, it was mainly a matter of maturity. To truly grown-up people in a civilized context, one could address serious art.

Libidinous aggressions in art as in life contribute to the destruction of the sensibilities on which art and morality, on which civilization, depend. The serious artist must, therefore, handle them with the greatest care and the greatest responsibility if he be not in some degree to commit suicide through them. The sensitive and extraordinarily civilized Howells understood this. But in the long run it is probable that even that was not the determining reason for his acquiescence in treating of the peripheral aura of sexuality rather than the deeds and details. Even now sexual detail strikes so powerfully into the midst of a novel's web of illusory appeals that almost no novelist can really control it. Repeatedly the "mystery" writer, the historical romancer, the exposé artist betray their art and their readers by irresponsible, commercial exploitation of that force. Long ago it got so bad that a leading censor-fighter threw up his hands: it had become obvious that authors and publishers were cynically tempting and baiting the laws in the hope of getting "banned" and reaping the resultant profits. But Howells' ideal was the fiction which could impower the reader's imagination to live intelligently in a world of keenly delicate perceptions, of fine-spun and therefore richly complex experiences.

It is long since the specific intellectual structure underlying Howells' response to the problem of sex in literature ceased to be available to most people. The esthetic sense of his artistic scruples is not likely to become obsolete so long as the novel lasts, however. The writer of the serious novel—as distinct yet from the romance, no matter how serious—will always have to take it into account. If he clubs the reader with big sensations, like overt sexuality, he will sacrifice his power to work in depth, to be taken seriously by the reader who has had his fill of the Big Bow-wow. Howells' ideal method demands serious effort from the mature reader. It deals in civilized and fine-grained subtleties. It neither denies nor excludes sex any more than it does tragedy. But it insists on its right—and justifies the right in its practice when it is successful—to deal with sex and tragedy in its own, nonromantic but yet civilized way.

V

After *The Shadow of a Dream* was done, Howells felt drained and weary. Moving into Boston, he and Mrs. Howells made a half-hearted show of reestablishing a home in an apartment on Commonwealth Avenue, but the reality was only painful. *A Hazard of New Fortunes* deceptively appeared to attract almost no attention as its length wound serially along in *Harper's*. Howells began to wonder if the public were as tired of him as he was of working for it. The sort of escape-dream familiar to creative people in that mood haunted him: he would get a big greenhouse and just raise English violets. As he would many times in the years to come—unreliably, because this was only a symptom of the tired mood—he began to complain that writing was a hateful business, and he did it only out of sheer economic necessity.

Yet actually, despite his fatigue—or even perhaps as a main source of it—his creative impulses continued to run freely. Whether they were released somehow by the dark agony of his prevailing inner weather or not, there can be no doubt about either the blackness or the pain of his thoughts. The sensibilities stirred up by the unknowable workings of his imagination had produced *A Modern Instance,* and were so concentrated by *The Rise of Silas Lapham* that "the bottom dropped out." They had been rising in a crescendo of intensity ever since and now reached their peak. Howells suffered through his grief and loss, quite naturally. But he was also moved to his most profound metaphysical soundings and to the most racking sort of self-examination. One document among many possibilities will do to illustrate his condition. In midsummer of 1890 he had a headache when it came time to pen his weekly letter home to his father. It made him think again of suffering and death, he wrote. He was willing to concede that suffering probably was good for him: "But think what mother suffered. And Johnny [his favorite brother], and Sissy [Victoria] and Winny ! And why? —That Why is so much on my mind that I wonder it doesn't show phosphorescently on my forehead, and still more on my bulging stomach."

It was in that frame of mind that he had struggled in the previous midwinter to begin *A Boy's Town.* As he progressed with it through the months of Boston cold, he found himself producing an autobiography extraordinarily charming and revealing as a "boy-book," and wonderfully evocative as social history. But it was also the volume S. Weir Mitchell found so full of terror and "haunting melancholy" that it made him "shiver . . . with interest." As Howells' reply makes clear, the baring of his psyche which had made the recovery of that haunted childhood possible was upsetting, if not frightening, to the man. The religious probings of his last two novels reflected the motions of his mind. "You speak of deepening convictions," he reminded Mitchell; "but I have none except of absolute helplessness. Sometimes this seems tragic, and then sometimes comic. This helplessness and the consciousness of a 'wild and whirling' constancy of change in all I think and feel appear at times to be all there is of me. But I am not unhappy, and I do believe that as far as I am responsible for myself, I am as well used as I deserve, and better. I doubt if anyone, however, is finally accountable; we are not really given into our own keeping—."

A natural result of this religious turbulence was Howells' recovery of his impulse to poetry. Sometime in the months after Winifred's death, he began to set down a kind of poetry almost completely different from the verse in tribute to Tennyson, Heine, and Longfellow with which his literary career had begun. This new rhyme was harsh, dark, and intensely metaphysical. Quite properly, his personal struggle with ideas is much more directly revealed in these poems than in his novels. He continued to write them from 1890, occasionally publishing them in *Harper's,* until some time short of the date in 1895 when they were issued, with portentous illustrations by his Swedenborgian friend Howard Pyle, as *Stops of Various Quills.* By that time the impulse had apparently dried up, for all his output of that sort of poetry seems to be in the volume.

There were profundities of metaphysical speculation, sharply shadowed by a sense of evil, and some of Howells' most effective social criticism in these poems. But the finest of them were the quick, poignant registerings of his shifting states of mind. The best of his several poems for what Winifred's fate had meant was:

Weather-Breeder

Oh, not to know that such a happiness
To be wished greater were to be made less;
That one more drop must make it spill in tears
Of agony that blisters and that sears;
That the supreme perfection of thy bliss
Alone could mother misery like this!

The depth of his self-judgment he recorded in a series of poems. Perhaps the hardest hitting, especially in its sudden ironical turn, was:

Calvary

If He could doubt on His triumphant cross,
How much more I in the defeat and loss
Of seeing all my selfish dreams fulfilled,
Of having lived the very life I willed.
Of being all that I desired to be?
My God, My God ! Why hast thou forsaken me?

Yet all this was mitigated to Howells by what he found at bed-
rock as he penetrated through to the bottom of his experience. He
possessed, at the very last of the ends, a redeeming sense of what
he had made Basil March call "the mystery of solidarity," a sense
of the ultimate reality of the unity and equality of all men as human
beings. This he communicates in the bit of cosmic drama he calls
"Company":

I thought, "How terrible, if I were seen
Just as in will and deed I had always been !
And if this were the fate that I must face
At the last day, and all else were God's grace,
How must I shrink and cower before them there,
Stripped naked to the soul and beggared bare
Of every rag of seeming !" Then, "Why no,"
I thought, "Why should I, if the rest are so?"

The ill-fated Professor Harry Thurston Peck had the critical
acumen not only to feel Howells' "profound melancholy" in these
poems but to see that the poet's "mental attitude" had also informed
A Hazard of New Fortunes and the novels which came after it.
Alden was more normally, for his age, Pollyannaish. "I see of
late," he wrote Howells about the poems, "that you walk frequently
on the chill and shadowed side of your Way. Come into the sun-
shine and dare to blossom." But it was Henry Van Dyke, in the
period when he was a genuine Presbyterian minister, whose Cal-
vinistic sympathies caught Howells' sense aright. Preaching on
"The Sin of the World," Van Dyke noted that Zola, Turgenev, and
Hardy wrote, in a way, commentaries on Jeremiah. It is "whole-
some and medicinal" to know "the saddest truth," Van Dyke insisted. No matter how "gloomy," a "sober, stern-faced pessimism
which looks the darkness in the face is sounder and more heroic

than the frivolous, fat-witted optimism which turns its back and shuts its eyes, and laughs."

For an epigraph to his sermon Van Dyke had taken Howells' quatrain, "Conscience":

> Judge me not as I judge myself, O Lord !
> Show me some mercy, or I may not live:
> Let the good in me go without reward;
> Forgive the evil I must not forgive !

Van Dyke had walked with Howells during a vacation in Maine and talked with him "of nature and art, of books and people, of love and sorrow, of life and death and life beyond. Speaking of his own poetry," Van Dyke recalled, Howells "called himself 'a sadder singer, full of doubt and misgiving.' Nothing on earth could be to him what it used to be before his daughter's death."

Now what Van Dyke, and no few of Howells' contemporaries, perceived, each after his own fashion, was that Howells had achieved, or perhaps had had inflicted on him, after Winifred's death his own variety of a tragic vision of life. As we have seen, that vision had come by slow degrees. It was not catastrophically imposed by Winifred's death. It had grown again out of Howells' temperament, reasserting itself from his youth and dissolving away the "tender-minded" optimism of his *Atlantic* period. It had been strengthened by his vastation over *The Rise of Silas Lapham*, by Tolstoi, and by the pilgrimage of his social conscience from *The Minister's Charge* to *Annie Kilburn* to *A Hazard of New Fortunes*. The fate of the Chicago Anarchists, like Winifred's death, had confirmed and established what *Stops of Various Quills* expressed. And yet, for all this thronging evidence, the invincible conviction clings to Howells' reputation that he was one of Van Dyke's blind and fat-witted optimists. That conviction founds itself on the fact that Howells once wrote something about "the more smiling aspects of life which are the more American." And, principally on this phrase, detached from context, he is generally denied whatever credit might attach itself to his really having possessed a tragic vision.

It is not easy to explain the vicissitudes of Howells' reputation in this regard. There is always the question of what one has read and in what context. The great majority of Howells' contemporaries felt his mature work to be tragic in its implications. Some applauded, as when the *Nation* reviewer found a new "sensitiveness to emotional tragedy" in *A Hazard of New Fortunes* and praised its catching "the cry of humanity . . . , the unbroken undertone of tragedy" in New York. But most of them resented what Theodore Roosevelt called Howells' "jaundiced view of life." A critic in 1897 pointed out that Howells "does not love his New York," and outrageously "finds the homes of the rich and of the poor almost equally squalid and disheartening." The reader, he continued, "turns away from Mr. Howells's impressions of our civilization, doubting their insight and sanity. They are too bad to be true, and have . . . a certain malign, narcotic influence, difficult to describe and ill to feel."

On the other hand, Henry James persisted all his life in finding Howells incurably optimistic and almost devoid of any perception of evil. Edith Wharton, who saw that *A Modern Instance* was "the forerunner of *Main Street,* of *Babbitt,*" felt that "Howells was the first to feel the tragic potentialities of life in the drab American small town. . . ." But she also felt that "incurable moral timidity . . . again and again checked him on the verge of a masterpiece" and spoiled "the logical conclusion of *A Modern Instance*"—though she does not intimate what that should have been, and it hardly seems clear that *Ethan Frome* is any more tragic or morally bold in its conclusion than *A Modern Instance*.

Obviously there is room for difference of opinion about the way one reads Howells' literature—or any one else's literature. But there can be little doubt that the use against Howells of his "smiling aspects" phrase—which has been used to denigrate him ever since the early Van Wyck Brooks's *The Ordeal of Mark Twain*—has been founded on a combination of misreading, ignorance, and an unknown variable. The misreading has been of the essay in which Howells used the phrase. The ignorance has been of Howells' temperament, the growth of his ethical sensibility and insight into evil, and of the whole context of imaginative and critical writing in which that essay appeared. The variable, requiring to be worked out for each user of the phrase against Howells, has been the particular motivation of the critic.

Howells, it will be recalled, began to write from his Editor's Study with the gay intention of "banging the babes of Romance about." In only the eighth of his series, for September 1886, he decided it was time to introduce the American audience to a great new Russian novelist to put beside Turgenev and Tolstoi—Dostoevsky. First Howells brilliantly summed up *Crime and Punishment,* the earliest of Dostoevsky's novels available in French, praising it highly for the right things, and both noting and defending the ghastliness of many of its scenes. His second little essay summarized Dostoevsky's life to date, especially the horror of his commuted execution and his sentence to Siberia. The third essay considers the lessons of Dostoevsky to the American realist. Howells notes that romancers like Hawthorne have lamented the unpicturesqueness of American conditions, the lack of "shadows and inequalities in our broad level of prosperity." And he proceeds to point up a contrast between Czarist Russia and America:

'. . . it is one of the reflections suggested by Dostoevsky's book that whoever struck a note so profoundly tragic in American fiction would do a false and mistaken thing. . . . Whatever their deserts, very few American novelists have been led out to be shot, or finally expelled to the rigors of a winter at Duluth; one might make Herr Most [the high priest of Anarchism] the hero of a labor-question romance with perfect impunity; and in a land where journeymen carpenters and plumbers strike for four dollars a day the sum of hunger and cold is certainly very small, and the wrong from class to class is almost inappreciable. We invite our novelists, therefore, to concern themselves with the more smiling aspects of life, which are the more American, and to seek the universal in the individual rather than the social interests. It is worth while, even at the risk of being called commonplace, to be true to our well-to-do actualities. . . . Sin and suffering and shame there must always be in the world. . . . We have death too in America, and a great deal of disagreeable and painful disease . . . but this is tragedy that comes in the very nature of things, and is not peculiarly American, as the large, cheerful average of health and success and happy life is.'

Now this was Howells in the midst of his earliest digestion of Tolstoi, with *The Minister's Charge* just finished. He is out to defend the American realistic novel as he understands and practices it. He has made a true and proper distinction between the social conditions, as he presently grasps them, which Dostoevsky must know and interpret and the "more smiling aspects" he knows. Except as this represents a historical perception (*vide* Robert Frost, "How are we to write/ The Russian novel in America/ as long as life goes on so unterribly?") valid to this present writing, Howells has done only two things. He has registered his sense of difference in view from the admired Russians. And he has registered his sense, as of about January 1886, of the status of the American Dream.

The crowding events of 1886–89 would alter Howells' view of the American Dream profoundly and deeply darken his view of the possibilities of tragedy and evil, as we have seen. The "Editor's Study" reflected that change, point by point, as the months marched on. By September 1891, Howells was cheering Hamlin Garland's *Main-travelled Roads* because "these stories are full of the bitter and burning dust; the foul and trampled slush of the common avenues of life: the life of the men who hopelessly and cheerlessly make the wealth that enriches the alien and the idler, and impoverishes the producer. . . . The stories are full of those gaunt, grim, sordid, pathetic, ferocious figures whom our satirists find it so easy to caricature as Hayseeds. . . . The type . . . is heart-breaking in its rude despair." He hails this as "fine art; though the material will strike many gentilities as coarse and common."

Some of the failure to understand or credit this shift in Howells may be laid to his impatient carelessness in editing *Criticism and Fiction*. The paragraph containing the "smiling aspects" phrase appears there, in an altered setting. It would be possible for a hasty reader to assume that this really represented Howells' thought as of 1891. Yet it is clear even there that the immediate sense of the phrase is directed to the comparison with Dostoevski; and a full reading of the volume finds Howells later on saying: "Especially in America, where the race has gained a height never reached before, the eminence enables more men than ever before to see how even here vast masses of men are sunk in misery that must grow every day more hopeless, or embroiled in a struggle for life that must end in enslaving and imbruting them." In the light of the evidence, neither the "smiling aspects" phrase nor any other can justify the view that Howells was too blind, too timid, or too fatly optimistic to feel or confront the mysteries of iniquity and of tragic loss in the world.

If Howells did have a view of tragedy, then, what was it? From characters' comments in *April Hopes, A Hazard,* and *The Shadow of a Dream* we clearly have some evidence on that question. Experience from the time of *A Chance Acquaintance* and *A Foregone Conclusion* had taught Howells to be cynical about his audience's— and therefore his publishers'—response to the tragic. Edith Wharton recorded with joy his "lapidary phrase": "Yes—what the American public always wants is a tragedy with a happy ending." But it was one of the hallmarks of Howells' integrity that he gave that public so many books with unhappy endings. As a realist, however, he insisted on the reduction of tragedy from supernal to human levels. Boardman in *April Hopes* pointed out that the difference between our literose expectations and our actual experience of tragedy was that the experience necessarily got reduced to "little steps." Twice in the "Editor's Study" Howells noted this point in his own person while discussing "real life" accounts of catastrophe. Sir Walter Scott's *Journal* discloses in his time of troubles that in life "tragedy is not incessantly tragedy." And a story of Arctic disaster reveals "how simply great things happen. . . . It is not all one uninterrupted course toward the catastrophe, spectacular, with an exterior of impressive dramatic unity. . . . What chiefly strikes one in it is that everything seems like everything else; that neither this thing nor that has projection or relief."

And if "real life" were this way, the realist must be faithful to its atmosphere. Howells was assured of the reality of tragedy in life, but he was equally sure how the loyal realist must convey his sense of it. A. Schade Van Westrum asked Howells about it in 1904 and got a fascinating summary answer in dialog:

' "Realism does not mean preoccupation with the common things of life," he says. "That was the initial misunderstanding of its opponents, and it still persists. On the contrary, realism makes all things its province, the uncommon as well as the everyday affairs of human existence, tragedy, disaster and crisis as well as the small round of daily events; but as these predominate, lead up to the climaxes and away from them again, their cause and result, realism holds that they, and not the momentary arrests of life, should be most important in the fiction that aims to reproduce that life with faithfulness."

"But are not the tragedies of life, its catastrophes, more productive of revelation of character, are they not more effective artistically?"

"That is a theory from which I differ most thoroughly. First as to the revelation of character, and secondly as to the artistic value.

"The culmination of a tragedy, its climax, does *not* reveal character to the full. It rather stuns all the faculties, all the emotions except a single one—defiance, perhaps, or fear, or despair. At such moments the interaction of life and human character ceases; there is no play as of sunlight upon the facets of a diamond. Life—fate, if you please—crushes the individual; the situation becomes supreme, character is passive under the weight it cannot lift or shift or move. Man is a creature of light; tragedy is darkness. In its presence he stands before the unknown, before the night, and the result is not revelation, but impenetrable darkness. There is but one color in the picture—black, dreariest gray at the best.

"Now, life in the aggregate is not black, and it does not stun character. In art, the catastrophe must be the close of the work, for otherwise there will be what is called an 'anti-climax,' a thing to be avoided. Life, on the other hand, is not afraid of anti-climaxes; it produces them daily. No tragedy in real existence but has its tomorrow, unheroic, perhaps, artistically, but unavoidable, inexorable. Art may stop where it pleases, life must go on. Realism endeavors to take note of the continuity which nothing can arrest for long, and considers it more important to the individual and humanity at large than the violent interruption.

"By all means, let us have tragedy in fiction as part of life; but the study of human character is best pursued in the normal daily round, with its endless variety of revelation of traits and formative influences, its gentle humor and gentler pathos, its ills for which it ever has its uses and its cures." '

Howells took the risk of daring to commit himself to a new kind of tragedy. To pluralistic, relativistic, contingent tragedy—not politically, metaphysically, or hierarchically "of a certain magnitude," but only emotionally and morally, *psychologically* so as it operated by the realistic standard. The risk was that readers habituated to classical and romantic tragedy would refuse him the hospitality of learning to read him on these his terms.

Personal tragedy and the contemplation of social tragedy were good for Howells as an artist, no matter how hard they were on him as a man. If he had tended toward smugness in the gay, great time of his 1870's, that was stripped away in the eighties. He became more alert and responsive both to people and their problems. His imagination deepened and darkened. It produced not only the themes of his published novels and the ever darker short stories of the nineties, but such Hawthornian germs in his notebook as a story to be called "Transfusion": "Old fellow who goes to a young friend for cheer when he is gloomy, and impoverishes his spirit. Friend expostulates with him; he stops coming; or on the way commits suicide. Perhaps young man's wife interferes." With fundamental dramatic and metaphysical accretions, that grew into the striking tale, "A Difficult Case," 1900.

At the base of Howells' memory, from which all his artistry sprang, there were his two earliest recorded impressions. A peach tree spread its warm and fecund blossoms in the security of his childhood's own backyard. A one-legged man lunged from his skiff toward the steamboat, missed, and slid silently forever beneath the rain-dappled, yellow water of a great river. And these visions may well be the symbols of a fundamental ambivalence in his mind. When he could, Howells sided with what Basil March called "civilization," with the Victorian conviction that the force of man's conscious mind, disciplined to science by logic and directed by good will, would solve the problems of mankind. Like Sir Leslie Stephen, for example, this Howells was an agnostic meliorist, progressive and realistic. Supremely gentle, idealistic, marvelously civilized, this was the domesticated Howells of the peach tree.

But out of the troubled childhood, up from the temperamental melancholia, there was always pushing the other man, the perturbed Howells of the drowned man. The confrontation of tragedy in the world, and then the irruption of tragedy upon his domestic heaven through Winifred, broke through his civilized serenity. These intimations of blackness kept Howells "tender" in the Quaker sense and prevented him from being "tender-minded" in William James's sense. They impelled him to his best and most mature literature.

If it really is necessary to interpreters of the immediate American past to support their various mythologies by finding someone to symbolize irresponsible optimism, that symbol should be some figure other than William Dean Howells.

THE WAY TO ALTRURIA

S ETTLED IN BOSTON FOR THE WINTER OF 1889–90, HOWELLS GOT a pleasant surprise to relieve the gloom of his own grief and his wife's prostration. For obvious reasons, once serialized to a national audience, his novels might retain commercial vitality for many years, but their sales in book form in the months just after serialization would be limited. In the eighties it is probably fair to guess that his sales averaged around 7,500 for any given volume in the first year after book publication. Before *A Hazard of New Fortunes* finished its serial run and appeared as a volume in November 1889, Howells had reason to be apprehensive. He had taken a bold chance, flaunting his new ideas and the linkage of his name with the Anarchists in his public's face. And the lack of public or critical response to the serial looked ominous.

But on book publication, *A Hazard of New Fortunes* suddenly boomed. It sold a 12,000 copy advance. Alden, belatedly, said that it was "the greatest novel you have written"; and the Harpers, belatedly, got out a second edition in two volumes that missed the Christmas trade. Even so, the novel pushed on through the year to the 20,000 mark—a figure impressive in that day before the trade was properly organized for best-sellerism.

Better yet, personal and critical response was ecstatic. William James raved over the book to Henry as well as Howells; and Henry was moved to write again, long, solemnly, and brilliantly to Howells about the theory of the novel. Lowell told Howells he was glad he had survived to see that achievement from his protégé, and confided to a friend that "I felt in reading some parts of it as I used when the slave would not let me sleep." Thomas Wentworth Higginson advised the Nineteenth Century Club in New York that this was Howells' first mature and great production, for which all else had

139

been preparatory, and that if they had not read it, they could not know Howells. Out in Kansas young William Allen White spent his summer "stark mad" over it. And James Parton, a self-proclaimed "pagan" theologically, thanked Howells for "this holy and august book" in the name of "our country and the whole English-speaking race." The Dryfooses, Parton exclaimed, ". . . the whole delineation of that unhappy family, slavered all over with their noisome and pitiable wealth for the Devil to swallow. O, by Heaven, it is pathetic beyond my power to express."

The magazines, of course, generally followed suit. Curtis set all the sheep to jumping in the right places with a canny review in the January, 1890, "Editor's Easy Chair." Howells' success was big and original, he said, and put the other critics on notice that the success could be used as a club in the Realism War, if necessary: it is "such a piece of realism as . . . at once illustrates and vindicates every principle which the Study has maintained and applied in its judgements of contemporary story." And so Horace Scudder, growling a little about Howells' "instinct" being better than his "theory," found himself in a substantial *Atlantic* essay accounting for this new power and vitality by tracing Howells' growth. At first Howells, a gay humorist, wrote fiction "altogether delightful and did not disturb our sleep," but now he "both charms us with his pictorial skill and banishes sleep from our eyelids," Scudder said, perhaps a bit slyly. Once Howells' "mind began to be stirred by problems," the *Atlantic* editor continued, he entered a transitional period the work of which, Scudder insists, was hard to read. But now, "the ethical and aesthetic glasses with which he views life . . . have the same focus."

The net result was personal vindication for Howells in both his war for realism and his right to fight for the American social conscience. His position was secured. Critics might continue hostile, but the best they could hope for was perhaps to damage his sales a little—and perhaps pick up a little notoriety for themselves. And there need be no fear now of retaliation over the Anarchists or retribution for continuing social criticism. Howells was speaking to the condition of the country, to the national conscience, and was being heard. He might or might not be responded to as he hoped, but he would not be crushed. He had taken risks and gotten away free. He could use that freedom to pursue his thought to conclusions. His limitations henceforth would be only personal.

1

At Howells' fiftieth birthday in 1887, efforts were made to let him feel and enjoy his fame. Letters, telegrams, and editorials praised and congratulated. And nowhere was this more strikingly done than in Boston. For suddenly, after fifty years of supremacy as the literary center of the nation in an age when literature alone among the American arts possessed maturity, Boston began to feel deserted. Neither in Concord, nor in Cambridge, nor in the Hub itself had any significant literary talent appeared since the generation of Lowell. Westerner, realist, democratic moralist, economic critic, Howells might be inconvenient. But he was about all Boston had left—if, indeed, she had him. Her young intellectuals were eager to claim him; his was the most stimulating mind in town. He constituted almost a last direct opening out of narrowing parochial concerns into the great mainstream of the nation's thought. And he was generously available to the young.

Hence the note of defiance in the Boston *Beacon* of February 26, 1887, as it congratulated the soon-to-be-fifty Howells: ". . . first, because he has always been a plain American with not an atom of the aristocrat or sectionalist in him; in the next place, because his private life has honored the literary fame he has won; in the third place because he has never published a line that could lower the tastes of his readers or degrade society." The proper gloss on that challenge to the anti-Howellsians was provided by Sylvester Baxter, realist and reformer, writing after Howells had left Boston for good. His first reputation came, said Baxter, from "that select and keenly appreciative element" which loves artistry. But when Howells dared enter "the broader world," he lost most of these "fastidiously narrow." What he gained in their place were "realists, modernists, veritists, caring nought for trappings and all for vital substance in the great, pulsating life of the world. . . ."

Energetic, radical, internationally controversial in his writing and fearless in the conversational expression and defense of his views, Howells became the nucleus of whatever was intellectually vital in the Boston of the later 1880's. He had long undertaken to repay some of his debts to the great of earlier generations by making himself at least equally open to young seekers. A co-founder of St. Botolph's Club, he had served with distinction as first president of the Tavern Club, an organization founded by young doctors, painters, and journalists. To these men, all born about the time he himself had commenced as a newspaperman in Columbus, Howells could bring not only his distinction and rare integrity of mind, but also his *savoir-faire* and the benefit of his contacts with the great. He always got along easily with painters and sculptors—J. Q. A. Ward, W. W. Storey, Frank Millet, St. Gaudens, and, of course, Larkin Mead were only a few of his friends. And this Tavern crowd, among whom Owen Wister was an early member, suited his humor as well as his ideas.

Though one of his last-minute acts on the threshold both of taking Winifred to Dansville and plunging into the Anarchist fight had been to resign his Tavern office—on the ground that he'd become "not a President but an Absident"—he by no means cut himself off from the young men of Boston. And at his returns he saw much of them in clubs, in society, at various meetings, in his own home. Louis Brandeis and Henry Cabot Lodge came in from Harvard. E. H. Clement, Charles E. Hurd, John J. Enneking of the *Transcript* and Edmund Noble of the Boston *Herald* were leading journalists in the circle. Very promising writers who died young, like George Pellew and Wolcott Balestier, belonged, as did writers who lived on and stayed minor like W. H. Bishop, Henry Harland, and Robert Grant. And then, tumbling and buzzing around Howells like a drunken bumblebee, there was Hamlin Garland.

Western farm boy and prairie sod-buster turned East in quest of the frontiers of the mind, Garland was expending his abounding vitality and magnificent intellectual drive in living one of the great, representative sagas of our cultural history. Nothing he spun out of his limited creative imagination would have anything like the impact or importance of his autobiography, especially the true central volume, *A Son of the Middle Border*. Hoarding his savings, Garland had spent a dizzying year engulfing modernity through the books of the Boston Public Library. Then he had begun to acquire a tiny income lecturing, giving elocution lessons, writing an occasional book review. As a fierce Whitmanian romantic, Garland had been taking an anti-Howells line in his lectures until he came to read enough Howells to grasp his import. Then Garland was resoundingly converted.

Despite various inconsistencies and discrepancies in Garland's dating, he seems to have met Howells during those months between

late October 1885 and February 1886 when Howells was living in
Lee's Hotel, Auburndale—the way to get the largest possible degree
of consistency into Garland's account would be to say that it was
in February 1886, just after the first serial installment of *The
Minister's Charge* appeared, just before Howells left for Washington. After that, Garland was Howells' disciple for years. He
hounded Howells with visits, letters, introductions, invitations, so-
licitations, appeals for criticism, appeals for help. He acted as
interpretor, adviser, and self-appointed public relations officer. He
tried to see to it that people met Howells, or Howells the people, or
at least that Howells read their books. He tried endlessly to convert
Howells to Henry George and the Single Tax. If sometimes offi-
cious, Garland was limitlessly enthusiastic, and for a period of ten
years or so he played an immensely effective part in redoubling
Howells' impact on the life of the mind in America.

For his part, Howells worked with the patient, sympathetic skill,
and the forbearance, of a great teacher to bring Garland along and
help him become, not a little Howells, but himself at his best. He
never would go along with Garland's devotion to the simplicism of
Henry George: "He is *one* of the great hopes, but not the only one,
it seems to me," Howells told Garland, "and I'm not sure that his
truth is the first in order." He had no hesitation in pulling strings
with publishers or reviewers for Garland's sake, and he did his best
to encourage that Western, Populist mood of protest against economic injustice and against the agrarian myth of the Happy
Farmer in which Garland did his best imaginative work. In his
brief tenure as editor of the *Cosmopolitan,* Howells ordered from
Garland, for instance, "a *personnel* study of the farmers' alliances
. . . their griefs and hopes, their minds and manners; everything
very realistic." There can be little doubt that if Garland had hewed
to that line instead of whoring off after *The Captain of the Gray
Horse Troop* and, eventually, spiritualism, his would have been a
much greater achievement.

As it was, Howells did his best to cheer and scheme Garland into
greatness. In the true vein, Howells told him, "you are one of the
great future men, I am sure. . . . Be fine, be fine, be not too fine,
and the game is yours." Up to a point, he would do almost anything
for Garland—but there also came the time when he thought Garland needed to be weaned, and he did it effectively. "A fellow who
stands as strong upon his legs as you, wanting a hand from a dotard

like me!" Howells jeered in 1893. "I think the public would say, 'Who is this doddering fool, who introduces Garland to us?' Get out ! Try to see us when you are East."

This, of course, signaled no ending of kindnesses or even detailed advice. Neither they nor Howells' affection for Garland were withheld when Garland drifted back into his apparently temperamental romanticism. The key to an understanding of Garland, or at least of his relations with Howells, seems to be the recognition of a tension between Garland's devotion to Howells and what he stood for and a more natively congenial Midwestern adaptation by Garland (much like Vachel Lindsay or Carl Sandburg after him) of the gospel according to Walt Whitman. Even at the height of Garland's allegiance to Howells, he climaxed his praise by calling Howells "a mystic" and, like John Burroughs, stressing Howells' kinship to Whitman. When Garland began, late in the nineties, to trend ever more strongly toward the mood of the "virile," Rooseveltian neo-romantics, Howells would play neither the hypocrite nor the heavy schoolmaster with him. "The Spirit of Sweet Water," he wrote Garland, "is *heroic,* and only bad, so far. But it is well done, and anybody else might be proud of it. You are you, however, and you have obligations to the modest truth. The truth in this *brags.*" And yet, "it will be well for you to print the story, and it will help many." In this, perhaps the most intimate of his many cordial relationships with the new writers coming up, Howells most fully exemplified the pattern and quality of his dealings with the young men.

Through Garland, Howells was introduced at a critical moment to James A. Herne, the pioneering realist of American drama. Howells had praised Herne's *Drifting Apart* in the June 1890 "Editor's Study," but unknowingly he had much earlier influenced Herne and the intelligent collaborator and brilliant actress who was Mrs. Herne. "I have met few people in any walk of life with the same wide and thorough range of thought," said Garland, who had taken the Hernes up enthusiastically after seeing *Drifting Apart.* "In their home oft-quoted volumes of Spencer, Darwin, Fiske, Carlyle, Ibsen, Valdés, Howells give evidence that they do not only keep abreast but ahead of the current thought of the day: Spencer is their philosopher, and Howells is their novelist. . . ." Herne's esthetic, in concepts and especially in vocabulary, derived directly from Howells: "I stand for art for truth's sake because it perpetuates the everyday life of its time, because it dignifies labor—reveals the divinity of the common man," Herne said, every word an echo of Howells.

When, probably in the winter of 1891, Herne had tried to go the whole, realistic way with *Margaret Fleming*, no Boston or New York manager would consider it. Howells invited Herne, Garland, and others out to lunch and, listening to Herne's woes, suggested he try what the experimentalists of Europe, like Sudermann in Berlin, were doing. Forget the managers—hire any common space, a sail-loft, a stable—and produce his own play. The result was the Chickering Hall performance of *Margaret Fleming*, shocking to many, exhilarating to others. Garland called it the first Little Theater performance in America. Howells threw and kept his great prestige behind it despite all the jeers and cries of outrage from neoromantics and squeamish moralists. Herne was grateful all his too few remaining years.

From Garland, but even more from two last surviving stalwarts of old Reforming Boston, Edward Everett Hale and Thomas Wentworth Higginson, Howells learned that other consciences were as active as his about social concerns. Hale had started a Tolstoi Club to enlist Harvard undergraduates in settlement work. Hale had brought Howells and Higginson into the orbit of organized Nationalism in Boston. Howells had long praised and supported Edward Bellamy as a writer. His review in the June 1888 "Study" had lauded *Looking Backward* perceptively and effectively. "Pure romance with a frank allegory" like this the prophet of realism accepted gladly. He pointed out boldly that this was "undiluted socialism" and found its literary charm effective beyond praise. Surprised at the popularity of Bellamy's ideas, he admired the Nationalists' hopefulness without really sharing it. It was too much to suppose that any such merely romantic impulse should last, as indeed it did not, more than a matter of months.

Such impulses were healthy, and the enthusiasm they stimulated might have long-term benefits—or might not. Old campaigners like Hale and quiet skeptics like Howells felt cooperative but not too eager. The quality of their response is registered perfectly in a story quoted in Arthur Morgan's *Edward Bellamy* on the organizational meeting of The First Nationalist Club of Boston. "I moved," said Cyrus Willard, "that we appoint a committee to bring in a constitution and by-laws. Edward Everett Hale got up, and in his peculiar hollow voice said, 'I had hoped that once before I died I might be a member of a body that had no by-laws to squabble over.' William Dean Howells was sitting on an empty wood-box in the corner, back of a tall stove about six feet high in the middle of the room. He kicked his heels vigorously against the wood box in applause. That made us all laugh, and I knew it was no use to press my motion. . . .''

Fascinatingly in this period, pressures developed to push Howells into conformity with the public impressions created by *A Hazard of New Fortunes*. People emerged who wished to play roles, and get Howells to play opposite them, imagined from his novel. That seems to be the likeliest explanation for Howells' having been drawn briefly into the Association of Christian Socialists in Boston. Under the general sponsorship, apparently of Phillips Brooks, an Episcopalian rector named W. D. P. Bliss was attempting to transplant Maurice's Christian Socialism from England to the United States via Boston. A tireless idealist, Bliss had founded his Association, a magazine, *The Dawn,* for propaganda, and a mission Church of the Carpenter. Howells, who had after all portrayed Margaret Vance and Conrad Dryfoos sympathetically as engaged in much the same sort of thing, attended the mission a time or two. But for all that Margaret's faith intrigued his creative imagination, he was far from ready to fall in behind Conrad. He went, he wrote his father on April 20, 1890, to the "organization of the Christian Socialists at their 'Church of the Carpenter.' It was like seeing the old faith renewed in the life."

The old faith, however, wistful as he might become for it at times, could not be Howells'. Nor could he function properly as an organization man. His next weekly letter home made it clear that his hope for reform lay ultimately in the American political system. "The *Dawn*," he told his father, "is edited by the pastor of the Church of the Carpenter. The Christian Socialists are more to my mind than the Nationalists; but I doubt if I shall openly act with either for the present. The C. S. have loaded up with the creeds of the church, the very terms of which revolt me, and the N. seem pinned in faith to Bellamy's dream. But the salvation of the world will not be worked out that way. . . . By and by labor will be so pinched that the politicians will have to put a socialistic plank into a platform, and then the party that stands on it will win." His hopes rested in secular democracy.

II

To a point, thus, Boston could stimulate Howells as well as he it. By the time he had finished this last Boston sojourn, in fact, he seems to have completed the essential structure of his thinking about socialism. In the mood of ironic self-deprecation appropriate to the friend and the occasion, Howells recorded a visit for his father's interest and amusement on February 2, 1890, ". . . I stopped to see Mark Twain at Hartford. . . . He and his wife and Elinor and I are all of accord in our way of thinking: that is, we are theoretical socialists, and practical aristocrats. But it is a comfort to be right theoretically, and to be ashamed of one's self practically." Joking aside, a profound core of truth lay at the heart of that remark. Short of hopelessly imitating Tolstoi's stultifying theatricality, Howells really did not know what to do personally and "practically" about his socialism. But he was sure that it ought to be a matter of conscience, that he and all men with him ought to be ashamed of social conditions, and that socialism must at least mean an enlightening analysis and diagnosis of those conditions. It must be critical.

Reading Tolstoi's *Que Faire?* in the spring of 1887 had simply left Howells "very unhappy." On November 27, 1888, he had written another unsendable letter to the editor of an unnamed newspaper which had been attacking him for socialism and defense of the Anarchists. Infuriatingly, they had also impugned his right, as a mere novelist, to speak out on such problems. Howells boiled over at being called "a sentimentalist, a promoter of bloody riot, a watering-place piazza novelist," as he (half-quoting?) summed it up. Bitterly he denied the dirtiest word of all: "from which of my books do you infer that *I* am a sentimentalist? . . . if my trade has taught me anything it has taught me to abhor sentimentality." He admires Tolstoi, he admits, and is "respectful" towards Gronlund. But he wishes to argue that socialism is "not a positive but a comparative thing"—anybody who believes in any degree of social cooperation is to that degree a socialist. The question is, to what degree? Then he told the story which would figure so effectively in *A Hazard of New Fortunes* of the starving foreigner scavenging food from the gutter and affirmed that the conditions which made this situation possible seemed "Christless."

He concluded with irony,

'I knew that there must be some occult connection between my "sentimentality" and the throwing of dynamite bombs; and that I, who abhor all violence and think that every drop of human blood shed in a good cause makes a bad one, must somehow be playing into the hands of the most murderous minded criminals. But for your reasoning on the subject, I should have supposed that the whole tenor of my literature and my life was counter to disorder of all kinds, and especially to disorder that in a free country applies the theories and methods of those who struggle against despotism [a razor-sharp, two-edged blade !]. I hope there will be some who will think it superfluous for me to have said this even in reply to your reasoning.'

It was not only superfluous but ill-advised, and so Howells did not send it. He had already said his say repeatedly in the Study and elsewhere, and could always do it again—on his own grounds and terms. It was, in fact, very likely the October 1888 "Editor's Study" which had drawn the editorial assault. There Howells had not only praised James to the skies and introduced another Russian, Stepniak, but had also dared to take up a pioneering muckraker's book, Alice Wellington Rollins' *Uncle Tom's Tenement.* In the slums, Howells observes, Mrs. Rollins shows that through "rapacity" the landlords have condemned the tenants to "savagery": "the former have accustomed the latter to squalor, till now they prefer it. . . . The abuses alleged are all undeniable and sickening enough; the extortions practiced are atrocious; the abominations and indecencies unspeakable." But, asks Howells, is there really "any hope of permanent cure while the conditions invite one human being to exploit another's necessity for his profit, or a bad man, under the same laws, may at any moment undo the work of a good one?"

He was developing a set of fundamental convictions about "the conditions" and the means necessary to cure them. One of the conditions he thought it most desperately needful for the people to understand was that they had permitted the foundations of the first American, the first modern, Republic to be subverted. Not Lindau's crazy violence, but many of his critical perceptions were shared by his creator, as the "Editor's Study" for 1890 made clear. In January Howells suggested a reading of *A Connecticut Yankee at King Arthur's Court* which, given his inside information on the author, has perhaps been too little remembered: "We see that the

noble of King Arthur's day, who battened on the blood and sweat
of his bondman, is one in essence with the capitalist of Mr. Harrison's day who grows rich on the labor of his underpaid workmen."
The next month he hinted at "the dangers which threaten to trans-
form us from a democracy to a plutocracy, dazzling us with dollars
to a betrayal of the best hopes and highest aims of the race. . . ."
And in October he warned solemnly that "unless something happens
to wean us from the love of money for the sake of power and station,
we shall go the gait of Europe, whose political tradition we have
broken with, but whose social and economic ideals we have clung to
and still cling to."

By late 1893, finishing just at New Year's time 1894, he felt
prepared to say with the utmost plainness just what he meant.
"Are We a Plutocracy?" he asked in an article brightly featured
in the *North American Review*. The answer was, yes. And he explained it forcefully. With style unusually direct and vocabulary
very plain, yet with much irony so obvious as to constitute sarcasm,
Howells argues that earning money to make a living is one thing
but "making money" is something else—plutocracy. The man who
works to acquire money for its own sake, and even more the man
who pays wages "for doing or making a thing . . . that he may
have some margin of gain for himself from it, without having
helped do it or make it," that man is a worshipper of Plutus, or
Mammon. It doesn't matter whether the man gives or takes the
wages, is lucky or unlucky, successful or not, rich or poor. If he
believes in the system and worships the God of money, he is a
plutocrat. Do most Americans do so? Do they permit business to
conduct society as a system of economic warfare for making money?
Do they acquiesce in the corruption of government by wealth for
gain at every level? He leaves it to the reader to confess, of course
they do. Then, says Howells, this is a plutocracy.

The material gains, he points out, are admirable. And yet, especially in the midst of the depression of 1893, there are those who
"say that the defects of our advantages are so terrible that the
wealth we have heaped up is like witch's gold in its malign and
mocking effects. If we have built many railroads, we have wrecked
many. . . . The tramps walk the land like the squalid spectres of
the laborers who once tilled it. The miners have swarmed up out
of the pits, to starve in the open air. In our paradise of toil,
myriads of workingmen want work; the water is shut off in the

factory; the fires are cold in the foundries. The public domain, where in some sort the poor might have provided for themselves, has been lavished upon corporations, and its millions of acres have melted away as if they had been a like area of summer clouds."

The depression would not last forever, the survivors of its suffering would prosper again. But even so, was plutocracy a good bargain? Howells concluded: "If the poor American does not like it, or if he does not prefer a plutocracy to a democracy, he has the affair in his own hands, for he has an overwhelming majority of the votes. At the end, as in the beginning, it is he who is responsible. . . . If we have a plutocracy, it may be partly because the rich want it, but it is infinitely more because the poor choose it or allow it."

Howells' diagnosis is, then, that the nation suffers from plutocracy—the pursuit and worship of money for the sake of power and prestige. His prescription is more and better democracy—democracy reimagined and freshly applied to the national ills. As a printer and a printer's boy, Howells easily sympathized with organizing labor, especially in the American Federation of Labor phase which succeeded the failure of the Knights of Labor after the Haymarket year of 1886. In the middle nineties he enjoyed sitting on the board of the Social Reform Club with Samuel Gompers, joining because it offered him "an excellent opportunity to become acquainted with labor leaders on terms of equality." But he never agreed with Gompers' notion that the unions should keep out of politics. On the contrary, while sympathizing with the needs and motives of strikers and their strikes, he insisted that the right recourse of labor was political.

"Strikes are only useful as a means of diagnosis," Howells said. "They are no remedy; they are merely symptomatic of the fact that the trouble must go on as long as competition goes on; they are themselves an essential part of competition." So far as the workingman struck for his own plutocratic reasons, he forfeited theoretical sympathy, however much he remained entitled to sympathy on human or practical grounds. Romantic-demonstrative and emotional reformers the realist rejected as he did all romanticism. To his father he indignantly repudiated "any admirers of mine" in Coxey's Army. "The whole thing strikes me as crazy," he wrote. "I hate all that theatrical kind of reform; it can only result in retarding real progress and giving the devil a fresh hold on hard hearts."

Obviously, a man with such an outlook was going to have a hard time finding organized groups to join with. In this sense Howells was what seems to be a fairly early example of the organizationally isolated "modern intellectual." His days of pulling like a wheelhorse for the Grand Old Party lay far in the past. "The Republican party is a lie in defamation of its past," he said in 1892. "It promises nothing in the way of economic or social reform, and it is only less corrupt than the scoundrelly democracy [his compliments to Tammany Hall]. The only live and honest party is the People's Party." In 1896 he voted "quietly" for Bryan, and after that hardly knew where to turn.

He might, as he would for a candidate he approved, "send a warm letter of encouragement with a campaign contribution" to a Socialist candidate for Congress. But there was no home for him in the Socialist Party. Howells might be classified as an adherent of what Howard H. Quint calls "Non-Partisan Socialism." Certainly the wild, conflicting winds of doctrine, the insane, often petty battles over leadership and personality, and above all the growing intransigence of the class-war-obsessed, "scientific," and Marxian, proto-Communist branch of the party gave no place to the agnostic, irenic, democratic Howells. He could be a critical and lower-case socialist, finding the socialist critique useful, the Populist-Progressive emotions largely admirable. He was too politically experienced (far more so than most "professional" reformers), too temperamentally skeptical, too devoted to his own art and creative way of life to become a party man or an active reformer.

On the other hand, Howells thought the public needed to have its eyes opened and its conscience sensitized and was quite willing to educate it. He became an effective spokesman for the socialist critique, particularly acceptable to the Fabian or gradualist group, though his recognition was by no means limited to them. In 1890, the General Secretary of the Fabian Society wrote from England to introduce the refugee Russian novelist and reformer Stepniak: "I am proud to be the connecting link between him and you." In 1898 *The American Fabian* announced that Howells' services "to the Socialist movement call for the warmest eulogy." It praised his realism as an art neither dark and vicious nor superficial: "He has pictured for us our own time, the struggle of mankind . . . the obligation of brotherhood." At real risk, it said, he "attacks the whole economic framework of modern society"; he is "the high-minded American gentleman."

As celebrity, humorist, and friend of the mighty, Howells the socialist was of course often enough the cause that wit was in others. E. C. Stedman thought this had contributed directly to enrich the American political vocabulary. As Stedman noted:

'Some years ago, Whitelaw Reid gave a luncheon at his beautiful town residence, on which occasion I think that Henry Irving was the guest of honor. The company was select, and composed chiefly of very rich men. Besides our host there were two other writers present, between Mr. Reid and whom, as his friends and colleagues from youth, a warm unbroken attachment has continued unbroken. One of these, Mr. Howells, by virtue of his rank, of his fellow-statehood with Reid, and of his slightly longer acquaintance, the host called to his right hand—when the seats were shifting, I, as the other earliest friend present, was assigned the place at his left. Mr. Reid then called upon the magnates present to drink the health of his friend Howells, "a parlor anarchist" and of myself, an "amateur socialist" . . . the pleasantry of regarding Mr. Howells, the sturdiest of men, as a parlor knight of any stripe, and Howells, the gospeller of peace and good will, as an "anarchist" with all that implies, was exquisite enough to travel far. Mr. Taft's "parlor socialist" apparently is a compound of these two types—now long known to the lexicon of attributes, but of which I remember no denotation earlier than the occasion of which I speak.'

A shaft of wit launched by a serious though friendly adversary, that joke originated in well-informed respect, not contempt. Howells had a formidable reputation in his day as a spokesman for reform, and deserved it. A friend of Henry Demarest Lloyd's went walking with Tolstoi: ". . . and he got to talking about certain American writers who interested him. Howells he seemed to like on account of what he called his 'fine spirit'; he also admired a number of his books as well as his manner of writing, he suddenly exclaimed: 'There are four men in this world that I should like to be the means of bringing together,' and my recollection is that three of the four were you, Mr. George, and Mr. Howells. The fourth was a clergyman in England, I believe, although I am not quite sure. The Count seemed to think that if all of you got together, and had a long soulful conversation, an advance would have been made toward the regeneration of degenerate humanity." Karl Marx's daughter, intensely conscious of her duty to her father's memory, wrote to introduce herself to Howells and praise him as "not only a true artist, and a great writer, but that even rarer thing, a brave and just man." And for all his frequent impatience with Howells, Theodore Roosevelt, when he thought he needed it, wrote to bespeak Howells' support for his efforts in restraining the "great fortunes."

TR's sense that Howells' support was worth having was doubtless sound. Howells had long since come to speak with an authority almost as great in the field of social thought as in literature. When *The Theory of the Leisure Class* came out, says Veblen's biographer, Howells not only "helped to make the book a sensation, but helped to set the fashion of interpreting it" which endured for decades. It was in recognition of that prepotency that Walter Hines Page wrote Howells in 1894. He could name his own length and price if he would write for *"The Forum* a statement of the tendency towards socialism and a formulation of a socialistic programme as far as you believe such a programme to be possible—putting into essay-shapes the suggestive tendencies shown in your *Cosmopolitan* Letters from Altruria." What Page got was entitled "The Nature of Liberty." It said what has since (mostly since the 1930's) become commonplace: liberty must be economic as well as political if democracy is to be meaningful in modern life.

In spite of the admirably clarifying interpretations pioneered by Newton Arvin and carried forward by George Arms and Louis Budd, among others, Howells' "socialism" has been fairly persistently misunderstood or misrepresented. Critics of a conservative cast of thought are blind to the depth and force of those ideas as they inform his novels, particularly. Marxists and their followers have often violently denied either the existence or the courage and relevance of Howells' social thought. C. Hartley Grattan went so far as to call Howells "the perfect exponent of the late Nineteenth Century bourgeois spirit in American literature," with a "view of America . . . scarcely distinguishable from Andrew Carnegie's" ! As with many a critic of Howells, one is left wondering what on earth he had been reading—if anything. The truth, as in almost everything Boyesen wrote about Howells, lies pretty exactly with that blunt interpreter's view. Howells, said Boyesen, is a "socialist" but not "violent." He "has an abiding faith in a slow and orderly evolution," in a "gradual change in men's sentiments toward a nobler and more universal altruism." He believes that "to socialism in some yet undeveloped form belongs the future."

Actually, Howells' socialism and social sensitivity formed a significant part of the emergence of a new kind of conscience in the world. One of the decisive events of the 1890's was the emergence of the Progressive attitudes out of what Richard Hofstadter has called the "Mugwump spirit" of an earlier, ineffectual generation. That Progressive crowd who came of age in the nineties knew and read Howells as the most vital novelist in America. No few of its members acknowledged direct debts to him. In them he helped foster the conviction that social and economic injustice is not tolerable in the modern world. It corrupts, embitters, and twists the victim. Long before Sherwood Anderson, Howells had recorded the plight of what Anderson called the "grotesques." Injustice is deadly for the oppressor, too. It enfeebles him morally, distends him with pride; perhaps worst of all, it makes him frivolous. And of course it poisons the culture which permits it, robbing it of vitality and inhibiting progress.

Howells shared this conviction with others, of course. But he lived it so profoundly that he could respond creatively to the imaginative impulses it set up within him, and this allowed him to speak it dramatically, and with the deepest intimacy, to his serious readers. One of the greatest achievements of modern American society has been to prevent class war and finally to set society on the road toward making class war permanently unnecessary and therefore impossible. That achievement would have been impossible without the creation of a condition of conscience and conviction within our culture which mitigated and diminished injustice and may permit us to be increasingly humane in the future. Howells contributed directly to the creation of that condition during the years when it had to be created or be obviated. He did so partly through the force of his critical socialism.

III

To Howells himself the most important thing about his socialism was its effect on him as a writer. The story of that effect tells itself in the story of the education of the realist's "eye," the deeper focusing power of his imagination as it threw up to the light of consciousness the images of persons and events from which the author could fabricate literature. That change in focus of Howells' vision could be recorded in several ways. But one of the most revealing is to follow its views of Boston. In the beginning, as in *A Chance Acquaintance* and *Out of the Question,* a Western democrat is eager to defend the common, middle-class American against entrenched Proper Bostonian snobbery. His eye fixes on the sterling qualities of the "unconventional" citizen to prove his innate worth and shame the "conventional" socialite into accepting nature's lady or gentleman on Jeffersonian terms. The author's eye focuses steadily on "nobility"—whether natural or factitious. He is mainly anxious to distinguish between the true and the false. In the first realistic novel, *A Modern Instance,* that focus has become unexpectedly leveled, the eye disenchanted. No glamor attaches itself to Equity, Maine. Bartley and Marcia Hubbard are only too painfully common, and only shreds of obsolete ideality cling to the bewildered socialites. In *The Rise of Silas Lapham* the author's vision has tilted downwards. Relevance in action and in moral choice, like vital hope for the future, lie only with the vulgar Laphams. But something more disconcerting is forcing itself upon the view. Howells cannot quite decide what to make of the slum and waterfront Boston he apparently cannot help seeing as somehow inescapably attached to the meaning of Silas' experience. In *The Minister's Charge* he explores that side of Boston life more thoroughly and makes a first decision about what must be done: at the very least everyone must recognise his "complicity" in the fate of everyone else, especially those outcast.

After "complicity" had been explored and extended to "solidarity" and brotherhood in *Annie Kilburn* and *A Hazard of New Fortunes,* it was a critical socialist who brought his eye to bear again on Boston. And what it now focused upon was a world the really imaginable existence of which the author of *Out of the Question* would have been ready to deny to himself. He imagined a young physician of Henry Jamesian tastes and sensibility, a specialist like Dr. Wingate in nervous diseases, who had been living in Italy for years. Having lost his patrimony in the financial wreck of the Union Pacific, Dr. Edward Olney has been forced to come home to Boston and compete in the American race for wealth. He returns to a July city deserted by that fringe of summer vacationing socialites who are his prospective patients and would normally establish the atmosphere of Boston for him. The real Boston, as it is without them, grates painfully on Olney's exposed, expatriate nerves. Olney finds that the real Boston consists, like Liverpool (or any other modern city?), of people belonging to "the proletarian type." Principally on exhibit in Boston are "primary and secondary Irish" generations of immigrants. Looking at them scientifically, Dr. Olney thought that "they might give us, with better conditions, a race as hale and handsome as the elder American race; but the transition from the Old World to the New, as represented in them, was painful. . . ."

The only Americans he can find who seem anything like as amiable as the Italians for whom he feels homesick are the Negroes who have been flocking in from the South. And in considering them, Olney—and Howells' work of fiction—come squarely up against a major American question. The huge advantage of the fact that Howells' imaginative focus had kept deepening was that it enabled him to discover possibilities for fiction both fresh and important. Sometime in this period he had quickly entered the germ of a story in his pocket notebook. "In Town Out of Season," it said. "—Might be a story in autobiographic form of a young man, rich, cultivated, well-born who notices all those handsome negroes we saw last summer, and falls in love with an octoroon."

In developing his story from that germ, Howells abandoned the "first-person narrator" and told his story "dramatically." Where *The Shadow of a Dream* had been a short, "autobiographic" novel, the new work became a genuine *nouvelle;* quicker, more condensed, decidedly tighter in movement than anything Howells had previously written. It pioneered in imagining frankly and dramatically two of the most central American problems—racial segregation, and miscegenation. And it dealt with them in their most immediate, crucial aspects—in Northern, urban, and what were then modern circumstances, though in terms which permitted no Howells reader to shield his prejudices from its impact. Perhaps mistakenly, Howells named it from the book's minor issue of morbid conscientiousness with which his readers were thoroughly familiar, and titled it *An Imperative Duty.*

Though the serialization did not begin in *Harper's* until July 1891, for reasons of Alden's editorial convenience, Howells, writing slowly this time, had finished his "novelette" by early September 1890. As a matter of fact, he must have been meditating it during the writing of *A Boy's Town,* for he told his father on December 22, 1889, that he had been visiting a colored Methodist church (used in a key scene in *An Imperative Duty*) and felt "softened and humbled among those lowly and kindly people." Almost certainly the impulse for this work came out of the author's time of painful reconstruction of his childhood. Now it is significant that there are no such intimate images of Negro playmates and personalities in Howells' memoirs as in Mark Twain's. Offhand, one recalls no Negroes at all in *A Boy's Town.* And it is not likely that there were many in bitterly proslavery, pro-Southern, antifreedman Butler County, Ohio, during Howells' boyhood there.

He could never know the Negro as Twain could, never write as a Southerner for the problems of the Southern psyche. But sympathy for the slave had been cardinal in Howells' childhood morality. For that his family had been hounded out of Hamilton, had suffered and failed in Dayton, had fought triumphantly in Ashtabula County. It was at least equally important to speak for the Negro to the Northern psyche and conscience. For this Howells had the background and credentials. As critical socialist he had the eyes to see that only the first problems had been solved in setting the slaves free, that perhaps even greater problems remained to be solved— and in the mind and heart of the white North. As artist he had the skill to present what his eye saw to the imagining eye of his reader. And as national figure he had and was willing again to risk the prestige to force his view on the public attention.

A *nouvelle, An Imperative Duty* has only three main characters. The few others are "business" characters who help move the action along and preserve the narrative illusions without counting for much otherwise. In his Boston hotel, Olney is called to minister to Mrs. Meredith, a lady also just returned from Italy, where he had met her socially. With her is her niece, Rhoda Aldgate, a bright, gay-hearted girl of warm temperament and unique beauty who again stirs Olney's interest. Mrs. Meredith is on the verge of a nervous breakdown. Olney knows her for a typically Howellsian feminine quixote—a literose romantic obsessed with ideals of absolute truth and duty. After several calls, however, it transpires that Mrs. Meredith has been living a lie of omission which has now placed her in a crisis. Rhoda's mother was an octoroon, and Rhoda has never been told. A clergyman named Bloomingdale, very blond and of a most conventional family, has proposed to Rhoda. Is it

Mrs. Meredith's imperative duty to tell Rhoda? She finally does, and Rhoda's reaction is so desperate that Mrs. Meredith commits suicide. Olney finds a home for Rhoda with Mrs. Clara Kingsbury Atherton (see *A Modern Instance*). When Bloomingdale reappears, Rhoda sends him away. Olney pays his court, talks Rhoda out of her melodramatic self-projections, marries her and takes her away to Rome to live.

Howells was scrupulously careful to give each character his point of view and let him speak from it. In the shifts of their views he developed much of the dramatic as well as thematic power of his work. He was quick to complain when readers did not appreciate the necessities of his method. The first pages, detailing Olney's first reactions to Boston raised, he told his sister Aurelia, an "Irish howl against me, and is likely to make noise enough. They can't see that it is not I who felt and said what Olney did." Yet he could not have denied—would not—that his was the vision that imagined Olney's, and it was after all he who introduced the topics his people talked about and envisioned their reactions to the events of the action he foreordained.

Before the crisis of Mrs. Meredith's duty has emerged, Howells lets Olney have his say on segregation. To the returning expatriate, the Negroes seem "the most agreeable, the most interesting feature of the social spectacle . . . the only people left who have any heart for life here; they all look hopeful and happy, even in the rejection from their fellow-men, which strikes me," he says, "as one of the most preposterous, the most monstrous things in the world, now I've got back to it here." Olney ends this discussion, which has been proceeding while he waits for a prescription to come up from the pharmacy and mixes a dose for Mrs. Meredith, by saying, "I believe . . . that if the negroes ever have their turn—and if the meek are to inherit the earth they must come to it—we shall have a civilization of such sweetness and good-will as the world has never known yet. Perhaps we shall have to wait their turn for any real Christian civilization."

As a man of science, he also rejects Mrs. Meredith's hysterical concern about genetic atavism—the "throw-backs" of popular mythology. Scientifically, he says, "The chances of atavism . . . are so remote that they may be said hardly to exist at all. They are outside of the probabilities, and only on the verge of the possibilities. But it's so thrilling to consider such a possibility that people like to consider it. Fancy is as much committed to it as prejudice is; but it hasn't so much excuse, for prejudice is mostly ignorant and fancy is mostly educated, or half-educated." Once again, romanticism is the villain.

When Olney learns that Rhoda is "of negro descent," he learns something about his own prejudice. His first reaction is "a turmoil of emotion for which there is no word but disgust . . . profound and pervasive. . . . His own race instinct expressed itself in a merciless rejection of her beauty, her innocence, her helplessness because of her race. The impulse had to have its course; and then he mastered it, with an abiding compassion, and a sort of tender indignation."

Olney argues that Mrs. Meredith should not tell Rhoda. But when she does, Rhoda's reaction is much like Olney's first one. Battered by a tornado of emotion, and without Olney's resources of intellectual cultivation, she ranges through every response of terror, resentment, self-pity, and self-loathing. She wanders out into the streets and down into the Negro section, all her earlier patronizing love of Negroes dissolving in jealousy—because they have always known of themselves what she has just discovered—fear, and hatred of the black skins, the Negroid features. She finds an old mulatto woman and follows her to church, there hearing a black, young divinity student who gives her the one ray of hope she *can* find. And it is, of course, Howells' Tolstoian doctrine.

In the midst of Rhoda's "whirling thoughts," she catches the young man's voice:

' "Yes, my friends," it went on saying, "You got to commence doing a person good if you expect to love them as Jesus loved us when he died for us. And oh, if our white brethren could only understand—and they're gettin' to understand it—that if they would help us a little more, they needn't hate us so much. . . . I believe it's the only way out of all the trouble in the world. You can't fight your way out, and you can't steal your way out, and you can't lie your way out. But you can *love* your way out. And how can you love your way out. By helpin' somebody else ! . . ." '

The other way to deal with the problems of segregation and miscegenation, Howells suggests, is to let the romantic steam out of them. They are, after all, only human problems susceptible of solution through good morals, common sense, and good will. When Olney finally can say to Rhoda, "I love you ! I ask you to be my wife," he gets the melodramatic response she has prepared:

'She let her hand seem to sink deeper in his hold, which had somehow not released it yet; she almost pushed it in for an instant, and then she pulled it violently away. "Never !" She sprang to her feet and gasped out, "I am a Negress !"

Something in her tragedy affected Olney comically; perhaps the belief that she had often rehearsed these words as an answer to his demand. He smiled "Well, not a very black one. Besides, what of it, if I love you?"

"What of it?" she echoed. "But don't you *know?* You mustn't !"

The simpleness of the words made him laugh outright; these she had not rehearsed. She had dramatized his instant renunciation of her when he knew the fatal truth.

"Why not? I love you whether I must or not !"

As tragedy the whole affair had fallen to ruin. It could be reconstructed, if at all, only upon an octave much below the operatic pitch. It must be treated in no twilight of gloom, but in plain, simple, matter-of-fact noonday.'

As a man of his age, Howells was at one with much of the scientific thought of the day in being a racist. That is to say, he took race seriously. He was proud of his own Welshness. He intimated that much of Rhoda Aldgate's trouble came from "that war between her temperament and her character which is the fruitful cause of misery in the world, where all strains are now so crossed and intertangled that there is no definite and unbroken direction any more in any of us." In Rhoda's sixteenths of ancestry there warred one Negro part against seven parts of white Southern oppressor (and therefore hater) of the Negro, and against those eight New England parts like those of Mrs. Meredith. These produced in Rhoda "that hypochondria of the soul into which the Puritanism of her father's race had sickened in her, and which so often seems to satisfy its crazy claim upon conscience by enforcing some aimless act of self-sacrifice." That, of course, was the question so familiar to Howells' audience from which he drew his book's title.

But if Howells was devoted to ideas about race which now seem outmoded, he was pioneering in applying them in the right direction. As so often in his work, where his careful studies of fact are now valuable only for the historical imagination and his intellectual ways and means seem obsolete, his moral intuitions for the United States of America remain thoroughly viable. The Irish have become the Americans Olney hoped they might. The Negroes have long since ceased to be childishly buoyant and flamboyant. It seems clear that continuing miscegenation will not "solve" the racial problem automatically. But it seems very clear that love and justice based on human solidarity, on common sense, and on mutual helpfulness can and will obliterate it. And that was Howells' fundamental prescription.

In his relations with Negroes both as persons and as a race, Howells apparently attempted to follow that prescription himself. As a result, he became the friend and patron of Paul Laurence Dunbar and one of the founding sponsors of the National Association for the Advancement of Colored People. The story of his relationship to the NAACP seems simple. When, at the centenary of Abraham Lincoln's birth in 1909 the situation of the Negro, segregated, disfranchised, uneducated, terrorized in the South and often in peonage, looked desperate, Oswald Garrison Villard issued a call for action which eventuated in the founding of the NAACP. One of the willing signers of Garrison's appeal was William Dean Howells.

But the story of his relations with Dunbar is the much more intimate, if familiar in Howells' life, tale of his encouragement and practical assistance of a young writer. Herne the actor, scouring the nation with a road company, stumbled across Dunbar's privately printed *Majors and Minors* in the spring of 1896 and sent it to Howells. To the astonished delight of the poet, the country's leading man of letters praised his work in his *Harper's Weekly* "Life and Letters" column. When Dunbar wrote a sincerely grateful but dignified and balanced letter of thanks, Howells busied himself on the poet's behalf. He put pressure on Ripley Hitchcock, the literary agent, to get Dunbar regularly published and wrote a carefully honest, illuminating preface for the ensuing *Lyrics of Lowly Life*. He set Major Pond, the Barnum of lectures and literary "readings," on Dunbar's trail, and Pond put Dunbar on the platform. Howells invited Dunbar to come and see him at the house he owned in Far Rockaway in 1896. And Dunbar was amused and amazed at the great man's lack of pomp. Dunbar opened the gate, as he told the story, "then from the verandah, and down the walk came running a fat little man with white hair, and halfway met me, seizing me by the hands, and exclaiming, 'This is Paul Dunbar !' It was Mr. Howells !" In the cold September night as he left, Dunbar was touched by Howells' insistence that he wear Howells' overcoat back to the city—and Howells, as Miss Mildred Howells records it, "was touched and shocked to find afterwards that Dunbar thought there was anything unusual in his doing it."

Such personal touches reveal the man Howells; but more important, perhaps, was the impact upon the sense of the nation of the exact and thoughtful words Howells spoke of the Negro poet in his introduction to *Lyrics of Lowly Life.* Quite properly, Howells begins by asserting that Dunbar's color and lowly employment as an elevator boy in Dayton, while interesting facts about a poet, are no good reasons for interest in the poetry—it must be art or not worth attention. But Howells feels "his merits positive and not comparative"—"in more than one piece he has produced a work of art." This taken as true by the critic's fiat, it remains to consider the significance of this art. He finds four items of significance. Dunbar is a "first." Negroes have achieved distinction in music and oratory, but "So far as I could remember, Paul Dunbar was the only man of pure African blood and of American civilization to feel the Negro life aesthetically and express it lyrically." And this he has done with the "most modern consciousness," studying the American Negro "objectively . . . with humor, with sympathy, and yet with what the reader must instinctively feel to be entire truthfulness." This is "an evidence of the essential unity of the human race, which does not think or feel black in one or white in another, but humanly in all." And, since the race has "attained civilization" in Dunbar, there is the hope that "the hostilities and prejudice which had so long constrained his race were destined to vanish in the arts; that these were to be the final proof that God had made of one blood all nations of men."

All very good, but there is a last significance perceived here which proves that Howells' views were not limited to those of Dr. Olney. Howells does not hope that the Negro will disappear into the general nation via miscegenation or any other route. For though all men be of one blood at the last, "Yet . . . it appears to me," said Howells, "that there is a precious difference of temperament between the races which it would be a great pity ever to lose. . . ." And that, Howells thought, Dunbar best caught in the humor and tenderness, the "finely ironical perception" of his "dialect pieces. These are divinations and reports of what passes in the hearts and minds of a lowly people whose poetry had hitherto been inarticulately expressed in music, but now finds, for the first time in our tongue, literary interpretation of a very artistic completeness."

How precisely right or wrong Howells was in these critical judgments is not to the main point here. For the main point is that, when Howells' was the most authoritative critical voice in the nation, for the first time a Negro writer found serious consideration in precisely the same way as any other writer, was treated neither patronizingly nor prejudicially: received, in short, by the regular lights of the critic, critical justice.

IV

One of the obvious temptations of publishing people dazzled by the success of *A Hazard of New Fortunes* was to imagine themselves playing Fulkerson, stealing Howells from the Harpers to play March, and winning success with joint magazine enterprises. Most liable of all to that beguilement was the dynamic pioneer of newspaper syndication, the buoyant Samuel Sidney ("S.S.") McClure. If Howells had imagined Fulkerson's personality from his old friend Ralph Keeler, he had also been mindful of McClure's imaginative coups in the publishing business, and McClure took pride in recognizing the fact. Howells had long cherished his dream of a first-class magazine of the realism of all nations to be called *The World of Fiction,* and by the spring of 1890 McClure was at him to try it as a hazard of new fortunes.

In May 1890 he sent Howells a contract (never returned) for signing. It proposed "an illustrated monthly magazine or purely literary miscellany of the highest class," to begin in December 1891, or whenever Howells was free. McClure was to provide up to $25,000 in capital. Howells was to be half owner and "Editor-in-Chief" with "absolute control" at a $5,000 per year salary. For what Howells contributed to the magazine he was to be paid $100 per thousand words for fiction and $50 per thousand for criticism, and $1,000 outright for plays or farces. Howells was to own his books and get royalties from them, McClure to have first right to publish any book. This offered Howells greater financial rewards than his contract with the Harpers, huge profits if the magazine were successful—and McClure's promotional prowess augured success. But it promised to monopolize his time and make devastating demands on his creative powers as well as his mere daily energy—and he was now fifty-three. Finally, it presented him with genuine hazards: he was to be paid only out of the net profits from the magazine; and residual profits were to be split (fairly enough) after McClure had taken his own $5,000 salary.

Howells signed neither that nor a subsequent contract offering to pay him percentages on sales of the magazine. He was interested enough by McClure to begin to wonder and waver over renewing his Harpers contract, however. And McClure did manage to finesse the serialization rights for Howells' next novel away from the Harpers. Essentially what Howells did was to supply *An Imperative Duty* to Alden for his 1891 novel, project *The World of Chance* for Alden in 1892, and write an extra novel for McClure to syndicate.

The result is particularly interesting because, by a lucky series of chances, the synopsis on which Howells sold McClure the novel—as he habitually sold novels to editors—has survived. This is what Howells wrote out for McClure to buy before Howells began to compose:

'I have thought of calling the story "The Mercy of God," or "The Grace of God," but I have not decided about that; perhaps either title would be too grave. But it would be the story of a man of great force, great apparent wealth and high social standing, who had worked himself up from simple New England beginnings, to the head of a great manufacturing interest. At the opening of the story, he is in the secret which cannot be kept any longer—that he had embezzled and muddled away the company's money to an amount that makes him a hopeless defaulter. Three courses are then open to him: to kill himself as Grey did; to stand trial and go to prison as Snelling did; to go to Canada as so many others have done. His lawyer, a man of conscience and certain original principles, advises him to stand his trial. A young fellow, not a very good young fellow, who has been sufficiently foolish in his own way, and who has not been very constant in his thoughts to the defaulter's daughter, finds himself made a man by the crisis, and agrees with him, too. She and the young fellow confirm their engagement in view of the calamity; and are ready to meet the worst together. But the defaulter himself has not the heart for it. He goes to Canada, and the story follows him to Quebec, on ground that I know very well. I should make a close study of his life and circumstances there, and try to show how without resources in himself, life must begin to pall upon him, there or anywhere away from his old interests. He goes back and forth to Europe, keeping out of the reach of extradition, but he is always an exile, always cut off from his old occupations, associations, and above all from his country place, where he used to find the highest pleasures— common ones, of course: horses, fine cattle, etc.—he was capable of. He is homesick, bored and lonesome. A detective appears, and shadows him; and he knows it, with a curious longing to make the man's acquaintance. He finds him, as I shall try to show him, not the conventional detective of fiction, but a human being with a family he is very fond of. They rather like one another, and I shall try to make the reader like the detective, without romancing him in the least, or blinking any of his professional characteristics. The defaulter begins to toy with the notion of going home and taking his chances; he and the detective talk it over, and the detective is enthusiastic about it; he tries to make interest with the defaulter to let him take him back and get the reward. The notion at first amuses the defaulter, but when he has fully made up his mind to return, he telegraphs for the detective and put himself in his power inside the American border. The detective is puzzled; in view of past kindnesses between them, he wishes to be magnanimous, and he gives him a last chance to escape (supposing the equivalent of the reward to be secured) if he has changed his mind. But the defaulter has not changed his mind. The idea of expiation has fully taken possession of it. He refuses the chance offered him and goes home. He is kept out of prison on bail, and while waiting his trial, suddenly dies.

I can give only a meagre outline of my scheme, without suggesting any but principal figures. I should try to have a strong love interest in the story, and I should try to give it humorous grace in the character of the detective and the Quebec people, and others. The whole design shows fantastic in some points, but I believe it to be thoroughly realistic, in the deep, interior way, where I should seek my strongest dramatic effects, while on the surface I should try to keep a constant play of incident for those who could not look below it. The subject is modern, immediate, such as I like to treat, and I feel the motive to be strong. But, of course, everything depends with me upon the working out, or rather the working in.

I should like this synopsis back again, for I expect to make no other memoranda for the story.'

McClure, naturally enough, was delighted. He had been given a unique glimpse into the creative process of a writer whose sophistication and maturity made him seem elusive to most readers. He confessed his surprise that the synopsis itself should stir his interest so strongly. But best of all, he could scent in advance the novel's appeal to his syndicate's readership. He was charmed to accept from Howells what "promises to be the strongest novel you have ever written," said McClure.

For Howells the actual writing turned out to be much tougher than he had anticipated. The massive flow of facility which had carried *A Hazard of New Fortunes* along seemed choked down to a trickle now. And here was no problem which could be solved with the elegant economies of his last two works. The defaulter's tragedy called for full-scale adventuring into unknown territories, and the explorer's way proved torturous. In February he was complaining to his father, "I find it more and more difficult to satisfy myself with my work; I seem to be always experimenting, always exploring a new field. But I suppose this is a condition of interest in the matter. . . ."

For stimulus and perhaps reassurance he sought family help with the look and feel of Quebec, especially in winter. He stirred up Sylvester Baxter to find out from fellow newsmen on the Boston *Herald* how reporters handled embezzlement stories. Howells personally investigated the Boston detective bureau, finding the chief "delighted" that he "was not going to take a melodramatic view of the detective's work" and zealous to cooperate with the realist. Yet the writing ground along slowly. Howells had to throw away the first 200 little manuscript pages of a "false start." When he began again, it went better. "But I never had material behave so before," he fumed. It was July before he could finish.

There may have been other causes, but at least one main reason for all this recalcitrance in his material was that Howells was groping through it toward important new understandings of American life and the meaning of the characteristics of the business community. In *The Quality of Mercy* he returned again to the setting and some of the characters of *Annie Kilburn*, but really he was working out one of the variations on the theme of *The Rise of Silas Lapham* natural to the critical socialist he had since become. Not until Thorstein Veblen published *The Theory of the Leisure Class* later in the decade would Howells get much conceptual help in clarifying the perceptions he was dramatizing in *The Quality of Mercy*. And it would be a generation before American writers in general would learn to work effectively with these explorer's cognitions.

Nothing shows in the texture of *The Quality of Mercy* to betray Howells' anguish in composition. His difficulties must have been intellectual, not technical. The structure is neater, the movement of events cleaner and easier than in *A Hazard of New Fortunes,* for all the demonically controlled ease of the latter's writing. *The Quality of Mercy's* structure is simplicity itself. Yet within it Howells was able to pack a dense complexity of events and reactions. His grip on the characters must have been deathly tight; for there is an unusually large number of them, and they are all—but one— solidly endowed with life and individuality. In their scenes, these definite characters mostly talk in their own expertly shaped styles. But when occasion demands, they act, or the main character thinks, in the midst of sharply pictured settings, which often stir up atmospheric and thence symbolic responses in the reader. And yet the relevance of all this is kept unusually clear by the simplicity of the novel's design. It has three parts, a long introduction, a long developmental middle, and a short, hard-hitting conclusion.

The first part was perhaps the most interesting segment of a novel Howells had yet written. Ever since he had opened *The Rise of Silas Lapham* by letting Bartley Hubbard interview Silas, he had toyed with the audience of his faithful readers by reintroducing characters from the past. Not only was that fun and creatively economical for an author whose best characters went on living in his imagination. It also lent a depth and definiteness of specification to his scenes and people hard for him to match by using the wholly new. Howells' loyal follower lived ever more richly in the author's world as he met old friends—and enemies—grown older and worse or better. The new or intermittent reader had only the present text to go on, and that created certain risks for him and for the author.

In *The Quality of Mercy* we find ourselves back in the setting of *Annie Kilburn,* in Hatboro and South Hatboro. Annie will appear, looking "handsome and very happy," for she and Dr. Morrell are married. Putney is there, with Gerrish and other old adversaries. Indeed, as the novel opens on a beautifully rendered scene of the coachmen and hackmen joshing and cursing over their cutters at the Hatboro station in February, it is an old enemy of Putney's who will get off the train, go home, open his safe, and take out his cache

of $43,000 to "skip" to Canada with. Northwick, the pompous
gentleman farmer of South Hatboro, a favorite target of Putney's
curses for his conspicuous consumption and corruption of the local
farmer, is Howells' defalcator. The wintry atmosphere takes us
back to *A Modern Instance,* and before we are done we will meet
again both Ricker of the Boston *Abstract* and the ghost of Bartley
Hubbard on the *Events.* Proper Boston, too, will be back. Charles
Bellingham, Bromfield Corey, and the Rev. Mr. Sewell, all a good
deal aged, appear.

To the Howellsian these familiar settings and people were intriguing. The mere practical skill of the artist at touching in his
views and atmospheres no doubt mattered. But neither of these
quite explains the sensation caused by *The Quality of Mercy* on
first appearance. "Your novel is taking splendidly. This is somewhat of a surprise to me, inasmuch as I had supposed that your
work would not attract the million," wrote McClure. "Mr. Nixon,
of the Chicago *Inter Ocean* was here yesterday, and he told me
casually that they had to print on Monday a second edition of the
Sunday which contained the first installment. . . ." The novel, he
continued, "will appear in the *Philadelphia Inquirer,* Chicago *Inter
Ocean,* Cincinnati *Commercial Gazette,* Toronto *Globe,* as well as
the Boston *Herald.*" The pull of Howells' name no doubt helped,
but the best explanation probably is that the material was more
inherently dramatic than any he had ever used—a millionaire criminal is in the act of absconding. He let Northwick "skip," exploiting
his emotional and psychological reactions perfectly. Then, with
technique and appeal extraordinary in Howells' work, he kept the
reader dangling in suspense while he moved laterally through a
broad sweep of action and implication with which to flesh his novel
out to full proportions and give it that potential of serious significance he had promised McClure to conceal below the surface for the
serious reader.

What Howells did was to put Northwick on the train for Canada
and then skillfully keep the reader guessing whether Northwick
had or had not been killed in a railroad accident while the author
went about developing the rest of the novel. The added interest for
us, which could have been shared then only by McClure and his
editors, is to watch Howells spin his work out of his mind, fulfill-
ing, adding to, and departing from his synopsis. What "showed
fantastic" in his "scheme" was discarded. And there lies the ex-

planation of Howells' throwing away his first 200 pages. Northwick had two daughters, old-maid Adeline and proud, gorgeous Suzette. In *Annie Kilburn* Sue was ambiguously courted by Jack Wilmington, who was also involved with his "aunt," the young wife of an old mill owner. Howells' first notion was to reconcile Jack and Sue over Northwick's dilemma. But that almost surely presented moral and psychological problems the solution of which would have pulled the novel far away from its major theme—and pulled it all out of shape to boot. So Jack was discarded.

In his place Howells imagined a family of Proper Bostonians: Eben Hilary, the President and Chairman of the Board of Northwick's company, who gives Northwick his chance to skip largely out of mercy for Sue, who is a friend of Hilary's daughter Louise; and Matt Hilary, their son and brother, who has kept on good terms with his quick-tempered but admirable father despite Matt's refusal to stay in business and his groping toward socialism. By letting Matt and Sue fall in love, Howells can give the promised "love-interest" to his tale and eat his cake by using their love and engagement as an essential vehicle for his serious themes.

The other problem was the detective. For all his research, Howells eventually found himself unable to imagine the detective. But he could easily imagine the sort of amiably vulgar "spaceman," that is, reporter who was paid lineage for what his paper printed rather than salary, who was always sleuthing around for a "scoop." So he sketched out Pinney, the perfect example of Bartley Hubbardism in newshawks (though Pinney is given an idyllically happy married life to contrast with Bartley's). In Pinney he could continue the study of "the counting-room in independent journalism" begun so expertly in *A Modern Instance*. Howells could also pay off some of the debts he had incurred to the journalism of the country out of the Realism War and the Chicago Anarchist case. Pinney, who would sell his soul for a by-line, was the perfect man for the *Events*. And "the *Events* continued what Bartley Hubbard had made it . . . a journal without principles and without convictions, but with interests only; a map of busy life, indeed, but glaringly colored, with crude endeavors at picturesqueness, and with no more truth to life than those railroad maps where the important centres converge upon the broad black level of the line advertised, and leave rival roads wriggling faintly about in uninhabited solitudes."

To balance Pinney, Howells found himself creating another and much more interesting reporter. Brice Maxwell, who writes for the more serious *Abstract,* is an aspiring poet and playwright, a "ravenous reader of philosophy and sociology." Frustrated and frequently ill as a result of his economic compulsion to do eight hours of often unsuccessful journalism to win two hours for his real work, Maxwell fascinated Howells—and the Hilarys. Matt Hilary takes him up, finding him "as completely at odds with life as anyone I ever saw. He has a great deal of talent and no health or money . . . the artistic type cynicised by the hard conditions of life—newspaper conditions, and then economic conditions." Life often imitates art. Perhaps Howells already knew a Maxwell in Boston. But when he put those words in Hilary's mouth, there was a young man hanging around the police court and New York Central station, fiercely playing baseball for Syracuse University, or scribbling at what may have been a first draft of *Maggie* in the Delta Upsilon house. His name was Stephen Crane. He differed from Brice Maxwell mainly in the fact that he had genius—and in a few years Howells would be influencing him profoundly. For the moment, however, Howells found Brice Maxwell so vital that he took time to initiate a romance between Maxwell and Louise Hilary and filed it away for future reference.

Holding everybody, readers included, in suspense over Northwick's fate, Howells is able thematically to dramatize the workings of "complicity." As Matt Hilary says, "there's really no measuring the sinuous reach of a disaster like this. It strikes from a coil that seems to involve everything." Northwick's disappearance brings grief to his daughters—who refuse to believe his guilt. It involves the Hilarys in a number of ways, several of them increasingly intimate. Through them, the great world of Boston is brought in. And in Hatboro, with all its well-tested levels, the reactions of most of the common people of America to Northwick's crime are registrable. Finally, in Matt Hilary the gentleman socialist and Brice Maxwell the struggling artist, Howells had created something special. Neither is quite an old-fashioned *raisonneur* nor quite a Henry James "sensitive observer." Each plays his own part and lives out his own fate within the novel. But they are both rebels, both seekers, both inclined to use Howells' socialist vocabulary for themselves rather than serve as mouthpieces for his ideas. They serve as a realist's—

and critical socialist's—chorus. Perhaps the best word for them would be "controls": against their standards the shortcomings of other characters and their ideas can be measured. By keeping the action suspended while he packed all this into Part One of his novel, Howells won the advantage of his dramatic opening and was able to get the same effect as the ancient *in medias res* beginning without having to resort to flash-backs.

When he opens Part Two, he has the flash-back ready in reserve and can throw it in to restore full drive to his novel again. Now we learn that Northwick was not killed but fled deep into wilderness Canada and has been deathly sick for months in a frost-isolated cabin. He writes a letter to the *Events* justifying himself. After the shock has been a little absorbed by the sisters, Matt proposes to Sue and is accepted. Then the Hilarys must take family responsibility for Northwick, and the conclusion of the novel is in sight. In Part Two the "love-interest" is developed. But below its surface, even, more triumphantly, in direct connection with it, Howells fully realizes his major thematic development and reaches the all-important turn which will allow him to round his novel off. In this his maturity, Howells was able to balance his fictional equations with a completeness not often matched by his fellow craftsmen. His way was to work from the intriguing cultural phenomenon toward social theory and then on through to the moral conclusion which for Howells represented the solution of his equation.

Snow and cold surround Northwick's defalcation, which takes place during a New England February cold snap. When Northwick enters his home, richly furnished, the air perfumed with living flowers from his greenhouses, the whole atmosphere warm with home and family associations, he looks in dismay at the bleakness out of doors. Yet it is into that he must go or suffer the penalty of his crime. Everybody complains about the cold. But Northwick is at the center of it, and fleeing ever northward into polar frigidity. Howells' pictures of Canadian towns and people, but most of all of the winter cold, are masterful. Cold becomes the symbol of Northwick's sin. As in many another work of literature, the no-color whiteness of the snow is an omen of evil. In letting Northwick slip away, fiery old Mr. Hilary calls him "you whited sepulchre," and as Northwick retreats into the bush he is ever more deeply oppressed by "the lifeless desert he had been travelling through."

He comes to think, more ironically truthfully than he is capable of imagining, that "he must die to the world, to his family, before he could hope to revisit either. . . ."

The physical cold nearly does kill him. It leaves him enfeebled, perhaps with heart disease, after his long illness. The psychic chill of exile paralyzes him and destroys his fond illusion of recouping in Canada and returning triumphantly to repay his victims. Howells works very carefully through Northwick's psychology, tracing the processes of his rationalizations. He shows Northwick refusing to face the knowledge both of his keen, conscious mind and of his deepest soul. His egotism keeps "sophistry" tacitly at work in him. "He contended," Howells observes, "from that vestibule of his soul, where he was not a thief, with that soul of his inmost where he was a thief. . . ."

As he dashes into the cold, Northwick's psyche is increasingly pulled apart by these tensions. His mind—rationally or irrationally? —wants desperately to quit, to give up, to hang his money belt at the altar of St. Anne de Beaupré, to confess to Père Étienne, but above all to go back home again: "the breach between his will and his mind seemed to grow continually wider." And, of course, as he stays away, home disintegrates. His daughters cannot keep it up. Even though they own land and buildings, the creditors eventually come and sell off the stock, the furniture, everything, and leave the house bare. His daughters suffer shame as well as grief after his letter to the *Events*. Adeline's mind begins to crack. Even as he lies delirious in Oiseau's cabin dreaming of home, home is ceasing to exist.

Meanwhile the world is deciding what to make of Northwick. Pinney makes a lurid, very personal nine-day's wonder of him, and then the *Events* and its readers go on to the next sensation. Defaulters are so commonplace—the AP wire averages a major one a day. But Brice Maxwell, working with Taine-like historicity, artistic "texture" and proportion, dignity, and "humane temperance," philosophizes him. Maxwell in the *Abstract* "accused the structure of society. There must be something rotten, he said, at the core of our society, when every morning brought the story of a defalcation . . . of officials, public and corporate, for whom we had no guaranty but the average morality of our commercial life." Though editor Ricker cut out of Maxwell's copy what Ricker thought its "rank socialism"—the hope that things might change—he let Maxwell say that "it behooved society to consider how it was responsible, which it might well do without ignoring the responsibility of the criminal." Matt Hilary, and Putney, thoroughly agree. "Northwick isn't the disease; he's merely the symptom," Putney says. "It's the whole social body that's sick. . . ."

And what it is sick of is commercialism, the worship of Mammon, of *making money*, of, as Howells would later say in his own person, plutocracy. This deprives a man of character. Northwick, says Eben Hilary, is an all too common phenomenon, "He's what the commonplace American egotist must come to more and more in finance, now that he is abandoning the career of politics, and wants to be rich instead of great." Through these voices Howells gets his phenomenon theorized in social terms. But there is worse to say. For all his luxuries, his fine library, his collection of pictures, his great houses, his horses and conservatories and all the rest, Northwick is simply empty. He is a barbarian deprived of barbaric splendor. The worship of Mammon had given him nothing but money. He had exchanged life for nothingness. Père Étienne the sensitive village priest, discovers in conversing with Northwick that he exists in "complete ignorance of the things that interest cultivated people. . . . He was merely and purely a business man, a figment of commercial civilization, with only the crudest tastes and ambitions outside of the narrow circle of money-making." Even in the vanished home for which he yearned, the luxurious "flowers were possessions, not passions. . . ." Before Père Étienne can extend Christian compassion to Northwick, he must swallow the fact that Northwick is "the creature of a civilization too ugly and arid to be borne." And insofar as it is indeed "commercial civilization," that is the truth of the world of Howells' novel.

But there is, after all, more to be said. Ancient Bromfield Corey, hearing Northwick discussed, agrees that his case is "commonplace." But every such case, he points out, "is preceded by a slow and long decay of a moral nature, and that is of a most eternal and tragical interest. . . ." Equally interesting is the question of Northwick's destiny. Can he be saved? And what will constitute salvation for him? What is the quality of mercy? Obviously it is not the selfish indulgence Northwick extended to himself in skipping. He finds his exile in the long run a worse prison than the penitentiary he has evaded. When Matt becomes engaged to Sue, noncommercial aspects of civilization reach out toward Northwick.

Mr. Hilary's love for Matt, his respect for Matt's love, his strong sense of decorum and family solidarity, those remnants of old abolitionist idealism which have made him tender of Matt's intransigeance, all are roused. He will resign from the Board, he will if necessary make Northwick's debts good—this is now a family matter.

But first Northwick must be found. Pinney, now a semiprofessional private detective (this will leave him free to make that essential last offer to Northwick) is retained to find him. And at this point Part Three begins. In beautifully characterized scenes he does find him and win his trust. Moved by his first knowledge that his daughters had long mourned him dead, Northwick takes the desperate chance of going home. Ghostlike he moves through the barren rooms of his old house at night. He finds his daughters and completely unsettles Adeline in the scenes of reconciliation, grief, and desperate parting again which ensue. He sneaks back to Canada to think. These stirrings of love and grief in Northwick, these first reachings outside his own egotism, are essential. They make his case more than sordid commonplace. They lend it a dignity of "deepening tragedy," as Matt Hilary observes. And gradually Northwick begins to acquire reality enough to get the point. "There began to mix with his longing for home a desire, feeble and formless enough, for expiation." He begins to see "rest and help in accepting the legal penalty."

Eventually he sends for Pinney, insisting that Pinney be ready to put him in handcuffs as soon as they cross the border. "I want the atonement to begin as soon as possible," Northwick says. Across the border, Pinney offers to let him escape if he wants to go back, but Northwick only demands the cuffs. Embarrassedly, Pinney slips them on without locking them. " 'That's good !' murmured Northwick." Those were his last words. When Pinney came to wake him from an apparent nap, he was dead. Pinney lifted his head, and "The loosened handcuffs fell on the floor." Northwick had atoned.

The last word goes to lawyer Putney—who has been fighting valiantly for the Northwick girls—in conversation with his best friend, Morrell:

' ". . . There wasn't the stuff for an example in Northwick; I don't know that he's much of a warning. He just seems to be a kind of—incident; and a pretty common kind. He was a mere creature of circumstances—like the rest of us ! His environment made him rich, and his environment made him a rogue. Sometimes I think there *was* nothing to Northwick, except what happened to him. He's a puzzle. But what do you say, Doc., to a world where we fellows keep fumbling and fizzing away, with our little aims and purposes, and the great ball of life seems to roll calmly along, and get where it's going without the slightest reference to what we do or don't do? I suppose it's wicked to be a fatalist, but I'll go a few aeons of eternal punishment more, and keep my private opinion that it's all Fate."

"Why not call it Law !" the doctor suggested.

"Well, I don't like to be too bold. But taking it by and large, and seeing that most things seem to turn out well in the end, I'll split the difference with you and call it Mercy." '

The two essential points here are Northwick's paucity of being and the neat reference back to the title of the novel. Aside from citations of Northwick's inner claim to the mercy of self-indulgence and escape and Mr. Hilary's reference to the mercy of the gentlemanly impulse, the "decent thing" in allowing Northwick grace, not much has been said about mercy until Putney flashes it as the last word of the text. The title of the novel functions like that of George Herbert's poem "The Pulley." When the work is done one begins to reflect on the meaning of the title, on the quality of mercy. Did Northwick deserve mercy? Did he get it? If one takes fate to mean character, as Howells readily did, one can sight back along the points set by Putney and Morrell to a reading of the ethical meaning of the novel. It was Northwick's Fate, as the Compleat Business Man, to have so little character as virtually to have none. That made him succumb easily to the temptations and opportunities to defraud suggested by the system on the one hand and his egotism on the other. And that made him "skip." But then the Law set in. Go or stay he must be punished. It turns out to be worst of all to fly and compound crime. But it is the quality of Mercy that there is another side to the Law. If through suffering Northwick can learn to love, to care, beyond his pride and greed, for others and for goodness, he may discover his soul in that love, and that will open his eyes to escape through expiation. He can discover the blessing of deliverance through accepting his suffering for his sins. So says the agnostic Swedenborgian-Tolstoian, not delivering it as a sermon but dramatizing it through his fiction on the stage of his reader's imagination.

This drama expressed Howells' established moral-metaphysical insights effectively. But there was nothing new about those insights. The newness came in the middle term of his equation, in the social theory, and particularly in the privative view of the necessary emptiness of the businessman's psyche. Thorstein Veblen would take the same view, and others would follow, agreeing or quarreling. But it remains a live question in America, discussed monthly in books and articles of opinion or of the imagination, whether "business civilization" is a contradiction in terms. Americans have not settled the question for themselves either in its individual or group aspects. Can a man give his heart and soul mainly to the business of making money and still create a self and a life intrinsically good, genuinely worth having? Can a society be composed of men who do that and prove itself a good society, creating a life for itself and for humanity which is worthy of respect and emulation? Nor is this a question merely for Americans.

Howells was by no means the first man or the first American to put these questions as he did in *The Quality of Mercy*. But he asked them at a time when almost no one who could command a major audience—like that of McClure's syndicate—was asking them publicly. It was a time when the nation needed desperately to face up to them. Further, he asked them in a fictional as well as sociological context and by a fictional technique which places him at the beginning of a line which runs through Dreiser, Sherwood Anderson, Lewis, Fitzgerald, and Dos Passos to Cozzens and beyond.

Does that make *The Quality of Mercy* a great novel? The answer, as for the short shelf of Howells' unmistakably major novels, seems to be Perhaps. This novel does not have the breadth or intensity of appeal lent by a "great" character. Howells believed in limited, contingent characters, and Northwick is necessarily very limited. Reviewing the novel, Horace Scudder in the *Atlantic* lamented its failure to exploit its opportunities for melodrama. But Scudder was missing Howells' point. The drama here was not melo- but moral. Northwick is by definition a man of almost nonexistent character. Nothing really melodramatic can happen to or through him. In honesty Howells must keep Northwick to his proper dimension. His problem is to work Northwick up to the place where his pathetic case may assume any tragic proportion. For the rest, Howells' task, superbly carried out, is to study the complicit environment without falling into the Clarence Darrow-like trap of deterministic futilitarianism. For the serious reader the "deep, interior" moral drama Howells promised McClure is there, and it is there with the force which comes from serious creative work maturely and originally consummated. Certainly *The Quality of Mercy* is major in artistry and significance. For the serious reader its depth of social and moral implication might well make it great.

At any rate, *The Quality of Mercy* marks the last true advance in the growth of Howells' mind. Henceforth he would yet write very distinguished novels. But they would re-explore territories already conquered. His imagination's grasp in Northwick of the privative effect on character of plutocracy was to be the last of the new impulses. He was past fifty-four. It would yet be long before it was time to take in sail, but he had reached the high point of a most extraordinarily vital period of late growth.

V

For all S. S. McClure's enterprise, he would never have succeeded in getting a Howells novel to syndicate if Howells' contract with the Harpers had not expired on January 1, 1891. For a decade thereafter he and the firm were to live in uneasy stages of negotiation and agreement broken by periods of relative estrangement during which Howells acted as a free-lance writer. Even the Harpers dramatized themselves in *A Hazard of New Fortunes* contexts, for Joseph Wesley Harper, Jr., apologized at one stage of his difficult bargaining with Howells for a misunderstanding that made him sound like "Dryfoos-père." A year of preliminary discussion did not settle things, and Alden wrote Howells on February 2, 1891, regretting his "wish to discontinue your Editor's Study at the end of the present year. . . ." In September Alden was anxious to reopen discussion, but not on the most flattering terms. Although the Study had not been "what could properly be called a popular success, . . . most cultivated readers would miss it," and the firm would like to see it guided into "less stormy waters" and made more popular.

From that tough bargaining position Alden resisted Howells' offer in October to continue the Study for $5,000 a year. If the Harpers thought Howells could not afford to leave them, that McClure was the only aspiring Fulkerson in the ocean, they were mistaken. On December 8 Alden was writing that he and the Harpers were shocked to hear that Howells was to become a magazine editor and write "fewer novels and no criticism"—but they wished him good luck. To bridge them over until they could settle on Charles Dudley Warner to continue the Study, Howells wrote perhaps a couple more. But he bade his enemies a fondly ironic farewell from the battered windows of the March 1892 Study. It was the same month in which, beginning on his fifty-fifth birthday, he became officially editor of *The Cosmopolitan Magazine.*

For all his writing about Lapham and Dryfoos, Howells had never had much real contact with the American self-made plutocrat. But now he had been hooked and landed by one who knew how to spot an opportunity and seize it. To be sure, this was a unique millionaire. "John Brisben Walker," as Howells explained to his father, "was born in Western Pa., brought up on newspapers, went to West Point, settled in Colorado, where he had ranches and mines. He is a millionaire and a Catholic, but he has very strong socialistic tendencies, and he got himself well scolded by the Catholic press for his address at Washington, preaching human equality and its duties of men to men. So far so good. Of course the affair between us is an experiment, and it may not work, but I shall do my best while it lasts. The money basis is good."

The tentativeness of Howells' outlook in that letter was partly temperamental, but it was sensibly prudential, too. The decisiveness with which he had been wooed and won surprised Howells. It pleased but also worried him. His relationship with Walker had started innocently enough. When a copy of a pamphlet Walker had printed of a lecture entitled "The Church and Poverty" had reached Howells, he had written his approval to the author. Walker's response was to note that he had heard it rumored that Howells was leaving the Harpers and to ask him to write a series of social essays for the *Cosmopolitan* of which Walker was the successful editor and publisher. On Howells' refusal to do that, Walker offered him, on December 4, 1891, $15,000 a year to give "your entire time . . . to the interests of The Cosmopolitan." Howells was to furnish either short stories or a novel of 60,000 words per year, and the *Cosmopolitan* was to have refusal of all his work after his current commitments had expired. Walker wrote on Friday, and Howells presumably gasped in surprise on Saturday when he opened the letter.

But on Monday he was confiding to his father that he had accepted the offer, and he must have notified the Harpers the same day.

The whole thing was so nearly too good to be true, that Howells naturally felt a little gingerly about it. Walker had been incredibly quick—but very complimentary as well as generous. Nevertheless, Howells found himself carefully detailing the facts to his father, and to Charles Eliot Norton, who had served as a practical aid and confidant ever since he had helped to make the Howellses' first little house possible to them in Cambridge in 1866. As he told his father, the *Cosmopolitan* job looked safe: "I am to have sole charge practically; and may end the engagement by six months' notice." His "life-long habit of being on a salary had somehing to do with it." He knew he could sell well as a free lance, but the constant business details were a nuisance. "The best thing about it is Mr. Walker's infatuation with his bargain; yet it is terrible, in a way, to have a man so satisfied with you. He couldn't be more so; he might be less."

If William Cooper Howells had any guidance to give, he was tacitly invited to give it. And so was Mr. Norton. To Norton it was urged that Howells would have "freedom from the anxiety of placing my stories and chaffering about prices, and relief from the necessity of making quantity, as well as full control of the time of publishing them, so that thereafter I can hope to finish each before I begin to print." Further, "the magazine is in such a state that I can hope to do something for humanity as well as the humanities with it. If I cannot, I can give it up, but the outlook is cheerful. . . ." And he asks Norton, as Lowell's executor, for Lowell's poem about Grant for Howells' first *Cosmopolitan* issue in May. "I mean to conduct the magazine so that you will be willing to print something of your own in it," he concludes. "I am to be associated with the owner, Mr. John Brisben Walker, a man of generous ideals, who will leave me absolute control in literature, and whom I think with in many other matters."

Thoughtfully and delicately, but characteristically, Norton answered Howells' unspoken question. The *Cosmopolitan* opportunity, "if you have a free hand," he said, "is superb. Any man might be glad to have such a chance of doing good." But he frankly spoke his doubts about that large "If." It will be "hard work to lift *The Cosmopolitan* out of the atmosphere in which it has flourished; an atmosphere in which there has been a large mingling of the nitrous oxide [laughing and anesthetic] gas of second-rate vulgarity." As a gesture of confidence, Norton let Howells have Lowell's "The Nobler Lover," secure in the recognition that he had done his duty.

AMERICA'S LEADING MAN
OF LETTERS

IF WILLIAM DEAN HOWELLS EVER REALLY DID EITHER DECISIVELY move from Boston to New York or take the literary center of America with him when he went, that event took place in the fall of 1891. The last two-and-a-half years in Boston had probably been as happy as those stricken years could have been anywhere. And certainly Howells had been creatively productive during them. The books of those years had confirmed his reputation as the nation's leading man of letters. Yet there were many reasons why, as he wrote to James in 1890, "I look forward to the winter in Boston with a feeling of satiety towards the place." Though Howells often yearned back nostalgically towards the great, old Boston, much of that greatness was now gone. And he knew that much of the nostalgia was only for his lost youth. Cambridge had not only similarly emptied but become, he confessed, "terribly painful to me, with all the ghostly past rising up at every step. . . ."

In the spring and summer of 1891, Elinor Howells' health seemed much firmer. Leaving his Commonwealth Avenue house in June, Howells wrote gaily to Aldrich that his address would be "simply, Solar System." But in the fall some kind of decision had to be made, and the Howellses drifted to New York. His reasons, and his feelings, were well expressed to his father: "I look forward to a winter in New York with loathing; I would so much rather be in the country; but it will be well for the work I am trying to do, and it seems the only thing for the children. Between the two cities I prefer New York; it is less 'done,' and there is more for one to see and learn there." His reasons for drifting to New York were personal and tentative. It was not until the *Cosmopolitan* deal came through that he decided definitely to move his things down from Boston, and that seemed an accidental and merely practical adaptation at the time.

His feelings about living in Boston, New York, or anywhere else were hopelessly beset by ambivalences. If it be true that the modern author does not really live anywhere, Howells had become in that sense "modern" perhaps as early as the date of his leaving his Beacon Street house in 1885. After Winifred's death, Mrs. Howells avoided formal "Society" completely, and Howells avoided it as well as he could. Yet he enjoyed the Author's Club (until a fight, apparently over Zola and the Dreyfus Affair, drove him out), the Century and other clubs, and association in general with the lively currents of mind and esthetics swirling in New York. Often he dreamed of moving to the country. Half in jest, he told one visitor, "I was raised on corn meal mush, and would like to live in the same simple way now, but my wife won't let me." Sometimes he told himself that "the city journalizes the mind," and dreamed again of living the simple life with axe and hoe for relaxation, calling back the skills of his boyhood.

With the country in mind, several times he dickered for houses in small towns and bought his Far Rockaway house in 1896. But the experiment didn't work. "It is much harder to settle ourselves than I supposed," he complained to his sister Aurelia. The emergent, pragmatic truth turned out to be that the best way was not really to settle at all. Some of the New York residences were elaborate and ostensibly permanent. But as time went on, the Howellses tended more and more to camp out in their apartments, renewing the spirit and atmosphere of their earliest Venetian life together. By the end of the decade Howells had reduced his professional impedimenta to "three cases of books . . . the volumes that I want to read over and over again, and the works that I most frequently consult . . . my necessary tools." These and his clothes he could move easily, and did move frequently. She had really given up housekeeping, Elinor Howells wrote an old friend about the end of the nineties; there just wasn't any point to it any more.

Eventually Howells became a sort of nomad. Garland blamed that on Mrs. Howells and her invalid's "notions." But there seems to be little evidence that Howells was troubled by it. He had long since learned to write regularly almost anywhere, and his moving around made it harder for people to interfere. In some ways his nomadism became the equivalent of "corn meal mush." As one acquaintance said, "During many years his habit was not to live very long in one place. I remember that he moved into and out of a single apartment home three times within a comparatively short period. Indeed one of his friends said, 'I don't care how often Howells moves, so long as he doesn't move into the same place ! That's when I get mixed up. . . .' " During the nineties, he was mostly in New York in winter, always elsewhere to flee the heat in summer, of course. After that, he was as often in Europe, Bermuda, or the South as New York, even in winter.

Did he move the literary center of America to New York in 1891? A good case could be made either way. In leaving, he certainly dimmed the prestige of Boston. "After Edwin Booth and Howells left, the Hernes and many others . . . followed," said Garland, "and Boston never seemed the same illustrious and permanent center it had been to me." He too went down to New York. On the other hand, Howells, who did not believe in a literary center for America, was emphatic in denying that status to Gotham: "New York is a mart and not a capital in literature as well as in other things." One might well argue that he had nonetheless confirmed its capital status by moving there—or rather that his judgment of the situation was correct—or even that he had hardly truly moved there at all.

I

There can be no doubt that Howells had become in fact the leading man of letters of the country. That, more than anything else, was what Walker was so willing to pay for. But before the *Cosmopolitan* job could be taken up in earnest, Howells had a debt to pay off to Alden and the Harpers. He owed them a novel for 1892, and one reason for going back to New York was that this was to be a second New York novel. It represented variations on certain major themes of *A Hazard of New Fortunes,* and so Howells called it *The World of Chance.*

Written at the height of Howells' powers and on themes profoundly interesting to him, *The World of Chance* was nevertheless artistically a failure—the author's first in the run of ten novels beginning with *Indian Summer.* It was impossible, of course, that this should be abject failure. At least three-quarters of the novel, and all of it concerned with the major theme, was brilliantly successful. The motives and settings of *A World of Chance* were original, many of the scenes and pictures as beguiling as anything Howells ever wrote. Even the reasons for his failure here are intensely interesting. And he packed into this novel his own considerations of all the major factors which were to characterize him in his decade as America's leading man of letters.

The fable of *The World of Chance* was typically uncomplicated. A romantic young reporter from the Midwest comes to New York with the manuscript of a first novel in his grip, seeking fame and fortune. Battling for survival in this chance-world, he struggles along as a free-lance hack and a journalist. Chance literary acquaintanceship brings him into contact with a family of Utopian idealists from whom he might easily have learned to read deeper into the significance of his gambler's existence. He falls in love with the *spirituelle* daughter of the family but is too youthfully egotistic either to learn her father's lesson or to win the girl. Through sheer luck his novel is published and has a flash success. At the end he gets on the train to go home, enjoy his celebrity, and wonder, what next?

In *The World of Chance* appears the first instance since *A Woman's Reason*—the first time since Howells' ascendancy to full maturity in *Indian Summer* and *The Rise of Silas Lapham*—when his "bulldog grip" on character, and therefore theme, slipped. It would be much too simple to say that anxiety to clear the decks for the *Cosmopolitan* job was responsible. Howells had been triumphing over far worse pressures to succeed in recent novels. The creative impulses basic to *The World of Chance* belonged to the Realism War and to two new resources being opened by his imagination. In his fifties, Howells began to mine the rich literary ores of his intense and fortunate youth. And he became introspectively fascinated with the psychological responses of his characters. Where once he had concentrated "dramatically" on what they did or said, now he began increasingly to imagine and project their psychic processes.

The creative impulse for *The World of Chance* had come from that vital period of 1889–90, and Howells' study of the adventures of young Percy Bysshe Shelley Ray was well founded. In September, 1861, newly fired from *The Ohio State Journal*, Howells had gone to New York with a never-published manuscript in his grip entitled, variously, *Geoffrey Winter,* or *Geoffrey: A Study of American Life.* Since then, he had profited as editor and sympathetic mentor from countless opportunities to study the literary neophyte, and his perception of New York's pre-eminence as the type and essence of that world of chance in which every new fortune must dangerously be hazarded was very fresh.

Consequently, Howells realized his vision of young Shelley Ray as a comic masterpiece. The paladin of realism joined with the expert *farceur* to convert Ray's romance, its plot, and aims into pure hilarity. At the same time, the serious artist and generous mentor remembered from what beginnings Howells' own art and wisdom had come, and the study of Ray's psychology probes deep. His egotisms appear natural to his youth, to his bad but popular romantic traditions, to the creative but self-centered subjectivity of his esthetic temperament, and, above all, to the hard necessities of the economic chance-world Ray must live in. Ray is pictured to be understood and forgiven. His generosity and sensitivity stand beside his folly.

While it centers in Ray and the other denizens of the literary mart, *The World of Chance* is vintage Howells. But it was in trying to broaden his grasp that the master slipped. He had written three tragedies in a row. He had also written, in three of his last four novels, important works of social criticism. Finally, as he'd confessed to McClure about *The Quality of Mercy,* he always had to face the commercial necessity to provide some kind of "love-interest" to satisfy the shallow reader and induce him to pay the bill for the possibility of deeper communication between artist and serious reader.

His notion of the way to get all three factors into *The World of Chance* was to introduce David Hughes, just returned from a long experiment of Utopian communitarianism, and his family. Intellectually, it was perfectly sensible to bring Hughes in. Young Ray needed to be educated to profounder depths of understanding than he could ever at his age see for himself. And in Hughes the author could imagine a spokesman, intriguing to the reader for his strangeness of Brook Farm and later Utopian background, to express the social ideas Howells had finally matured. Hughes's ideas, in fact, are exactly those of the author whose next book would be *A Traveler from Altruria.*

It was easy thus to endow Hughes with a stock of appropriate

ideas. And it was not difficult to convey the pathos of his family
wrenched away from the secure ideality of their community to share
the chaos—symbolized by the fearful racket in an old house up
against the El—of life in New York. Howells must have congratulated himself on his success in meeting the demand for a noble
woman, wise, spiritual, and devoted, as he created Peace Hughes for
Shelley Ray to love ignorantly and lose. But the frustrating and
finally damning fact was that he could not make Hughes and his
entourage truly organic with Ray and Ray's development.

Honestly confronted, Ray had to be supposed naturally insensitive
to Hughes's tragic social vision. Buoyant young Ray had to see the
world of chance as a field of fortune. Howells' genuine creative impulse for the novel was toward the comic-ironic study of a romantic
provincial in New York. He could not make Ray bear any genuinely
tragic weight without uselessly disintegrating him. Given Ray's
youthful impercipience, Howells' effort to teach him tragedy through
complicity was foredoomed. And in his desperation the author was
shamefully, for a realist, reduced to impotent melodrama in the
scenes of Denton's madness and suicide. His only consolation after
the fact could have been that his theories were vindicated by his
failure. Howells had no business playing with a theme from
Charles Brockden Brown's *Wieland*.

In trying to make *The World of Chance* tragic, as in trying to
give it overt social significance, Howells was permitting his ideological commitments to thwart and confuse his true creative impulse.
In completing his exploration of the social problem, he had proceeded from perception to idea. His search was done, the end of
understanding attained. Significantly, there were to be no more
novels of social criticism. While exploration had proceeded, the
author's perceptual findings were available to his fictional imagination. Raised to the level of abstract ideas, these findings became
excellent resources for propaganda but, as *The World of Chance*
proved, no longer usable creatively. A period in Howells' artistic
life had ended.

His significant creative life had, of course, by no means ended.
There would be major novels yet, and enviable literary achievement
of other sorts. But there would be no new major growth. The
coming decade of service and prestige as the nation's leading author
would be a time of exploitation, sometimes major, sometimes minor,
of resources already discovered. The decade's themes were all im-

plicit in *The World of Chance*. Howells would be much concerned
with the coming generation, with young men somewhat like Shelley
Ray. As the leading man of letters he would mean much to them
and the nation. His unprecedented career would constitute both
inspiration and challenge. That career was paradoxical in its
worldly success poised against its Altrurian message. Howells
would say and symbolize much about the man of letters as a man
of business. He would become increasingly the bridge back to the
great past as he alone knew it personally, and as literary memorialist he would become both a master craftsman and a symbol. Yet
as realist he would represent the voice of modernity to many. As
Altrurian he would voice the hope and inspiration of many toward
the future.

II

For some such neophyte as the Stephen Crane who moved like
Shelley Ray to New York (possibly with the first draft of *Maggie*)
in September 1891, just as Howells was getting well into it, *The
World of Chance* could easily have served as a writer's guide to
professional know-how. Nobody knew the business of authorship
better than Howells. His experience was long and exhaustive, and
he could exploit it brilliantly. In the opinion of the most careful
student of the business of authorship, Howells was the best businessman of them all. He had discovered, certainly like no one
before, and possibly like no one after, how to make writing pay
steadily, fully, even handsomely without selling out either his artistic or civic conscience. In this, too, he was the nation's leading
author.

It seems not to have damaged his status at all that his *Cosmopolitan* venture foundered quickly. At the beginning there was no
indication that it would be anything but clear sailing. Walker's
infatuation with his bargain increased, if anything. The February
Cosmopolitan "Barnumized" Howells with a vengeance. A special
full-page portrait served as frontispiece, with the cutline below
it: "On March the first, Mr. Howells will take editorial control of
the Cosmopolitan Magazine conjointly with the present editor."
And the faithful Boyesen printed a strenuously prorealistic article
on "Mr. Howells and His Work" in the main body of the issue.
Walker himself seemed to mean more than "conjointly" in discuss-

ing the conduct of the magazine. On February 16 he wrote Howells of his delight in being able to go on vacation secure in the knowledge "that before I return you will be fairly installed and that the Cosmopolitan will have started upon the higher career." All contributors had been advised to submit their manuscripts through Howells.

With *The World of Chance* not quite finished but started as a serial in *Harper's,* Howells went to work for Walker on March 1. He had already begun to solicit manuscripts, and he had already begun to write for the *Cosmopolitan.* Walker paid him for the first installment of *A Traveler from Altruria* on March 13, adding somewhat dubious praise of "the magnificent work you are doing —work which will go down into the centuries when your books have become memories of the catalogues. . . ." Walker continued cordial, even solicitous, through April. A note of April 27 is personal and friendly. But his next surviving message to Howells, of June 21, is curtly businesslike and formal. Obviously some rift had occurred. On June 30 Howells informed his father that his connection with the *Cosmopolitan* ended that day and gave the cause as "hopeless incompatibility."

What happened? Probably we shall never precisely know. The eccentric Walker was a notoriously hard man to work for. Ex-editors of the *Cosmopolitan* became so common that Howells, sitting with two others at the Player's Club once greeted a current one with, "Here comes a candidate for the club of ex-editors of the *Cosmopolitan.*" Charles Hanson Towne's story that Walker sent Howells a note directing him to appear at his desk at 8:00 A.M. daily seems too improbable—unless Walker chose that as a device for firing his colleague. It was understood that Howells' writing, his most valuable contribution, was to be done on his regular morning schedule at home.

The secret probably lies in the literary quality and quantity of what Howells put into the *Cosmopolitan.* Walker had built circulation spectacularly by using the formula Charles Eliot Norton thought so vulgar. As editor Arthur Sherburne Hardy recalled, Walker's theory was: "Supposing the average number of articles in each issue to be X and the products of the pen to be classified roughly into groups, as fiction, travel, sport and adventure, natural science, history, etc., then, since the magazine speaks but twelve times a year and its object is to attract the greatest possible number of readers, it should as far as possible have in each issue an article appealing to readers interested in each of the subjects." Howells and Walker had agreed on a "higher career" for the magazine. But apparently they did not have entirely the same thing in mind. Walker was thinking of Altrurianism; Howells cherished his dream of the great literary magazine, *The World of Fiction.* He raised the amount and quality of fiction and belles-lettres sharply.

Whether the circulation dipped correspondingly or not, the day came, as Howells told Ellery Sedgwick, when Walker stalked into Howells' office "with a bundle of accepted manuscripts under his arm and a look of suppressed fury.

' "Mr. Howells," he said, "be so good as to return these to your contributors." Mr. Howells thought a moment, and then replied: "Mr. Walker, I will prepare the bill of fare for your dinner but I will not wash the dishes." '
His working tenure on the *Cosmopolitan* was exactly four months.

Parting with Walker brought Howells more relief than pain. He was in no danger of penury, and he had not quarreled with Walker, who continued to buy his Altrurian pieces and pay well for them. The experience mainly served to launch him on what proved to be a thoroughly profitable period of free-lancing. As the leading man of letters, Howells wrote voluminously through these years, was published (through reprints) a good deal more than he wrote, and made substantial amounts of money.

Between the expiration of his contract with the Harpers at the end of 1891 and the time when, toward the end of 1900, he made a new and lasting deal with them, Howells' publication is worth listing. In 1892 the Harpers published six books for him: *The Albany Depot,* a farce, reprinted twice; *An Imperative Duty; The Quality of Mercy; A Letter of Introduction* (farce); and *A Little Swiss Sojourn* (reprinted from the 1888 *Harper's*). He also finished "The Editor's Study," published a couple of poems, a couple of literary essays and a farce in magazines, and introduced a book. He began to serialize *A Traveler from Altruria* in the *Cosmopolitan* and *The Coast of Bohemia* in *The Ladies' Home Journal.*

And so it went. In those years Howells published six novels: *The World of Chance,* 1893; *The Coast of Bohemia,* 1893; *The Landlord at Lion's Head,* 1897; *The Story of a Play,* 1898; *Ragged Lady,* 1899; *Their Silver Wedding Journey,* 1899. Also three novelettes, *The Day of Their Wedding,* 1896; *A Parting and a Meeting,*

1896; *An Open-Eyed Conspiracy,* 1897; and two children's books—
Christmas Every Day, 1893; *Stories of Ohio,* 1897; a Utopian romance—*A Traveler from Altruria,* 1894. There were three memoirs
—*My Year in a Log Cabin,* 1893 (reprint from *Youth's Companion*
in 1887); *My Literary Passions,* 1895; *Literary Friends and
Acquaintance,* 1900—a volume of poems, *Stops of Various Quills,*
1895—a volume of sketches, *Impressions and Experiences,* 1896—
nine separate publications of farces, and two editions of poems set
to music by various composers. The miscellaneous items are numerous, including reprints, introductions, special essays, and sketches.
Miscellaneous periodical pieces were not numerous, but there were
hard-hitting social essays, some excellent short stories, and two
series of essay-review columns: "Life and Letters" in *Harper's
Weekly,* March 30, 1895 to February 26, 1898; and "American
Letter," *Literature,* May 14, 1898, irregularly to November 10,
1899.

Despite the occasional attacks of continuing neoromantic or
Gospel of Wealth opponents, the net result of all this was a new
place for Howells in the eyes of his countrymen. According to
Samuel Hopkins Adams, who was one of them, the young Manhattan
newspapermen began to think of Howells as sacrosanct, above criticism. However wrong it was in its fatuous conclusions, the
following portrait of Howells for the June 26, 1892, New York
Tribune represents pretty accurately the impression the nation
formed of its leading author—especially insofar as it did not read
his serious works of the imagination seriously. Mr. Howells, said
the interview,

'is of medium height and is quite stout, round, and con-
tented looking. His face is round. Nearly all the lines of his figure are
curved. His hands are fat and dimpled. His round face has the look of
refinement, experience of the world, the good-natured indifference and
the cynically happy disbelief of a diplomat of experience and high position. His eyes are dark gray, and deeply set. His forehead is broad and
high, covered nearly to his eyebrows with iron-gray hair, combed down
it in what might be called a bang, if there were not a semblance of a
parting to destroy the character of such a definition. An iron-gray
mustache shades his firm-lined mouth. The nose is straight and not
large. His chin is smooth shaven and forceful. His voice is very agreeable. There are certain notes of contentment in the tones of his voice

which argue that Mr. Howells is satisfied with his career and with the success he has made in life.'

The interviewer, who was running true to all the worst Howells had ever said about his despised race, could not have been more false to the psychological facts. No doubt he saw in Howells what he came predetermined to see—but that is just the point. Celebrity, wealth, and kudos were flowing in on this Howells. Why, in the popular view, should he not have been just as unguently complacent about it as any millionaire? He was good copy for any interviewer, good material for any periodical article. When McClure finally launched his magazine, "Real Conversations I. A Dialogue Between William Dean Howells and Hjalmar Hjorth Boyesen" led all the rest, and nine portraits of Howells were printed. This was the Howells whom Theodore Roosevelt begged to help get Henry Cabot Lodge elected to the Senate. Edward MacDowell set his poems to music and "loved" the man. Richard Le Gallienne became his fan. E. C. Stedman called him "the best American since Lincoln." But the ultimate public cachet came from the company of George Harris and Sons of Chicago which begged and received permission to use Howells' name and portrait "on a handsome Cigar Box Label."

It was in a meaningful sense true, as the more serious view of Harry Thurston Peck had it, that Howells had "swept the whole horizon of his time," and become the "most eminent" American writer, whose every book was "a literary event." Contracting first *The Coast of Bohemia* and then *My Literary Passions* for his magazine, Edward Bok hugged himself with joy. Somewhat incautiously he supposed that he "had completely tied up the leading novelist of the day for his next two years' output."

In 1899 the *Critic* carried a real hymn of admiring affection from Gerald Stanley Lee, who was happy at the news that

'the last stronghold of bashfulness in American letters has capitulated to Major Pond, and that W. D. Howells is to go on a tour of fifty lectures in the leading cities of the United States. . . . We want to hear Mr. Howells in America today because he particularly belongs to us and because we particularly belong to him and because we are both proud of it. Judged from the ordinary standard of advertising and reputation-pushing that obtains today, it certainly must be admitted that Mr. Howells, though he created Silas Lapham and loved him, has never allowed Silas Lapham to brag about him. His work has never been pushed like the Persis Brand. He has stolen his public. There is nothing striking or picturesque or showy in his entire career . . . we never celebrate Mr. Howells. He is part of our literary climate. We breathe Howells—most of us. It never occurs to people to hold an Anniversary for Oxygen. . . . The things that belong to us, that are really a part of us, in any great and vital and beautiful sense, are the things that we take for granted. It never occurs to anyone to attempt a Parade in honor of the American Climate. . . . We cannot reduce Mr. Howells to the celebrating stage. We cannot get him far enough off. We cannot untangle him from ourselves. His art belongs to us. Our common American lives are the warp and woof of all that he has brought. In his large and sane and noiseless way he may be said to have done more for the self-respect of American fiction than any other living man. Under these circumstances it is no small occasion—the announcement that we are to be permitted, in any general sense, to hear his voice on the lecture platform. There is something about Mr. Howells that makes a public—his own particular public —almost blush not to be as modest as he is himself. Going to hear him lecture is as near a celebration as we can get. We know him too well.

Many of us would find it interesting to follow Mr. Howells about from one hall to another. We would find it still more interesting to watch Mr. Howells, who is always a spectator and an artist, following himself about. He will be cheered by seeing the Rev. Mr. Sewell and Lemuel Barker in the front row in some places, sitting unconscious side by side. Mrs. Corey will be there. Mr. Corey will want to know what it was like when she gets home. Mrs. Pasmer will not fail to say something delightfully not to the point. Bartley Hubbard will write it up, and all the Silas Laphams in the East and West will go home wondering how it is that a gentle, quiet, unnoticing-looking little man like this should understand them so much better than they understand themselves.'

Such a position was, of course, not only enviable but profitable. Howells made money—at a rate which, what with taxes and successive inflations, was probably the real equivalent of $100,000 a year in 1958. As he periodically cast up his net worth in the nineties, it rose steadily in spite of depression, his robust standard of living, and his consistent generosity with far-flung relatives. The figure rose from $60,000 in 1890 to $68,000 in 1892, $84,000 in 1894, $93,000 in 1897. He had made investments and still owned his houses in Cambridge. But almost all of this had been earned with his pen, and the continuance of his prosperity depended on it. No comparable literary career had been forged—Twain's far larger income depending on his unique power to sell well through the door-to-door "subscription" sales system, on his publishing house while it lasted, and on his unique attractiveness as public performer—and it is worth while to see what the structure of Howells' money-success was, why he was at once the model and despair of the young men.

By this time, of course, part of his prosperity came from backlog. In 1892 he figured on $2,000–$2,500 a year in royalties from old books. Houghton Mifflin as successors to Ticknor were paying him 20 per cent on *A Modern Instance, A Woman's Reason, Indian Summer, The Rise of Silas Lapham,* and *The Minister's Charge* (on all of which Howells owned the stereotype plates) and 16⅔ per cent on plays and paperbacks. He had begun with Osgood, as far back as *A Chance Acquaintance,* to pay for and own his plates. That raised his royalty rates and also gave him leverage in the horse-trading, at which he was expert, to raise them still further. Later it provided good business for brother Joe Howells in Jefferson, Ohio. With that leverage, Howells was able to renegotiate his contract favorably with Houghton Mifflin in 1889. Perhaps owning plates gave him added copyright protection and brought him extra consideration—as it still might even now for any plates which survived World War II—in reprint deals.

For all his occasional complaints about it, Howells clearly adored dickering. In 1892 he made a new book contract with the Harpers, giving them first consideration on books for five years, getting 20 per cent on retail of the first 5,000 sales (after paying for the plates) and 25 per cent thereafter, and raising royalties to a flat 20 per cent on *April Hopes, Annie Kilburn, A Hazard of New Fortunes, The Shadow of a Dream,* and *An Imperative Duty.* Thereafter his correspondence shows Howells not only renegotiating but often initiating ideas for the design, variation in editions, reissue, pricing, and the timing of publicaton of his books.

The real meat of his income came, however, from fresh enterprise. In a moment of self-examination on March 31, 1893, he totted up his opportunities and responsibilities in his notebook. His prospects at that moment included eight contracts with separate publishers for a total of $29,400. Free-lancing had upped his market value substantially. When Edward Bok paid Howells $10,000 for

My Literary Passions and Curtis spent $50,000 advertising the fact, the Harpers began to reconsider. Alden was commissioned to try to lure Howells back to the Harpers, offered him a new department, "Editor's Table-Talk," almost hooked but then lost him in spite of the added inducement of a new $5,000 per annum contract and guaranteed succession to Curtis in the Easy Chair. Alden ended by paying him $9,000 for magazine rights to *Literary Friends and Acquaintance*. In 1899, therefore, Howells could command bids from Alden of $7,000 to serialize *Their Silver Wedding Journey* and $10,000 for the never-written *History of Venice*.

With his depth of experience in the business of authorship, Howells had learned to be philosophical. One young man who tried to collaborate with him in dramatizing *A Hazard of New Fortunes* was anxious to broach the money question, and began by stammering, "I have been told that Mr. Barrie's royalties from *The Little Minister* run as high as $1500 a week." Howells, who knew it would be time to talk money when they knew they had achieved something salable (which they never did), smiled, said, "It's enough to rouse all our very worst passions, isn't it?" and changed the subject.

That philosophy was not entirely proof against his chagrin at being by-passed by the innovating tides of best-sellerdom, however. Howells formed one pole in the opposition between his kind of fiction (the only serious genre for which there was then a market in America) and the variants of neoromantic best-sellerism. He felt the polarity just as the young writers did. Like James, he could and would not compromise. But, as he told James, "it galls me that I should sell only as many thousands as the gilded youth of both sexes are selling hundred-thousands, and largely as I believe for want of publicity—that is the new word for advertising." If there was a certain hyperbole in his figures—elevating theirs and depressing his in that monstrous ratio of a hundred to one—that did not keep Howells from goading the Harpers.

It was not until they issued *The Kentons* as a trial in 1902 that he was satisfied. There had been no serialization; the Harpers, he agreed, had gone all out; and it had, he admitted to his sister Aurelia, "only the usual sale of my novels, after all the puffing and blowing of the publishers. My public is a curious one: neither the birth rate nor the death rate seems to affect it. During the last ten years all my books have sold about the same." Allowing for the fact that *The Kentons* had not been serialized, that probably, in fact, shows how the audience for Howells' fiction had begun to taper off in the decade after the nineties. But his admission that the book sales were all about the same—probably at a median figure of about 10,000—helps establish the dimensions of his career. At his royalty figures, Howells was making about $5,000 per novel out of book publication. When he serialized, as he almost always did, he got at least that much more.

His value to the magazines was unique. The dependability of his faithful audience was a sound asset. His enmity toward the sources of appeal to the big public market was a liability. It is also probable that his high magazine price and very high royalties—20 and 25 per cent on the retail price of a book—discouraged publishers from plunging on big advertising budgets for him. In the long run Howells depended on keeping the value of his name high through the cumulative prestige of his total career. That, and his steady productiveness, preserved his marketability. His system denied him flashy commercial success. But it gave him security and an excellent living together with freedom to do his own real work as he understood it.

Did he overwork, overproduce, and compromise for the sake of his system? It could be argued that he did, and quotations from Howells himself could be adduced to show that he confessed that this was so. But equal and opposite quotations could be cited from Howells tired and depressed to Howells strong and confident which support another argument. He wrote two kinds of fiction in the nineties—his fifties and early sixties. One is clearly second-rate; in it Howells seems tired, unable to lift his work to solid, organic unity and artistic success, derivative in that Howells sometimes imitates himself. It is not bad; he is far too much the master of his art for that. But it is not like his first-rate fiction, which deepens, or relumes major themes and insights, vitalizing them artistically into powerful works of the imagination. Howells' own method of dealing with such an argument would have been to observe that probably both contentions are true. He would probably also have urged that the first-rate work was produced by the same system as the second-rate—a system long professional practice had made inevitable for him—and that one judges an artist, in the long run, by his first-rate work: so few practitioners ever produce any.

III

But what right had the socialistic Mr. Howells to be making so canny a living from the business of authorship? As his social ideals took mature form, Howells found himself thinking that through, and he confided both his expert knowledge and the gist of his conclusions to the public in a brilliant essay sold to the October 1893 *Scribner's* and called "The Man of Letters as a Man of Business." As a practical guide to the business of authorship in the 1890's, this essay is rivaled in fascination and in usefulness only by the revelations of *The World of Chance*. But Howells' conclusion about the fundamental morality of the relationship was ruthless. The subject, he wrote his father while meditating the essay, "is of course anomalous, since literature should no more be sold than the ministry of religion."

Here, as in the Altrurian papers he was writing for the *Cosmopolitan* (and this essay may well have been originally intended for what was so briefly "his" magazine), Howells tried to say something unmistakable to the aspiring young men:

'I think that every man ought to work for his living, without exception, and that, when he has once avouched his willingness to work, society should provide him with work and warrant him a living. I do not think any man ought to live by an art. A man's art should be his privilege, when he has proven his fitness to exercise it, and has otherwise earned his daily bread; and its results should be free to all.'

In the business of the arts, "there is something profane, something impious . . . something false and vulgar." The artist can say "that, as the thing is, unless he sells his art he cannot live, that society will leave him to starve . . . and all this is bitterly true." The artist must in "dishonor" submit "to the conditions which none can escape; but that does not justify the conditions, which are none the less the conditions of hucksters because they are imposed upon poets":

'The poet must use his emotions to pay his provision bills; he has no other means; society does not propose to pay his bills for him. Yet, and at the end of the ends, the unsophisticated witness finds the transaction ridiculous, finds it repulsive, finds it shabby. Somehow he knows that if our huckstering civilization did not at every moment violate the eternal fitness of things, the poets' song would have been given to the world, and the poet would have been cared for by the whole human brotherhood, as any man should be who does the duty that every man owes it.'

The one hopeful thing is that "at present business is the only human solidarity; we are all bound together with that chain. . . ." But Howells was increasingly anxious to be rid of that chain. In the fall of 1890 he had seen his $6,000 worth of Atchison and Topeka stock fall from $1.13 to 24 cents and commented to his father that he hoped such things would persuade the country to nationalize the railroads. He wouldn't mind, he said, losing his earnings that way; he hated to lose them to the rascality of Jay Gould. Criticism and standard of comparison now fall into the pattern of thought Howells was terming "Altrurian." Altrurian ideals were much to the forefront of his thought in these years. The nation's leading man of letters was at once a critical socialist, a practical success, and a constructive social idealist. It gave the young men something to contemplate.

It was not only good fun for Howells to give full rein to his ideas in the Altrurian papers he did in two series for Walker, it was doubly fun to cut loose on a romance. The tradition in which he should work was obvious. The time-proved instrument of critical fantasy was the alien observer, Oliver Goldsmith's Citizen of the World—the "man from Mars"—and if the object was Utopia, why then the observer came from there. Howells enjoyed his release from stern realities and even played at ornamenting his fantasy with curlicues of romantic irony. *"A Traveler from Altruria,"* he reminded himself in his pocket notebook, "Sometimes seems wholly subjective like one's own consciousness of better things. Bring this idea in towards the end."

The complex publishing history of the Altrurian sketches was neatly worked out by Professors Gibson and Arms. Howells wrote two continuous series for the *Cosmopolitan*—"A Traveler from Altruria," November 1892 through October 1893; "Letters of an Altrurian Traveler," November 1893 to September 1894. He thought the reception of the sketches good, but apparently the Harpers did not agree after *A Traveler from Altruria* was published in book form in 1894. Though Howells contemplated a second volume, to be called *A Visit to Altruria,* in 1895, it was to be almost thirteen years before his second series went between covers.

He cannibalized a couple of sketches for *Impressions and Experiences.* But not until 1907 did the Harpers feel that a revival of interest in Utopias warranted encouraging Howells to write up "a visit to Altruria" and add that to the earlier sketches of Aristides Homos in New York to make the two parts of *Through the Eye of the Needle,* 1907.

The structure of *A Traveler from Altruria* is obvious enough. At the beginning a snobbish and Bertie Woosterish little neoromantic novelist meets the distinguished traveling observer from the newly discovered island-continent of Altruria and takes him up to the New England summer hotel where the novelist is vacationing. Utterly democratic, outgoing, sympathetic, genial, yet scholarly in his determination to understand the strange world he finds himself in, the visitor from Utopia is a considerable embarrassment to Mr. Twelvemough. Homos is always lending a hand to porters and waitresses, shaking hands with headwaiters—treating people as his equals. Twelvemough finds himself involved in all sorts of ironies —innocent for Homos, but agonizing for him—as he attempts to "explain" the United States to his guest. After two chapters of that there follow seven in which a panel of vacationists—a fine, candid banker, a bluff industrialist, a drily cynical lawyer, a mean-spirited professor of "political economy," a dreadfully embarrassed minister, and a colorless doctor—engage in a series of conversations which expose to Homos the true condition of the American "democracy." A society woman and later a family of poor but literate local farmers add scope to the talk. This climaxes with three chapters leading up to a "lecture" by Homos in which he explains Altruria to the Americans.

As might be expected, the fantasy of Altruria is used here as a foil for the United States. Once again the issue most in question is the American Dream. Altruria glows in the distance as the standard of what America might become if she were truly and thoroughly democratic. When America as it now is appears to the pitying view of Aristides, however, it seems obvious that the nation has become a plutocracy, that rich and poor are slaves of that greed and iron necessity which mutually produce one another, that the farm problem is pushing the farmer to the wall, that Labor is at war with Capital—and both are absurdly stupid about it—that, indeed, the conditions of all life in America are those of warfare. The summer hotel is like a great ship docked by the shores of a backward country. The passengers and natives trade warily and grudgingly with each other, but the "class" hotel people and "common" natives are at least as alienated as if they belonged to different nations, different cultures. The only wonder, Homos says repeatedly, is that human affection and good will can cross the awful barriers to mitigate this warfare at all. The kindliness and humanity one does see among Americans seem to Homos a magnificent but monstrous illogicality: the human heart triumphs over the logic of the "conditions."

This all climaxes beautifully in Homos' lecture. Taxed with their brutalities and absurdities, the Americans Homos has met have taken refuge, with damnable iteration, behind the observation that "It's human nature, and you can't change it." Now he sets out to show them how, given the chance in right conditions, human nature changes from egotism to altruism. In the emergent view of Western history popular with Utopians in this period, Homos traces the Evolution which had saved Altruria. Just like the United States, Altruria went through an industrial revolution which led to intense economic warfare. This had culminated in a general but unstable Monopoly—inefficient, tyrannous, and subject to panics and failures. At last, in a burst of inspiration, the voters of the country had crystallized into decision, and the Accumulation had been voted into public ownership at one swoop. Thereafter the logic of the situation had led toward Utopia.

In Altruria everyone works three hours a day and is thereafter free for his usually creative enjoyments. "The artist, the man of genius, who worked for the love of his work, became the normal man, and in the measure of his ability and of his calling each wrought in the spirit of the artist." Daily life became decentralized, the life of an idyllic country town, though swift, electric transport made the governmental and intellectual centers readily available. Poverty and greed disappeared. Equality and brotherhood became normal. The nation became a great family. Egotism was converted into the ideal of service.

As Homos concluded,

'We are still far from thinking our civilization perfect; but we are sure that our civic ideals are perfect. What we have already accomplished is to have given a whole continent perfect peace; to have founded an economy in which there is no possibility of want; to have killed out political and social ambition; to have disused money and eliminated chance; to have realized the brotherhood of the race, and to have outlived the fear of death.'

The first part of *Through the Eye of the Needle* powerfully reinforces the critical analysis of its predecessor. This is an epistolary novel, with Homos writing home his "study of the plutocratic mind" from New York—"how Americans live in the spirit, illogically, blindly, and blunderingly." The darkness, dirt, and "uproar" of New York's living conditions are again recorded. The stuffy stupidities of the comfort civilization of the upper classes, the dreadful expense of the Society "standard"—of conspicuous consumption— the practical and psychological brutalities from the employer to the servant classes, and all the "hideous nightmare" aspects of New York are noted.

There is no lack of humor. Homos' "understanding" of Thanksgiving Day is bitterly funny. He jots down, dead-pan, the fact that "Brooklyn is always a joke with the New-Yorkers." But the real emphasis is on tragic, not comic, incongruity. Homos sits in the brilliant luxury of a millionaire's apartment and listens to the gay persiflage about charities for the poor. "They tossed the ball back and forth with a lightness the Americans have," Homos wrote, "and I could not have believed, if I had not known how hardened people become to such things here, that they were almost in the actual presence of hunger and cold. It was within five minutes' walk of their warmth and surfeit; and if they had lifted the window and called, 'Who goes there?' the houselessness that prowls the night could have answered them from the street below, 'Despair !' " The heart of the matter is "that bedevilment of the entire American ideal through the retention of the English economy when the English polity was rejected. But at the heart of America there is this ridiculous contradiction, and it must remain there until the whole country is Altrurianized."

But how to bring the reader to Altruria? Since this is a romance, that will be easy. Homos shall meet the unique American society woman who has a real social conscience and, appropriately, the name of Eveleth Strange. They shall fall in love and, after an illustrative quarrel over her abandonment of her money, shall go to Altruria. Thence she shall write letters back to America, and Howells' lovely, neo-Greek pastoral idyll can be communicated through the eyes of a plutocrat slowly converted to true Altrurianism. If America is a hideous nightmare to Homos, Altruria is a lovely dream to Eveleth. At the end of this, as of his first Utopian romance, Howells obeyed his own injunction to make it seem sometimes "wholly subjective." He meant to insinuate into the reader's imagination the idea that, though fantastic, Altruria could be real —real "like one's own consciousness of better things."

It was natural that the climactic references in the two Utopian romances—which are really one book—should be religious. If one made the mistake of assuming that Homos was Howells, he could show that Howells had at last achieved the rest and consolation in a mystical but liberal Christianity which he had obviously long sought. But that would be a mistake. Perhaps Howells did take personal comfort in the certitudes of natural piety among the Altrurians to which Homos and later Eveleth testified. That was only possible, however, in Altrurian circumstances. Among Howells' plutocratic "conditions," religious faith was naturally like that of Eveleth Strange in New York.

The woman with whom Aristides fell in love had "a charm in her, different from that I felt in other American women, and impossible in our Altrurian women," he found. "She had a deep and almost tragical seriousness, masked with a most winning gayety, a light irony, a fine scorn that was rather for herself than for others. . . . In fact, this generous and magnanimous and gifted woman was without that faith, that trust in God which comes to us from living His law, and which I wonder any American can keep. She denied nothing; but she had lost the faith to affirm anything. She no longer tried to do good from her heart, though she kept on doing charity . . . always with the ironical doubt that she was doing harm. . . ."

Howells himself was no more Eveleth than Aristides, but his religious state was much more like hers than like the Altrurian's. As Professor Arnold Fox has conclusively shown, Howells was more radical than Eveleth Strange. There were many things that he denied—creedal formulations, a "hireling ministry," and ecclesiastical institutions in general among them. His experience showed that metaphysical enterprises always ended up in doubt. In one of his most moving short stories, "A Difficult Case," a faithful and honest minister fails completely, after temporary success, to convince an old man that there is any point to life whatever. Yet the final implication of the story is that the minister has received a divine sign. Howells found within himself a permanent and significant will to believe in the enduring efficacy of love. Life was not just a question of wearing out through experience in time the basic passions of "love, hate, greed, hope, fear," as old Hillbrook argued. Ewbank the minister affirmed that love triumphed over greed, cast out fear, and so eliminated hate.

At the end of still another first-class short story of the period, "The Circle in the Water," Basil March came to a moment of affirmation. The problem concerned Tedham, a released convict, and the question of whether evil and complicity for it were not endless, spreading indefinitely, to the mechanical view, like the circles on a surface of water after a splash. But Tedham's daughter's love saves him. Basil concludes:

'So far now as human vision can perceive, the trouble he made, the evil he did, is really at an end. Love, which can alone arrest the consequences of wrong, had ended it, and in certain luminous moments it seemed to us that we had glimpsed, in our witness of this experience, an infinite compassion encompassing our whole being like a sea, where every trouble of our sins and sorrows must cease at last like a circle on the water.'

Perhaps Howells was thinking of his grandfather's prophet, George Fox, whose crucial illumination came at a moment of visualizing an ocean of death and darkness spread over by an infinite ocean of love and light.

For Howells religion remained a serious but baffling matter. Many of the poems in *Stops of Various Quills* were religious. It troubled him that, despite the moral progress of the ages, "civilization has remained pagan." It may have been true, as one contemporary critic supposed, that his realism had brought on a tragic sense of things—"a deepened perception of pain and discord, and an inevitable sense of 'the pity of it.'" It seems more probable that this sense came rather as a response to his total experience than as a reaction merely literary. His efforts to recapture Swedenborg were not successful—at least not theologically so. The prophet, Howells said to his father after a course of rereading, provoked in him "mingled astonishment and weariness." His thought was "true" but mechanical. Swedenborg was too much "in bondage to the old dogmas . . . if he lived now he would reject them." Perhaps Howells was stiffened in this reaction by his wife's faithfulness to her lifelong Unitarianism.

He recognized the responsibilities his dealing with religion in public brought him. If he had not, the public would have reminded him. His Altrurian lecture, "Thy Kingdom Come," at Boston's Twentieth Century Club on Ash Wednesday, 1900, won fame as "the best Lenten sermon in this city." A British scholar on colonial sick-leave wrote to bless him for relieving "terrible days" with his art and praised his humanitarianism "full of the spirit of the Christ, its perception, its sympathy, its delicacy." To these and many similar expressions Howells' response could only be conscientious. He could not feel worthy: "I am all the time stumbling to my feet from the dirt of such falls through vanity and evil will, and hate, that I can hardly believe in the self that seems to write books which help people," he said to Edward Everett Hale, who as a good minister had to take it the right way.

All he could do was be honest. If he must "lament an incompleteness and uncertainty in my life," he could reflect that his vision perceived "that in all life on earth, which is a mere fragment." Howells' metaphysical anguish, not infrequent in these years, was, as we have seen, a source of his finest creative powers. The highest praise is due the honesty and the often heroic success with which he struggled to face up to himself and to do his very own work in thought but above all in art. It is by no means clear that the utmost theological certitude has any higher humane—or even divine—value than the candor of such a confession as this to his father:

'The whole of life seems unreal and unfair; but what I try to teach the children is to be ready for the change that *must* come in favor of truth and justice, and not to oppose it. . . . In the meantime Elinor and I live along like our neighbors; only we have a bad conscience. Sometimes, however, the whole affair goes to pieces in my apprehension, and I feel as if I had no more authority to judge myself or to do this or the other, than any other expression of the Infinite Life, say a tree, or a field of wheat or a horse. The only proof I have that I might to do right [*sic*] is that I suffer for my selfishness, and perhaps this is enough. I dare say God can take care of all the rest. I wish I could once leave it to him.'

It seems certain that this represents something very close to the center of Howells' religious experience.

Howells thought the reception of his Altruria—the best of his social gospel, with its ideal of the "inclusive society"—was excellent. There were some very favorable reviews, especially that in the *Atlantic*. Reformers were delighted. The famous Miss Frances

Willard addressed him as "Dear Brother: (For since *Altruria* you are that). . . ." His mail was full of grateful letters—more than from almost anything he had ever done. He found his corner news-paperman reading it in Yiddish "in a Hebrew workingman's paper," and the hero-worshiper showed Howells his picture in the paper, surrounded by a text of his work in words he could not read. "Wasn't that fine?" he crowed to his father. *A Traveler from Altruria* was used as a text in the State Normal School at Oswego, New York, and the Union Reform League's correspondence-school "College of Social Sciences" offered a course in "Literature—Social Ideals in Literature, or Utopia's from Plato to Howells." He could feel that the country was listening, even if the Harpers were slow to be impressed.

IV

Yet if the country, or one part of it, would listen to him as visionary radical, a voice of the future, it was still another paradox of his significance as its leading man of letters that the country, or per-haps another part of it, was eager to hear him as the voice of the past. The nineties were a self-conscious decade, accumulating force to break out violently with imperialistic self-assertion on the inter-national scene at the end of the period. If anyone could tell Ameri-cans what their cultural nature and achievement were, it was Mr. Howells. Sometimes he told them decidedly unpalatable things about their present and what they must do to be saved for the future. Yet he was uniquely the heir of the greatness of the past. He was the past, in a sense, and his countrymen could put up with his foibles, as they often had and do with their great men, and admire him yet because he embodied the greatness of the nation. He had known the giants, many of them intimately and, among living men, uniquely. When he turned back to the past to explain his own emergence, or when he testified to the wonder of the men who had brought American literature (and therefore culture) into mature being, they were anxious to listen. The substantial invest-ments of Edward Bok for Curtis and Alden for the Harpers were well worth while when Howells turned memorialist.

My Literary Passions was intriguing autobiography. For one thing, it told the great American success story. The almost incredi-ble tale of Howells' emergence—how the printing office educated him, how he found Cervantes and began to study Spanish all alone, how when his family moved into a dilapidated, backwoods log cabin he discovered Longfellow's lyrics in a barrel in the attic, how he fought his way upward with blind earnestness to learn an art and master a world of specialized knowledge, how at last, out of the commonest of American journalistic backgrounds he burst out into the great world, how he found that American cultural achievement matched and dovetailed with that in the other parts of the Western concert of nations—all this was exhilaratingly familiar in one way to Americans. The great men of the age, from Lincoln down to Rockefeller and Carnegie, had like histories. It was the great American boast.

But it was much more familiar in the statesmen, generals, and tycoons than the artists and intellectuals. In applying the great success story to their men of mind, Americans had always been a bit queasy. With all the notable exceptions, American heroes of culture had generally had unusual advantages of wealth or college breeding, or both. And there was an uneasy suspicion of the genuineness of their stature and achievement. The insincerities attendant on patriotic and parochial reputations in the arts or the life of the mind in nineteenth-century America often proved a real bar to recognition of genuine achievement when it came along. And, indeed, it was not clear that mature American achievement, worthy of full recognition, national and international, had appeared except sporadically, as in a Franklin or a Bowditch, in any field except the literary prior to the 1880's. It was clear, however, that American literature had not only come of age but developed a strong and self-sustaining life of its own. Howells became pre-eminently the representative of that life. Americans felt sure of the national cultural achievement in his art and in him as its avatar. They could enjoy wholeheartedly his being the first received American artist to tell the story of the development of his mind. For his part, Howells got extra mileage out of *My Literary Passions* by carefully and progressively exploiting his opportunity to turn it into an even more effective weapon in the Realism War than *Criticism and Fiction.*

Working on both more or less interchangeably, while he wrote *My Literary Passions* for Bok he also began for Alden what eventually became *Literary Friends and Acquaintance.* Though Howells rejected Alden's bait of a memorializing "department" for *Harper's,*

Alden was successful enough in horning in on Bok's show to get "My First Visit to New England" for his May through August 1894 issues. Spotted through 1895 Alden printed three more chapters, and got the Holmes study and "The White Mr. Longfellow" for 1896; but it was not until 1900 that Howells painfully finished the last two parts and had the book ready for the Harpers.

There were unique advantages, as Alden saw, in having Howells write of the giants, great, middling, and small, he had known. His knowledge of them was unparalleled. As he said at his seventy-fifth birthday dinner to the assembled dignitaries, "if I missed the personal acquaintance of Cooper and Irving and Poe and Prescott, I was personally acquainted with all the others in whom the story of American literature sums itself. I knew Hawthorne and Emerson and Walt Whitman; I knew Longfellow and Holmes and Whittier and Lowell; I knew Bryant and Bancroft and Motley; I knew Harriet Beecher Stowe and Julia Ward Howe; I knew Artemus Ward and Stockton and Mark Twain; I knew Parkman and Fiske." It is worth remarking that this list was illustrative, not exhaustive, and mentioned only the dead—and that the majority of these were more than acquaintances.

The audience appetite for intimate gossip about literary men, in an age when writers were the principal public entertainers, was insatiable. Revelations on so high a level were priceless. On the other hand, there were real dangers for Howells in this. He guarded scrupulously against descending even slightly toward gossip-columnist "revelations." He had to be wary of literary reputations and critical partisanship. Above all, with his horror of egotism, he had to fight against establishing the postures which once made effective criticism of the popular wisecrack that William Lyon Phelps's autobiography ought to have been titled *Great Men Who Have Known Me*.

Both of these literary memoirs of Howells' are, each in its own way, masterpieces. They constitute moving and revealing autobiography. They provide unique insights into American literary and cultural history; they often open the reader's eyes to bright critical insights. *Literary Friends and Acquaintance* is a prime biographical source for a number of its figures. Even so, one feels stubborn constraints in both, especially in the necessarily incomplete *Literary Friends*. The Howells of his major novels, Howells writing with the right hand that later shaped *My Mark Twain* into greatness, could have produced greater memoirs than these. And this impression is confirmed by the record of his growing distaste as he worked at them.

At first he felt sanguine. "Why, in fact, should I not make a Personal History of American Literature for the thirty years since I have been part of it?" he asked in October 1892. By January he was encountering the inward resistances which kept his Personal History finally incomplete. "I think I shall stop the reminiscing business for a while," he told his father. "I use up material which I could turn to better account in fiction, and perhaps enjoy better doing in that form." He didn't, of course, stop, and a month later he could see the practical end of *My Literary Passions* (though not the theoretical). "The selection is rather puzzling, but I let myself go, somewhat, and trust to what comes first," he explained. On the whole, however, "I prefer to write fiction. Then I feel quite free, and have no sense of trenching upon my own intimacy." By the time he had finished *Literary Friends* in 1900, he felt that all his memorializing was being "tormented out of me, in spite of the small pleasure and pride the past gives me. 'It's so damned humiliating,' as Mark Twain once said of *his* past."

His guess that better fiction could be made of his autobiography was wrong. He could not let himself go enough to give *The Flight of Pony Baker* the vividness of *A Boy's Town* or really to write for boys in it. Throughout it sounds like somebody's uncle, a very distinguished man of letters, telling stories to his nephews. His proposal in 1893 to begin again, after what was then twenty-five years of false starts, on what finally became *New Leaf Mills* (1913) was again aborted.

If it can be guessed that, with a more ruthless egotism, Howells might have made his literary memoirs still greater, it must be recognized that the books he did write are both uniquely informative and very moving. They stand in the front rank of their kind in American literature. And that fact constituted a substantial portion of his stature as the nation's leading man of letters in his time. First as major novelist, then as critic and champion of realism, then as moralist, social critic, and Altrurian, then as professional success, then as miscellaneous magazinist, *farceur*, poet, and belles-lettrist in general, and finally as custodian of the past, How-

ells towered over the crowd. He presented an extraordinary figure
to the young men as model, as mentor, and as father-image to emu-
late or rebel against. The one certain thing was that they could not
ignore him.

V

Full coverage of Howells' relations with the rising young men and
women writers of his age would fill a large book in itself. Here one
can hope only to examine representative examples of his dealings
with those who were learning their trade and coming up into public
view during Howells' tenure as the leading man of letters. From
the time when in 1860 he had first acquired status as a Poet of the
West, he had for 30 years exercised as colleague, editor, critic, and
publisher's consultant his genius for helping other writers fulfill
their promise. Now, as champion of realism and reputedly his
nation's most distinguished author, he was perfectly placed. His
power, his convictions, and his habit of glad generosity united to
permit him to influence the development of his country's literature
by promoting the work and success of the authors he believed in.

The list of "his" men and women in this new generation, quite
ignoring the long line of elder writers he had affected, is impressive.
It includes George Ade, Abraham Cahan, Madison Cawein, Charles
W. Chesnutt, Stephen Crane, Richard Harding Davis, Harold Fred-
eric, Henry B. Fuller, Robert Grant, Robert Herrick, James G.
Huneker, Edwin Markham, Brander Matthews, Meredith Nicholson,
Frank Norris, Booth Tarkington, Octave Thanet, William Allen
White, and Brand Whitlock. These were all among his admirers,
beneficiaries, or followers, even disciples—they were from one to all
four of those, the combination varying with the case. There are
surprises in the list. At a late turning point in his career, Thomas
Nelson Page wrote quaintly to acknowledge that he was striving to
be more contemporary and truthful, was now reading Tolstoi and
finding there the same things Howells had: "I should be unduly
stupid if I had not got something of your spirit out of our association since that long time back," Page wrote, "when you walked
into my office in Richmond and did me the honor to say we were
'chips from the same block.' The Negroes had a saying that 'De
chips don' fly fur from de stump,' and, maybe, we have both lain
in the same pile these many years. At least, I have recognized the

chip from the heart and tried to be like it somehow." And early in his career, thus spanning a wide gap, Henry Seidel Canby inscribed his novel *Our House*, 1919, to Howells "in gratitude for what he has meant to our younger generation."

As his study of Shelley Ray's experiences in *The World of Chance* revealed, Howells had taken the trouble to become precisely informed about the life, prospects, and problems of the writing younger generation. He knew his power to attract and influence them, and he meant to use it well. His crusades for literary and social sanity were, like Emerson's lectures, aimed at the young. In the final "Editor's Study" (March 1892), he summed up his advice to "the young Writer desirous to Form a Style":

' "Go first of all and be a man, in the widest and deepest sense of that much-abused word; a man so genial that tolerance, which is as modern as music among the arts, is a birthright and not an acquisition with him, and whose impulses are all as kind as they are wise; who finds the bewildered spirit of humanity in vulgarity itself; whose smile never wounds, and whose brows are lifted in patient deprecation when other brows would frown; who knows too much ever to despair, yet who is himself trying to learn from every lesson he teaches. Be that kind of man, young Writer, and all the rest shall be added unto you: beauty of phrase, refinement of manner, subtlety of perception, delicacy of touch, all that you admire and that you have been told can be acquired by the study of good models, you will find in yourself; and they will clothe you like your own flesh and blood, and not like those slop-shop things that you have got ready-made from the Chatham Street pullers-in of the schools." You will say that it is extremely difficult to be a man of that kind. Well, we own it is; we perceive the obstacle in your way; and yet it is not impossible. The supreme counsel was a counsel to perfection.'

It should be pointed out that nowhere in this, or any of his other advice, is there any call to "Follow me. Write like me. Be my disciple." Howells' last wish was to make little Howellses out of the young. All he wanted from them was full and honest work, and he would tolerate any amount of variance from his notions, even defiance of them, so long as he thought true work was forthcoming. He saw no reason to muffle his own convictions when a serious young writer flouted them. But he did not retaliate, either. The furthest length he would go, and that in the face of what seemed to him extreme provocation, was to withhold his reputation-making word. The point is made precisely in a letter to Robert Herrick in 1909 concerning Herrick's *Together*. Has the treatment there of sex been intended "as simply a picture of certain sides of American life, usually blinked, by an impartial observer whose sole business was to get them to the reader's knowledge; or . . . as in some sort a polemic for wider freedom in the sexual relations than the accepted ethics now grant?" If it is a matter of art, "You are within your rights as an artist," Howells tells Herrick, and his respect for Herrick's "serious and conscientious mind" and "literary quality" stands unimpaired. But if it is propaganda for attitudes Howells thinks immoral, he must dissociate himself from them. "If I bring you to book it is not with bell and candle. If you wish to straighten me out . . . this is the moment. Or if you would rather on the whole that I should not write of your books I shall not misunderstand you, or depreciate you."

Howells' alertness and receptivity to new talent became famous. He would have loved the humor of the desperate youth who, after many rejections, wrote the *Century*, "If you do not take some of my contributions, I shall have to resort to the humiliation of being discovered by William Dean Howells." For the discovered, however, that "humiliation" could be the most exhilarating of triumphs. It was partly the fame, partly the reassurance, but much of the joy came from Howells' tact, simplicity, and sympathy. Young William Allen White blew in from Kansas, looked Howells up and found him in the midst of packing to leave for the country. The great man sat down on a trunk with Allen, drumming and scuffing the heels of his short, nimble legs on its side, and talked to Allen as if he'd known him for years. He took the Westerner to the Century Club, and to keep him from being abashed by the gray-beard dignitaries as they entered the dining room, "said in a soft, merry voice: 'You know, Mr. White, the Century takes its name from . . . the average age of its members !' "

It is not hard to find testimonies to Howells from emerging writers which verge on the abject. "You have always been my literary master," wrote Alice French (Octave Thanet). "I . . . am as uncompromising a realist as lives." Brander Matthews, a major critic who also tried the novel, agreed at first to disagree creatively with Howells: he could not write realistic fiction, but "from no American author have I learnt as much as from you of the ways, customs, traditions, thoughts and characters of my fellow citizens."

After Matthews had achieved *Vignettes of Manhattan* and *His Father's Son,* he said, "I was trying to tell the truth according to your precept and I was hoping that you would like the tale." And again, "So far as I am conscious of the masters I modelled myself on . . . they are Turgenev and you." Brand Whitlock, the reform politician turned novelist, grew almost tearful. "Your kindness to me during all these years has been in many ways the most wonderful thing in my life. . . . Your approval of some of the things I have done has meant more than almost anything else could possibly have meant; I can do nothing but assure you of my devotion. . . ."

It was not in Howells to be callous or arrogant toward this sort of testimony, of course. But he did not feed on it nor maneuver to get it. He took it as kindness for kindness and kept his eye on the main chance—the production of fresh, vital American literature from the only source whence it could ever come, from the new, young writers. When they were really new and really big, they would not be likely to call anybody "master." Nevertheless they could be substantially helped if spotted in time. Howells made it his business to look for them, and he was rewarded by the appearance of a powerful but tragic triumvirate on whom he staked his bets. They were Stephen Crane, Harold Frederic, and Frank Norris.

Born in 1856, Frederic antedated Norris by fourteen and Crane by fifteen years, and naturally came into Howells' view sooner. He had early declared himself a realist and follower of Howells, making a pilgrimage to meet him in 1888. Yet Howells' first mention of him was in an adverse critique which then swung prettily around to become an admiring salute in the October 1890 "Editor's Study." Howells began by illustrating "the fatuity of the historical novel" in the inevitable anachronism of its characterizations from Frederic's "uncommonly well written" *In the Valley,* 1890. But then he turned about to make Frederic's contemporary reputation by regretting that he had hitherto neglected such "artistic and important books" as *Seth's Brother's Wife,* 1887, and *The Lawton Girl,* 1890. "It is a loss not to have known till now two books so robust, so sound, so honest," he said. He praised their "metaphysics and ethics" and the depths of the author's acquaintance with human nature. Particularly fresh was "Mr. Frederic's fidelity to conditions not much understood by people out of politics, which are managed by ambition rather than by money, as a general thing. Next to this in value is the truth, almost as novel, with which farm life, inside and out, is painted. . . ." Howells apparently never reviewed *The Damnation of Theron Ware,* though in 1899 he listed it as one of the major serious novels of which Americans could be proud.

The potency of Howells' word to make a reputation is illustrated by Theodore Roosevelt's reaction to this. He apparently read *Seth's Brother's Wife* at once and wrote Howells on October 20 to second his praise of the political insights of the novel and rejoice that the truth about American politics was gradually becoming available to the literate public. But Howells had methods for promoting his protégés besides supporting them in print. He had already put Garland onto Frederic, and, as he was writing the Study on Frederic, he stirred up another faithful henchman, recommending that Sylvester Baxter read Federic and look for his "indirect groping toward the new economic as well as artistic truth." A man like Baxter could help Frederic not only as a journalist but by alerting the circle of Howells' Boston friends to the new author.

Frederic's reaction to all this was just right. He had been Howells' grateful scholar; now he would be Howells' grateful ally—but his own man. "I am the richer for having come to know you—and the stronger for having gained a closer insight into your beliefs and feelings. It by no means follows that I see all things as you do, or that the work I am going to do will wholly please you, but I am sure both the vision and the performance will be helped by the fact of my knowing you." That was a statement of fact exactly as Howells would have wished. That it was perfectly acceptable to him may be evidenced from Frederic's lasting friendship and allegiance. In the year of Frederic's premature death he wrote in response to an invitation from Howells, "With you I will belong to any hose-company or target-shoot that takes your fancy—and be happy."

Like everything in that life so dazzlingly turbulent and abruptly quenched, Stephen Crane's relationships with Howells were more complex and less conclusive. Howells obviously played a number of significant roles in Crane's development, but it is not easy to isolate them definitively—partly because that development was cut off so early. He understood Crane's problems and struggle for existence as a young writer in New York, having sketched the circumstances exactly in *The World of Chance.* He seems not, however, to have been aware of the bitter privation, so graphically painted in Corwin Knapp Linson's *My Stephen Crane,* which resulted from Crane's tough-minded refusal to play the pliant hack. But, then, Crane's pride concealed that suffering even from his brothers.

His official version of their personal relations Howells wrote out for Cora Crane after her husband's death—obviously, from the style, intending it to be published in her projected biography of Stephen, or anywhere else she wished. At the beginning, Howells said,

'. . . Garland first told me of *Maggie*, which your husband then sent me. I was slow in getting at it, and he wrote me a heartbreaking note to the effect that he saw I did not care for his book. On this I read it and found that I did care for it immensely. I asked him to come to me, and he came to tea and stayed far into the evening, talking about his work, and the stress that was on him to put in the profanities which I thought would shock the public from him, and about the semi-savage poor, whose types he had studied in that book. He spoke wisely and kindly about them, and especially about the Tough, who was tough because, as he said, "Everything was on him." He came several times afterwards, but not at all oftener than I wished, or half so often, and I knew he was holding off from modesty. He never came without leaving behind him some light on the poor, sad life he knew so well in New York, so that I saw it more truly than ever before. He had thought wisely and maturely about it, but he had no plan for it, perhaps not even any hope without a plan. He was the great artist which he was because he was in nowise a sentimentalist. Of course I was struck almost as much by his presence as by his mind, and admired his strange, melancholy beauty, in which there was already the forecast of his early death. His voice charmed me, and the sensitive lips from which it came, with their intelligent and ironical smile, and his mystical, clouded eyes.

Inevitably there was the barrier between his youth and my age, that the years made, and I could not reach him where he lived as a young man might. I cannot boast that I understood him fully; a man of power before he comes to its full expression is hard to understand; it is doubtful if he is quite in the secret of himself; but I was always aware of *his* power, and nothing good that he did surprised me. He came to see me last just before he sailed for England the last time, and then he showed the restlessness of the malarial fever that was preying on him; he spoke of having got it in Cuba. But even then, with the sense that we were getting at each other less than ever, I felt his rare quality. I do not think America has produced a more distinctive and vital talent.'

What that extraordinary letter does not say, of course, is that Howells did a great deal more for Crane than invite him to tea. Crane apparently sent *Maggie* to Howells sometime in March 1893, in his second year in New York, for his "heartbreaking note" was dated March 23. Howells replied promptly that he would read it as soon as he could. By April 8 Crane was apologetically stifling his "humiliating misgivings" and asking for a recommendation to Godkin of the *Evening Post*. On the same day Howells wrote back, "You know how well I think you handled that subject, and if I could not agree with you on all points of theory, I thoroughly respected your literary conscience, and admired your literary skill." He apparently included the desired note to Godkin. A week later, since he then had no regular reviewer's channel, Howells used the convenient outlet of a newspaper interview to announce his discovery of "a remarkable writer" and to praise *Maggie*. From that point forward Howells worked tirelessly to get *Maggie* regularly published until in 1896 he finally succeeded and launched it on the public with a hosannaing "Introduction."

From April 1893 forward, relationships were close between Howells and Crane for as long as Crane remained in New York. Howells read the manuscripts of *George's Mother* (Mrs. Howells thought that the best of Crane); of Crane's poems; of *The Third Violet*. The one exception appears to have been *The Red Badge of Courage*. Crane began it as a desperate potboiler and saw it turn into a work of unpremeditated greatness under his hand. Though Howellsian ethical ideas affected it, *The Red Badge* was certainly not realistic; and if Crane thought Howells might not like it much, he was right.

But Howells' practice was to treat his young men as equals. Each should have the right to disagree with impunity. Howells had gone out of his way in *Harper's Weekly* for June 8, 1895, to plug the "grim, not to say grimy truth" of *Maggie* and lament that "all its conscience and all its art could not save it" from neglect. When he reviewed *The Red Badge of Courage*, however, he did his best to help it without compromising his own principles. Crane had struck a "fresh note," but the reviewer (quite justifiably) was not impressed by the authenticity of the combat scenes. More surprisingly, he could not find any warrant in his own aural observation for the dialect. He praised the "subjective" effect of the novel, its "conception of character," its potent presentations of that "human

commonness (which we cannot shrink from without vulgarity),"
and he registered perfectly its ethical implications, the ideas so
much like his own. ". . . In commending the book I should dwell
rather upon the skill shown in evolving from the youth's crude
expectations and ambitions a quiet honesty and self-possession man-
lier and nobler than any heroism he had imagined. There are divinations of motive and experience which cannot fail to strike the
critical reader, from time to time; and decidedly on the psychological side the book is worth while as an earnest of the greater things
that we may hope for from a new talent working upon a high level,
not quite clearly as yet, but strenuously."

When Crane seized the opportunity of New Year's Day and wrote
to thank Howells for all his help and for "your kind benevolent
life," Howells also exploited the chance to show that there were no
hard feelings. Thanking Crane for "your New Year's greeting,"
he went on warmly, "I have been enjoying for your sake your English triumphs. I am glad you are getting your glory young." Personally, however, Howells was convinced that the popularity of *The
Red Badge* as against the neglect of *Maggie* was an accident as
absurd as fashions in hats. Howells never registered at all the
aspects of *The Red Badge* often glorified as "mythic." As he continued to Crane, "For me, I remain true to my first love, *Maggie.*
That is better than all the Black Riders and Red Badges. You have
a lot of good work in you, and the whole of a long life to get it out.
I wish you would come sometime to see me."

Replying the day he got Howells' letter, Crane expressed the same
fears he was announcing to Nellie Crouse of being corrupted by
success: "If they would only continue the abuse," he said to Howells, "I feel able to cope with that, but beyond I am in great doubt."
If it was tempered criticism Crane was hoping for, he got it at once
from Howells' review of *The Black Riders.* As Howells had told
Crane after reading his poems in manuscript, he thought them
"striking" but formless. Howells was permanently unable to appreciate free verse. "These things are too orphic for me," he had told
Crane on October 2, 1894. "It is a pity for you to do them, for you
do things solid and real, so superbly. However, there is room for all
kinds—and if you like ! I do not think a merciful Providence meant
the 'prose-poem' to last." These objections he raised in his review,
even printing a poem he intensely admired as prose to make his

point. But he quoted generously and appreciatively to illustrate his main thesis that Crane had done "the most striking thing of the year."

Howells continued to back Crane up. As the eventually successful campaign to drive Crane out of New York as an undesirable character proceeded, Howells, unlike Hamlin Garland, refused to be impressed by the vicious gossip. He had seen and read his man, and he stuck to his own judgment. Crane is "a good boy," Howells said repeatedly. He personally nominated Crane for the Author's Club, for as Howells said to Ripley Hitchcock, "I believe in him thoroughly. I'm not afraid of his spoiling. But he's necessarily in his own hands."

Consequently, when Howells wrote a gorgeously headlined feature for the New York *World* on Crane and Abraham Cahan as New York writers, Crane was deeply moved—and to wonderfully characteristic expression:

'It is of course the best word that has been said of me and I am grateful in a way that is hard for me to say. . . . I always thank God that I can have the strongest admiration for the work of a man who has been so much to me personally, for I can imagine the terrors of being indelibly indebted to the Chump in Art or even to the Semi-Chump in Art.'

Howells' response to this was to invite Crane down to Far Rockaway, urging him to stay overnight so as to get in two swims.

If Crane felt so "indelibly indebted," what was he indebted for? As we have seen, for friendship, encouragement, and for a skillful, untiring effort both in print and behind the scenes to get the audience and reputation Crane deserved. For, in spite of Howells' disclaimers, he exhibited a greater measure of understanding than there is evidence to show came from any other critic in Crane's lifetime. Howells' introductory "an appreciation" for the long-delayed true publication of *Maggie* places an indicative finger precisely on some of Crane's rarest qualities: "The wonder of it is the courage which deals with persons so absolutely average, and the art which graces them with the beauty of the author's compassion for everything that errs and suffers," Howells said; ". . . it is notable how in all respects the author keeps himself well in hand. . . . He never shows his characters or his situations in any sort of sentimental glamour; if you will be moved by the sadness of common fates you will feel his intention; but he does not flatter his portraits of people on conditions to take your fancy."

The reasons for the accuracy and ease of that understanding of Crane, which is profound though not complete, was the same as the reason why Howells was *not*, to Crane, the "Chump"—or even the "Semi-chump in Art." Crane's honesty, his courage, his negative capability were, so far as they were more than temperamental, the result of what he credited to Howells in inscribing a copy of *The Red Badge:* ". . . a certain re-adjustment of his point of view victoriously concluded some time in 1892." Crane was proud to call himself a realist, and to feel that he was one of the few people who really understood what the word meant. And he did understand Howells almost uniquely well. Crane's interview of Howells for the New York *Times*, October 28, 1894, elucidated Howells' theory more plainly and effectively than perhaps any other single statement— including Howells' own.

Crane's own account of where he stood and how he got there at midpoint in his career, February 29, 1896, after the success of *The Red Badge*, is unusually high-flown for him. He was writing to impress an early flame who had turned him down, and his mood was the obverse of that in which he wrote Howells and Nellie Crouse. Here he makes the boast (improbably, though he may then have thought it true) that he had early "developed all alone a little creed of art which I thought was a good one." The commonest humiliation of the intellectual young is to respond to the current climates of opinion by "inventing" ideas which are later found to have belonged to prominent figures. "Later I discovered," Crane continued, "that my creed was identical with one of Howells and Garland and in this way I became involved in the beautiful war between those who say that art is man's substitute for nature and we are the most successful in art when we approach the nearest to nature and truth, and those who say—well, I don't know what they say. Than that they can't say much but they fight villainously and keep Garland and I out of the big magazines. Howells, of course, is too powerful for them. . . . The two years of fighting have been well-spent. . . . We have proved too formidable for them, confound them. They used to call me 'that terrible, young radical,' but now they are beginning to hem and haw and smile—those very old coons who used to adopt a condescending air toward me. There is an irony in the present situation that I enjoy, devil take them for a parcel of old, cringing, conventionalized hens."

Thus Stephen Crane on the Realism War. But he was soon to learn how temporary was his victory over the "old coons," how right he and Howells had been in fearing the realists must wait. There is no reason at all to doubt that Crane, who made a fetish of veracity, was a realist. Nor that his extraordinarily firm grasp of what realism was fundamentally affected his writing. Neither is there any doubt that the influence of Howells' ethical ideas can be traced in *The Red Badge of Courage* as in "The Blue Hotel" and a number of other Crane pieces. On the other hand, it would be absurd to intimate that the essential Crane was a little Howells. "He's necessarily in his own hands," Howells said. And in his own keeping Crane exercised certain literary powers entirely other from Howells', not dreamt of in Howells' philosophy. Conceivably Crane might have grown into entire rebellion against all Howells stood for, had Crane lived to maturity. On the other hand, he might have gone on, in full realization of his magnificent potential, to confirm by extending and transcending all Howells' doctrine and practice precisely as Thoreau and Whitman, each in his own way, did Emerson's. One aspect of the tragedy of Crane's youthful death is that we shall never know: unique possibilities for the continuity and upward reach of American culture were cut off.

Something of the same thing was true, and again in part with relation to Howells, in the equally tragic, almost equally early death of Frank Norris. A year older, but less precocious than Crane, Norris did not come to Howells' attention until the publication of *Moran of the Lady Letty*, 1898. What Howells' subsequent delight in Norris and consistent promotion of Norris proves is that Howells demanded no discipleship from his young men at all. Norris never pretended to be a follower, nor a "Realist" either. All he ever pretended to strive for was genuine seriousness in the novel, real fidelity to his own vision of the world. And with that, exercised through Norris' obvious gifts for literature, Howells was richly satisfied. As always, Howells never abdicated his right to hew to his own lines, and he gave Norris the same right. As a result Norris proved eminently teachable.

Above all, Norris proposed to be deadly serious. The novel had become "the great bow of Ulysses" in the modern world, he said. It had replaced the Church and the Press as the essential vehicle of contemporary expression and communication. Therefore the novelist had "a heavy duty to perform, and tremendous responsibilities to shoulder . . . with earnestness, with soberness, with a sense of his limitations, and with all the abiding sincerity that by the favor and mercy of the gods may be his." He shared with Crane this young man's fetish of sincerity, and he shared with some of the other young Harvard men of his era the conviction that it was all up to them. Somehow American culture did not exist, and they had to start from scratch to create it. Surveying the past, or indeed the present, Norris could find no school, for instance, of really American fiction. Everybody was colonial, or provincial, or corrupt, an expatriate, or a failure. "Mr. Howells alone is left, then, after the elimination is complete. Of all producers of American fiction he has had the broadest vision, at once a New Englander and a New Yorker, an Easterner and—in the Eastern sense—a Westerner. But one swallow does not make a summer, nor one writer constitute a 'school.' Mr. Howells has had no successors. Instead, just as we had with 'Lapham' and 'The Modern Instance' [*sic*] laid the foundation of fine, hardy literature, that promised to be our very, very own, we commence to build upon it a whole confused congeries of borrowed, faked, pilfered romanticisms . . . and I cannot allow this occasion to pass without protest against what I am sure every serious-minded reader must consider a lamentable discrowning."

If Norris, however, hoped to become a "successor" to Howells as an all-American novelist, he emphatically did not propose to do so as Howells' man. He could agree in despising "faked, pilfered romanticisms." But he thought responsible, modern Romance (like Zola) far superior to Realism. The trouble with Realism, Norris said, is that it "confines itself to the type of normal life" and "stultifies itself" because it notes only the surface of things. "Realism is minute; it is the drama of a broken teacup, the tragedy of a walk down the block, the excitement of an afternoon call, the adventure of an invitation to dinner." Norris craved something mightier and more intense than that. He proposed, Whitman-like, to end the Realism War by transcending it. Neoromanticism, he agreed, was contemptible, but true Romance far outshone Realism with its focus on "the ordinary, the untroubled, the commonplace." For, as he saw it, "to Romance belongs the wide world for range, and the unplumbed depths of the human heart, and the mystery of sex, and the problems of life, and the black, unsearched penetralia of the soul of man. . . . Romance, too, is a teacher, and if . . . she wears the camel's hair and feeds upon the locusts, it is to cry aloud unto the people, 'Prepare ye the way of the Lord; make straight his paths.' "

Much is revealed about Howells as critic and mentor in that he was quite willing to accept this, and its fictional results, from Norris for the sake of Norris' seriousness, freshness of insight, and talent. Under no compulsion to review anybody's book and internationally recognized as conferring a large favor on any writer, especially a new or little-known one, he chose to mention, Howells treated *Moran of the Lady Letty* in very interesting style. *Moran,* he said, was a "romanticistic story"—meaning the same things as Norris' "faked, pilfered romanticism"—and Howells compared it unfavorably with *The Money Captain* by Will Payne, a minor Chicago realist. Yet Howells apparently scented true promise in young Norris; he apologized for knocking his book and called it "a clever little story . . . boldly circumstanced in the light of common day," a "fresh and courageous invention, which has some divinations of human nature, as differenced in man nature and woman nature, and some curious glimpses of conditions."

Norris' letter thanking Howells for the review must have been intriguing. For Norris said he knew *Moran* was "full of faults" and might "justly" have been damned. He admitted that he had been "flying kites" and "showing off a bit," but he thanked Howells for encouraging him to "attempt the bold and unconventional." He now had in press, Norris continued, *"The People of Polk Street"* *(McTeague).* "It is as naturalistic as *Moran* was romantic and in writing it I have taken myself and the work very seriously. I earnestly hope that if you ever have occasion to review it I will be more deserving of your encouragement than I am afraid I was in the case of *Moran.*"

Howells' review of *McTeague* treated Norris as a mature and arrived novelist. Between this and *Moran,* Howells said, the author had shifted to realism "suddenly and with the overwhelming effect of a blizzard." Despite its obvious debts to Zola, this was both Californian, therefore indigenously American, and vitally original with Norris. This is the new fiction, fitted to the new Imperial, expansionist mood of the nation. It expands from the territory of "the old-fashioned American novel," which had been devoted to the "hypocrisies" in which "civilization" begins, to "the passions and the motives of the savage world which underlies as well as environs civilization."

Howells noted vestigial romanticisms in *McTeague* and was the first to object to the bathos of the ending. But he applauded the good points of the book, accurately charted its movement, and found its artistic power beyond the ordinary terms of admiration. He praised Norris at the end, while striving to educate him, by comparing him headily with the men he had in *My Literary Passions* called the greatest of novelists: "Mr. Norris has, in fact, learned his lesson well, but he has not learned it all. His true picture of life is not true, because he leaves beauty out. Life is squalid and cruel and vile and hateful, but it is noble and tender and pure and lovely too. By-and-by he will put these traits in. . . . In the meantime he has done a picture of life which has form, which has texture, which has color, which has what great original power and ardent study of Zola can give, but which lacks the spiritual light and air, the consecration which the larger air of Tolstoi gives. It is a little inhuman. . . ." Norris in thanking him for the review which "encouraged me more than anything that has ever been said of my work," gladly accepted all the strictures, except "the anticlimax, the 'death in the desert' business." And revealed the plan of his *Wheat* novels, "a big epic trilogy . . . that at the same time would be modern and distinctly American."

Howells' presentation copy of *The Octopus* was inscribed "most sincerely and gratefully," and, indeed, the elements new to the novel show that Norris had made good use of his instruction. And Howells, in his turn, was lyrical from the "Editor's Easy Chair" which he had at last inherited. Norris, he said, was "a poet among the California wheat-fields" who had "woven a prodigious epic . . . of Zolaesque largeness; but Mr. Norris is a poet of native note, and he owes to the great romantic realist nothing but the conception of treating a modern theme epically." Though Howells had some reservations about Norris' tricks of method and deplored his weakness for "melodrama," he felt "something vital, something primeval in his people," and "the stir of dumb, cosmic forces . . . of great imaginational consequence." With whatever little defects, he concluded, "it is a great book, simple, sombre, large and of a final authority as the record of a tragical passage of American, of human events, which, if we did not stand in their every-day presence, we should shudder at as the presage of unexampled tyrannies."

A year later the robust Norris was suddenly dead of appendicitis, and Howells was left to celebrate his worth—". . . he was in the divine secret of the supreme artists: he saw what was before him, with things in their organic relations, and he made life live"— and to mourn his loss: this death "has bereft us of a hope in fiction which no other now promises fully to restore."

In Crane and Norris, Howells knew that he had been given two potential successors to help and educate into what he hoped would be a greatness higher than his but resting on his achievement. Less noticeably, perhaps, Harold Frederic was a third. And all had died tragically young, with fine work done but almost indubitably greater work *in posse*. The great tragedy, of course, was for American letters and the flowering of their continuity. But there was real loss here for Howells, too. Now he would never see what the logic of his life's development might have come to had the young men of genius lived to whom he had devotedly transmitted it in the moment of his greatest strength as the country's leading man of letters. Directly after Norris' death, Howells mourned his loss of both Crane and Norris together in an article entitled "Frank Norris." As between Crane the "vibrant," the "electrical," "lyrical spirit, whose freedom was its life" but who "was the absolute slave of reality," and Norris, the strong master of "the full music of his own aspiration, the rich diapason of purposes securely shaping themselves in performance," Howells preferred Norris. But with Crane gone first, Norris' death left an absolute void. Howells was not stripped of young followers. He could look around at the end of his lament and name Brand Whitlock. William Allen White, Robert Herrick, and Will Payne as men who had all done "good work" and would do it again. He might have named others. But there was no one to whom he could now look for greatness in his line. It was a strange and bitter stroke of fate.

Chapter Seven

THE DEAN IN THE EASY CHAIR

A S RECOGNITION OF HOWELLS' PRE-EMINENCE AMONG THE MEN OF
letters of his day became increasingly a matter of fact, the
temptation to the obvious pun on his name was increasingly
irresistible. William Dean Howells became the "Dean of American
Letters." Nobody seems to have been proud enough to claim the
paternity of the coinage. It just drifted into casual use.

It cannot be denied that during the era of his elevation to his
post, the Dean experienced a marked falling-off in creative power.
Without being able to date many of his fundamental creative impulses to fiction, one suspects that he had begun to live off creative
capital—that the ideas for almost all the fiction after about 1892
had come from the previous six or seven years of extraordinary
creative richness. Much of his writing became autobiographical,
either as memoirs or in a return to the travel writing from which
he had originally graduated to the novel. Or he wrote criticism,
essays, sketches. He began again to dream of his long-abandoned
history of Venice, and even of that childhood's fancy, the biography
of Cervantes.

When he did essay fiction, he showed that his hand had lost no
cunning. His power to command all the effective techniques of illusion was as great as ever. But the shaping power of his imagination now sometimes failed him. *The Coast of Bohemia* is a good
case in point. Taking hints from Beaton of *A Hazard of New Fortunes* and from Shelley Ray of *The World of Chance*, Howells re-
verted to the theme which had defeated him in *A Woman's Reason*
and *Dr. Breen's Practice*—the feminist problem of the place of
women in a man's professional world. But now his heroine was an
Ohio girl, from Jefferson as a matter of fact, with fine artistic

talent who came to New York's world of chance to study at the Synthesis of Art Studies in hopes of a career.

Much of *The Coast of Bohemia* is brilliantly done. Important themes of feminism, of problems of art education, of Americanism in painting, of the problem of the artist in the modern world, of art and popular culture, of Bohemianism, and of the artist in relation to the monied culture-vulture are not only introduced but incarnated into vivid characterizations and actions which Howells supported with a number of masterly scenes and settings. But the major action of the novel develops into love-interest patterns of discovery, crisis, and happy ending which are lamentably irrelevant. To be sure, there had to be a love interest for this *Ladies' Home Journal* novel. But Howells at his best had long been expert at forcing the shallow reader's love interest to serve the serious reader's thematic and intellectual concerns. This time, even worse than in *The World of Chance,* that publicly necessary action failed to work organically with the themes. Instead, it cut across, snarling the essential thematic lines and, even worse, violating the character of Cornelia Saunders, his most interestingly imagined Ohio woman artist.

I

Something of the same weariness of the author's central novelistic imagination was to doom much of Howells' subsequent fiction to comparative unsuccess. In the 1894 interview with Crane, Howells had spoken of his plans for *Ragged Lady,* 1899. If that was one the little-reading Crane had sought out, it may well have been the one he said had disappointed him. On the other hand, occasionally the old fires flamed up magnificently in the Dean, and his full powers returned. Some of the short fiction of the nineties is superb. And right in the middle of the decade he produced another major novel, unquestionably first-class and uniquely his own. This was *The Landlord at Lion's Head.*

One of the six volumes published in the *Library Edition* aborted by a publishers' feud in 1909, *The Landlord* then got one of the most amusing and revealing of Howells' introductions. He remembered working so hard at it, "It made me feel at times as if I should never learn my trade, but so did every novel I have written; every novel, in fact, has been a new trade." But his "very good grip" on the characters enabled him to break "through into the daylight" and thoroughly succeed with it. He recalled the far-flung sources of his materials: the title came long before the book—when he had seen a lion form in a mountain on Lake Champlain in 1891. The hero's name, Durgin, "had been waiting for his personality ever since I got it off the side of an ice-cart many years before." Throughout a decade he had been meaning to write a summer hotel story, and he had accumulated an experience of them "extending over a quarter of a century, and scarcely to be surpassed if paralleled." Finally, between his twelve years' residence in Cambridge and John Mead Howells' recent years at Harvard, he felt that he had acquired a sufficiently reliable "intimacy with the university moods and manners."

Only enriching textures and effects had their sources in such details of Howells' outward living, however. The real power of the novel came from a sharp insight into the cultural and thence psychological experience of New England. Contrary to the impressions garnered by some hasty readers, Howells, he confessed, "liked the hero of the tale more than I have liked worthier men, perhaps because I thought I had achieved in him a true rustic New England type in contrast with urban life under entirely modern conditions." Below that, he had sought and found something still more interesting in Jeff Durgin: "the realization of that anti-Puritan quality which was always vexing the heart of Puritanism" in the life of New England.

Around Jeff Durgin, Howells organized his long-standing research into the plight of civilization in modern American life into its most solid pattern. At first blush the novel looks like another in the line since Angus Beaton of artist-studies. But Jere Westover, the painter, figures in the novel primarily as a person, not an artist. Howells handled him, in the end, very skillfully indeed. So much so that one suspects that the problem of just what to do with Westover was the wall against which the author had to beat and beat until he broke through into the fine formal success of his novel. Westover's technical function is the Jamesian service of "register," "sensitive observer," and "center of revelation." Most of what cannot be performed scenically by the characters comes to the reader through Westover, and he is the catalytic performer or listener in many of the key scenes.

Thematically, however, Westover escapes the blank personal futility of the mere observer. Howells lets him represent civilization and stand at the end as the one character who can incarnate values which really call Jeff Durgin's success into doubt. Howells-like, Westover observes the state of modern civilization in New England from the outside. Westover had been a gifted child in the frontier-wilderness forests of Wisconsin whose talent was recognized and valued early enough to save him. In Europe he had acquired both professional competence and, through honest personal cultivation, civilization. He had returned to paint and teach in Boston, accepted, for his worth, as an outsider in Proper Bostonian Society. At the start of the novel he has tramped deep into Robert Frost country, into "almost primitively solitary and savage" New England mountains where the starving, decadent Yankee farmers are waging the last of their losing battle against rocky soil, bitter climate, tuberculosis, and the ruinous price competition of the prairie West. There, at the homestead of the Durgins, he finds the ideal spot from which to paint the fascinating Lion's Head mountain.

Year after year Westover fights to capture the incredible play of light on that mountain, "as imperative and importunate as the Great Stone Face itself" in all weathers, until his paintings of it become his trademark. And as he returns, he becomes increasingly drawn into the affairs of the Durgin family and their neighbors the Whitwells. He watches Mrs. Durgin, robust and hearty in contrast to her frail husband and (all but one) phthisic sons, spurred by need into developing her farm step by step into a summer hotel. And he watches Jeff Durgin, the one son who takes after his mother, grow up, struggle reluctantly through Harvard, find himself in the world, and become a swank-hotel operator.

The patterning of social and moral relationships throughout the novel is extraordinarily complex. Jeff, with all his natural buoyancy, rugged energy, convivial charm, is a born anti-Puritan. He inherits from his maternal grandfather, an ancient tavernkeeper, hell-raiser, slave-catcher, and Copperhead, his good-looking blond strength and three innate characteristics. It is born into him to be, in the repeated country phrase, a "comical devil" always in some sort of roistering trouble; to know instinctively how to "keep hotel"; and, as "the law of his nature," always to return evil for good by retaliating whenever anyone tries to guide or discipline him toward goodness. He must always revenge "the stress put upon him for righteousness." He was, in defiance of all the generations of Puritan inheritance, born to be what the founding New England divines meant by "the natural man."

As such, Jeff, for all his compensating attractiveness, is a bully, a "blackguard," and a savage—completely beyond the reach of discipline from within or without. The problem of the novel is to see what it will mean that Jeff becomes the landlord at Lion's Head. How will this natural man, coming out of the savage bleakness and beauty of his isolated mountain country, make terms with the modern world? And what kind of terms will the world make with him? At home he has only the futile remnants of Puritan tradition, dryrotted into the decadence of spiritualism, the decadence of eccentric though salable "character," or the decadence of women's inherited but unphilosophical scrupulosities. From boyhood he has known that he could vanquish these with contemptuous force of will.

Beginning with Westover, Jeff finds the outside world, as it comes in ever increasing waves to Mrs. Durgin's hotel, thoroughly puzzling. The easy integrity of Westover's civilization baffles Jeff. He respects and admires yet profoundly resents it. And he finds the same qualities in the guests who create the first real success of The Lion's Head Inn. As Westover observes:

'The people who can afford to pay ten dollars a week for summer board, and not much more, are often the best of the American people. . . . They are apt to be middle-aged maiden ladies from university towns, living upon carefully guarded investments; young married ladies with a scant child or two [it's taken for granted that the husbands have stayed home to work] . . . ; college professors with nothing but their modest salaries; literary men or women in the beginning of their tempered success; clergymen and their wives away from their churches in the larger country towns or the smaller suburbs of the cities; here and there an agreeable bachelor . . . hosts of young and pretty girls with distinct tastes in art. . . . Such people are refined, humane, appreciative, sympathetic; and Westover . . . was glad to find himself in the midst of this unrestraint, which was so sweet and pure . . . the first aspects of society at Lion's Head seemed to him Arcadian.'

Unfortunately they did not continue Arcadian. As the hotel prospered, its prices went up and its clientele's prosperity followed. There came the day when Jeff, all good style, good nature, and buoyant good will, led a picnic party out in the woods and the most stylish of the ladies dished him out his food first so he could go and eat it with the horses. With a jolt he learned that the society which pretended to be civilization was just as savage as any of his own most blackguardly impulses. In summer hotel society, and then at Harvard, where he suffered the penalties for being a "jay," and on the fringes of Boston society as he came to know it, Jeff found that the law of Society was really that of the savage tribe. If you were In, or if you could charm, buy, or force your way in, all was well. If you were a "jay," you were Out.

For himself Jeff learns the same things about American life, whether in higher education, Society, or elsewhere, that Aristides Homos learned. When Westover, as the voice of morality and civilization tries to teach Jeff "what a savage you are," and that "You can't do a wrong thing and prosper on it," he finds that Jeff has learned his own answers:

        ' "Oh yes, you can," Jeff interrupted, with a sneering laugh, "How do you suppose all the big fortunes were made? By keeping the Commandments?"

"No. But you're an unlucky man if life hasn't taught you that you must pay in suffering of some kind, sooner or later, for every wrong thing you do—"

"Now that's one of your old-fashioned superstitions, Mr. Westover," said Jeff.'

Further on he tells Westover: "Prosperity and adversity, they've got nothing to do with conduct. If you're a strong man, you get there, and if you're a weak man, all the righteousness in the universe won't help you. . . . I shall be blessed if I look out for myself; and if I don't I shall suffer for my want of foresight."

In the all-too-practical world around him, Jeff has already proved his point to his entire satisfaction. The touchstone of his own barbarity has found its response in the plutocracy. He has wooed and won the heart of Genevieve Vostrand, of the international set, but lost her to parental ambitions to have her marry an impoverished Florentine nobleman. He has exposed the emptiness of Proper Boston in Bessie Lynde, who has an affair of sorts with him for the same decadent reasons which make her brother Alan an alcoholic. And in the plutocratic race he wins. This hereditary anti-Puritan and savage prospers mightily as the man of the present. He turns Lion's Head into a huge success, wins back Genevieve Vostrand, and joins the international set himself. "I tell you, Jeff's the gentle-

man now, and his wife's about the nicest lady I ever saw," says old
Mr. Whitwell. The landlord at Lion's Head "got there."

The only thing Jeff has lost is the pure and lovely Puritan maid,
Cynthia Whitwell, whom Westover eventually wins. The question
remaining is whether Jeff is also the man of the American future.
If a Jeff can so prosper, can there be "any moral government of the
universe?" If a society of Jeffs can prosper, what then? Westover,
as the man of civilization, is sure of the answer:

'A tree brings forth
of its kind, as a man sows he reaps. It's dead sure, pitilessly sure. Jeff
Durgin sowed success in a certain way, and he's reaping it. He once said
to me, when I tried to waken his conscience, that he should get where
he was trying to go if he was strong enough, and being good had nothing
to do with it. I believe now he was right. But he was wrong, too, as
such a man always is. That kind of tree bears Dead Sea apples, after
all. He sowed evil, and he must reap evil. He may never know it, but he
will reap what he has sown. The dreadful thing is that others must
share in his harvest.'

Yet that is, within the confines of this novel, only Westover's
faith. To the thriving landlord, it may remain merely old superstition. The reader is, as Barrett Wendell admiringly noted, left "free
to philosophize" for himself, not told what to think.

Thus Howells had written yet another major novel. It was artis-
tically strong. Owen Wister related how, when he visited Henry
James at Rye in 1896, that stammering master had fallen to praising
The Landlord at Lion's Head:

' "It's—it's—it's," he began, "Well, I think
it's possible—yes, I'll go as far as possible—that—that six-and-a-half
Americans know how good it is."

"Counting me?"

"Yes, my dear Owen, you're the half !" '

And it spoke to the condition of Americans. The vast bulk of
middle-class Americans were invited to consider why their ambitions should be the same as Jeff Durgin's. Some of them responded
just as Howells might have hoped. Young Mark Sullivan, matricu-
lating as a freshman at Harvard, read *The Landlord* because a lady-
friend had told him it dealt with his college. He finished it elated
at the view of amazing new horizons, rushed to the library to ask
how many books he was allowed to withdraw, and took out that
number of volumes by Howells.

II

One of Howells' almost constant activities was writing for and about the stage. According to Professor Walter J. Meserve, between the translation of D'Aste's *Sansone* in 1874 and the publication of *Self-Sacrifice* in 1911, Howells wrote probably thirty-six plays. Of these thirty were published—twenty-four one-act farces; *A Sea Change,* musical comedy; *Out of the Question,* and *A Counterfeit Presentment,* two comedies; *The Mother and the Father: Dramatic Passages;* and *Samson.* Unpublished were adaptations of *A Foregone Conclusion, The Rise of Silas Lapham,* and *A Hazard of New Fortunes:* a collaboration with Twain on *Colonel Sellers as a Scientist;* the translation-adaptation of Tamayo y Baus, *Yorick's Love,* a fairly popular tragedy; and perhaps others.

Altogether, this is a respectable volume of writing. Together with a certain amount of theatrical criticism, ardent, lifelong theatergoing with an equally enthusiastic wife, and an inevitably substantial amount of time and anxiety invested in the practical worries of the playwright over production, performance, contracts, casting, and the like, this adds up to still another career for Howells. As historians of the stage seem agreed, that career possessed real significance for the development of an American theater. Yet it is curious that it should have had so little real effect either on Howells' major work, his fiction, or on the course of his life as a whole.

Perhaps one reason for that comparatively small effect was that for Howells the playwright the times seemed out of joint. He could really score only with the delicious farces which, however expertly he fashioned them, had mainly to succeed as antiromantic jokes. At a popular level Howells' farces deserved their great success. "They began to be acted everywhere within a week or two of their publication," said Booth Tarkington, recalling his Indiana youth, "and a college boy of the late 'eighties and 'golden 'nineties' came home at Christmas to be either in the audience at a Howells farce or in the cast that gave it." Nor was that popularity merely sectional. Part of Kate Douglas Wiggin's *My Garden of Memories* included glamorous hours in Santa Barbara, California, where the community took a "lively" amateur interest in Howells' farces, and she was "cast for the verbose, light-hearted (and lighter-headed !)

heroines of *The Register, The Parlor Car,* and *The Sleeping Car.*"

Nor was that success merely amateur. Augustus Thomas, who wrote more than 60 plays, was traveling with a troupe of actors cross-country when he "found our boys in the smoking-car roaring with delight over a little comedy in *Harper's Magazine* . . . the smart dialogue of *The Elevator* by William Dean Howells. That was my first knowledge of him as a dramatist," Thomas confessed. "The effects that he achieved in that little play . . . and in others . . . were very educational suggestions to a young writer as to what could be done in the theater with restraint joined to precision." The success was also international. Howells' farces were performed in London, sometimes by distinguished people. George Bernard Shaw, in 1895 a drama critic, crowed with hyperbolic delight over *The Garroters:* "The little piece showed, as might have been expected, that with three weeks' practice the American novelist could write the heads off the poor bunglers . . . our managers [get] when they want a small bit of work to amuse the people who come at eight. But no doubt it is pleasanter to be a novelist . . . to be independent of time and space, than to conform to the stern conditions of the stage and fight with stupidity before and behind the curtain."

But of course it was no mere callous preference which kept so fond a theater-lover mainly to the novel. He would have adored a playwright's full success. But farces could not win it. As Augustine Daly pointed out in urging Howells to write a full-length play for him in which to star Ada Rehan, "One-act plays bring no profit and give very little lasting satisfaction to authors, actors, or managers." Howells tried repeatedly but could never really ring the bell. Much of his playwrighting history was told in capsule form in the letter he wrote to his father after the stage version of *A Foregone Conclusion* was performed at the Madison Square Garden in March 1886. The house was "splendid," the applause "incessant," but the reviews were bad "without a dissenting voice": he was hard at work on *April Hopes.*

There is no way of knowing whether Howells could have written himself into eminence as a playwright the way he did as a novelist —by dint of constant practice and steady growth. He never had the chance. And for that as well as more objective reasons, he found the theater of his day impossible to respect. In *Silas Lapham* he let Bromfield Corey say of the theater, "from what I've seen of it I should say it was intellectually degrading." But for the most part, Howells tried to reform it through satire, to laugh it toward intellectual respectability. In America, he observed in the "Editor's Study" for July 1887, "We have no drama and only the faintest promise of a drama, but we have a dramatic criticism which surpasses that of other countries as much as our fire department. A perfectly equipped critical engine stands in every newspaper office, with the steam always up, which can be manned in nine seconds, and rushed to the first theatre where there is the slightest danger of drama within five minutes; and the combined efforts of these tremendous machines can pour a concentrated deluge of cold water upon a play which will put out anything of the kind at once."

These critics, he said later, "whose discipline is so perfect that they often seem to think as one man, and sometimes as no man at all," can see only the lifeless ideal of the French well-made play. And they so corrupt the public and intimidate the managers that all realism, all reflection of real American life, and all earnest concern with social and psychological questions are barred from the stage. A heroic idealist like James A. Herne fights for the future. But perhaps the true hope lies in the directions opened up by Edward Harrigan, Denman Thompson, and Charles Hale Hoyt. Actors and managers as well as playwrights, these men could win public success with their gropings toward the common life, however vulgar, of America. When they should evolve toward treating serious intellectual problems "in the spirit of their liberal art," there would emerge "a national drama." In the meanwhile, Howells suggests, we might look toward freeing the stage from the fears and necessities of the manager by instituting "a municipal theatre in every city and town, sustained by a tax. . . ."

With these outlooks on the drama, it was not surprising that Howells' theater novel, *The Story of a Play*, 1898, should be a comedy. Another in Howells' 1890's series of studies of young artists, this one revives Brice Maxwell and Louise Hilary from *The Quality of Mercy*, marries them against the will of her paradoxically liberal-Proper Boston family, and studies the working out of their marriage. Henry James as reviewer was right in praising the "world of wit, perception, and intellectual curiosity" in which it moved and in suggesting that it might well have been entitled *The Story of a Wife*. For we see the action from Louise's point of view. Through her we learn to comprehend and respect Brice Maxwell's personal and creative integrity. We see how theatrical people can be at once pompous, enthusiastic, impulsive, idealistic, arrogant, sacrificial, grasping, and, above all, unstable. We witness through Louise the gradual education of a Boston lady to an understanding of artistic duties and processes, to reconciliation with the demands of living with a truly creative man who will never become Proper no matter how well her society accepts him for his literary distinction.

If there is a serious flaw, it inheres in the fact that too much space goes to Louise's difficulties and not enough to Brice and his work, not enough especially to Godolphin, the wonderfully pictured actor-entrepreneur on whom Brice must rely. Godolphin's oscillating reactions and communications, probably based on Howells' experiences with Laurence Barrett's tours with *A Counterfeit Presentment* and *Yorick's Love* in 1877–79, make marvelous satire. Living the Theater, Godolphin perfectly expresses, especially in contrast to Maxwell's grim integrity, the point Howells wanted to make about drama in America. Perhaps Henry James was still too close to the agonizing trauma of his own theatrical defeat, perhaps he knew too little about the American conditions Howells was attacking, perhaps he was a prisoner of his theory of Howells. At any rate, he was wrong in suggesting that *The Story of a Play* should have been a tragedy. It was no less a weapon in the fight for a serious drama because it satirized the state of the theater in America.

III

Once his craft is learned, an author as artist is absolutely dependent on only one thing. Out of the depths of his psyche must flow that strange force, the mystic troubling of the waters of the imagination, which provides the artist with the special stuff out of which only he can make his kind of art. The creative impulse cannot be commandeered. Sometimes it flows with incredible richness. Sometimes it is slow, and sometimes, disastrously, it dries up. During the decade 1881–91, it welled, even spurted up like a wilderness fountain for Howells. Throughout his forties and well into his fifties, he was generously endowed. But the flow slackened toward his sixtieth birthday and sprang up only intermittently after that.

Therefore he turned again toward journalism. He tried such desperate expedients for stimulating a flow of creativity as *Their*

Silver Wedding Journey. In 1897 the Howellses went abroad, and he conceived the idea of refining on what was once the organic growth of *Their Wedding Journey* and *A Chance Acquaintance* from the travel book to the novel. The Marches, now firmly resurrected, would live and talk a new *genre*—the travel in a novel frame. As a novel *Their Silver Wedding Journey* was a nonentity. But it sold well enough to convince Howells and the Harpers that the continued vitality of the youthful travel books was no accident. Howells retained a solid audience as a travel writer.

For this and many other reasons, he became indispensable to the firm in the years which followed. The vicissitudes of the world of chance hit Harper and Brothers hard. The firm was forced into receivership, and on November 28, 1899, George Harvey, then the young owner and editor of the *North American Review,* was appointed "agent" by agreement with banker J. P. Morgan. Howells had a large stake in the rehabilitation of the Harpers. And they plainly thought him essential to the firm's recovery. S. S. McClure, who seems to have failed in a last, desperate play to prevent the bankruptcy, had begged Howells in October to come and talk about the "very great" help Howells could give him. Through the succeeding winter other firms were at Howells "in view of the probable liquidation of Messrs. Harper and Bros." But he made no move, and when Harvey sent the annual royalty check in the spring he opened a negotiation which eventuated in Howells' return to the Harpers on terms which made him financially secure for the remaining twenty years of his long life.

For $10,000 a year the Harpers were to take all Howells wrote. He was to revive the "Editor's Easy Chair," contribute occasional short stories to *Harper's Monthly,* articles to Harvey's *North American Review,* and serve the firm as literary counselor. In that last capacity he was to continue his natural work with young writers —but for the benefit of the firm if possible—and solicit manuscripts. Naturally he would take all the advantage of this he could to promote serious fiction, and realism.

Unlike Walker, Colonel Harvey and his amiable colleague Frederic A. Duneka proved easy to get along with. For a while they even persuaded Howells to keep an office in their fabulously hideous old Franklin Square Building. It was "lost in a dreary backwater of small business establishments, corner gin-mills, and third class restaurants. The trains on the elevated structure made a continued reinforced by the din of the traffic on the Brooklyn Bridge only a uproar just outside the windows, and these distracting noises were stone's throw away," said Joseph Henry Harper. It was a very allegory of the world of chance, and Howells must have felt like Aristides Homos anew every time he struggled up its crowded, slippery cast-iron spiral staircase.

But it represented the security he felt he had a right to give himself in the chance-world. He could feel his creative energy and his resiliency for daily living shading off as his sixties advanced. There would yet be major novels, but he could not be sure. Too much of what he now essayed would not come right. Of all his many complaints through this period perhaps the most character-istic was that to S. Weir Mitchell in 1907: "I am as usual busy making my gold-brick, without straw, buried in prosperous slavery to a salary and dreaming of some great achievement hereafter, well knowing that if any achievement of mine has greatness it [is] of heretofore." Yet anyone who read into that or any of a dozen sim-ilar plaints in the period the inference that Howells had quit, that he would no longer be trying to produce fine work, would misread the man. It was normal for him to undervalue himself: he feared and fought egotism as the deadliest sin. It was hard to be patient with diminished creative resources. But he was a devoted artist and an honest thinker. When the resources were available, when the wells of creative impulse flowed, he would make the very best of what they gave him. If he is to be criticized in this final period of his Deanship, it should be for pumping too hard at the wells, not for neglecting them.

Despite his occasional complaints, the forceful quality of his copy shows that Howells returned to magazining with zest. For *The North American Review* he wrote some of his most extended and judicial works of true literary criticism. Reviews and commentary on topics of current interest he could toss into lesser Harpers publications like the *Weekly* or the *Bazar*. The *Monthly* he reserved for practicing his own theory of the grand tradition of the occa-sional essay in direct line from the revered Curtis.

Simultaneously reviving the Easy Chair for Howells and the Study for Alden, Harvey had the magazine make a big splash. Above the first Easy Chair "The Editor" devoutly recorded his hope that Howells was "the man who, of all living writers, is the fit master to conduct it on the old and familiar lines that ensured its prosperity in the thoughts and affections of readers." In the neighboring Study, Alden penned a curious little opening. He called on all readers to rejoice with him in the "wise and genial strain" of the new "guest" in the Easy Chair "—since the appreciation of Mr. Howells' writings has become a part of our American culture." He promised a "vital charm" in these essays from the author who "brings us strange gossip of ourselves, probing our modern mood and consciousness." He wondered if Howells would not speak out with the "more zest" after years of "self-denial for the sake of art; and the restraint put upon himself in fiction." He wanted in short to promise, without saying it, that Howells would "unbosom himself" but not revive either the Realism War nor the attendant social polemic of the old Study. And so he concluded, "For while it is the unwritten law of this Magazine . . . to avoid the . . . 'burning questions' and . . . themes that divide sects in religion, parties in politics, and classes in society, yet there is no periodical in which more value is set upon the writer's individuality."

What Howells did in the Easy Chair was take Alden at his word. He launched no polemics, conducted no campaigns. And yet he spoke his constantly individual, often radical mind firmly. Though *Harper's* would carry reams of neoromantic trash, replete with sadism, swordplay, and intimations of rape, Howells continued his attack, often with irony but sometimes openly. In his inaugural Easy Chair essay, he said that in fiction and drama "there never was a more imbecile time, perhaps." Both prospered hugely as parts of a mass entertainment industry "upon a single formula of blood-shed and arch-heroism." The only source of hope was that in the midst of all this ephemeral but commercial tripe, true writers like Henry James, and the Misses Wilkins and Jewett still produced, "and against a night as cheerless for the friend of serious fiction as any that ever was there has risen in the name of Mrs. Edith Wharton a star of literary conscience and artistic ideal, pure, clear, serene." Finally, since this first was also a Christmas number, he managed to ring out clearly the talismanic name of Tolstoi.

Twelve familiar essays a year were simply more than Howells cared to write, however. He was at his best when he invented characters with which to conduct the little scenes typical of those collected in the happily titled *Imaginary Interviews*, 1910, or when he wrote editorials. The interviews were often wryly funny and evocative of nostalgic reflections; but they tended to be bland. The editorials could be caustic.

The subject on which the early Easy Chair—or any other editorials Howells could find opportunity to insinuate into his many outlets—was most caustic was the revolutionary American imperialism which followed the Spanish-American War. He had never had any use for the ideal of the White Man's Burden. As early as the October 1891 Editor's Study, he had been saying that, while no doubt conditions in Japan might be improved, "our own are so far from perfect that we could wish that charming and gifted people, when the change comes, something better and wiser than our status." We ought to hope "that if they are left to work out their own solution they may achieve one yet that will not involve so much social and moral damnation as ours, and that if they finally achieve Christianity it will be in the form of a life as well as a creed."

Hispanophile and Altrurian, he felt disaffected toward the yellow press's war from the start and said so. Eventually "our war for humanity" became openly "a war for coaling-stations," the plundering peace was made, and the subjugation of the Philippine Republic by the United States Army began. Then Howells found many of the Americans he most admired enlisted on his side as "anti-imperialists." The best-loved and most intimate of these, of course, was Mark Twain. Howells had no such gift of overwhelming invective, nor any such place in the hearts of his people, as Twain. He produced nothing comparable to Twain's masterpiece, "To the Person Sitting in Darkness." But he could and did throw the weight of his name and the broadside force of his battery of journals into the fight.

The finest and most enlightening of all these writings was the January 1902 Easy Chair which reflected, with prophetic accuracy, on the meaning of events between the sinking of the *Maine* and the assassination of McKinley. Almost nothing is known, he began, about the laws of change in nature or history, and often it comes so slowly that no one notices. But sometimes it happens dramatically; and, "We are mystically aware that the Americans since that war are not the Americans they were before it. . . . The nation that looses the passions of its people in a foreign war must pay for the debauch; a state which refuses to control the industrial strifes within itself must suffer the effects of the hate left alike with the winning and the losing side."

The courage, dignity, simplicity, humility, and mercifulness of McKinley in death were sublime, Howells continued. And yet "an epoch came to an end with that deed . . . an order of things which has prevailed with us for more than half a century." The order, the "ideal of the common man" which had prevailed from Jackson through McKinley, now gave way again "to an older order which it superseded, and which has now become the newer order." This, he said, carefully maintaining the space between the two words, was the opposite "ideal of the gentle man." The great presidents out of the people had "vindicated" the common man. "Their great lives hallowed the notion of humility of origin and condition in the hearts of most Americans as something humanly dear and sweet, as something almost divinely sacred." But what would become of us under Roosevelt, "this new man of that old order," an honest and dutiful man, "a democrat *de facto*, though he is inalienably an aristocrat *de jure*"?

It remained to be seen, he suggested. Surely we stood in perplexing new circumstances: ". . . beside the European powers which never credited the maxims and principles of national conduct which we have now openly discarded. We are conquerors like the rest; we have an imperial empire, with a Constitution that does not cover that empire. . . ." Perhaps it was as well to leave the situation "in the keeping of those who brought it about." Common Americans had better hope that the new gentle man's generous fervor would help him to imagine his duty correctly, and they had better back him up. "Let the American people in their vast commonness be worthy of the faith which such a man puts in them, and there can be nothing to make them uneasy. They are always their own masters, when they will, and they are his."

With the best of his critical essays going into the *North American Review* and ordinary reviews often in *Harper's Weekly*, Howells made the Easy Chair no such center of contemporaneous literary excitement as he had the Study. Yet his last great critical triumph was scored from the Easy Chair as he analyzed the New Poetry in September 1915. His performance was by no means perfect, of course, and he made no pretense of having read all the contributions to the new "poetic sunburst," nor even all of what volumes had come his way. Yet even if he had not been seventy-eight at that writing, his recognitions would have had to be called brilliant. True to his convictions of sixty years, he remained hostile to the "formlessness" of *vers libre,* reminding its apostles how Martin Tupper, Whitman, and Crane had used it before them. He saw, however, the "extraordinary worth" of the perceptions of human nature in Masters' *Spoon River Anthology,* and nothing comparable in Amy Lowell.

Howells liked the "fine, manly *go*" in what he had sampled of E. A. Robinson's *Captain Craig,* cared less for Conrad Aiken and John Gould Fletcher, and, in properly descending order, less still for a group of now much less known poets. His deplorable weakness was for "Uncle" Walt Mason. But his great admiration was reserved for Robert Frost and, after him, Vachel Lindsay. His grasp of *A Boy's Will* and *North of Boston* was perfect. He thought Frost a "strong, sweet musician" with "very distinctive power. . . . Dirge, or idyl, or tragedy, or comedy, or burlesque, it is always the skill of the artist born and artist trained which is at play, or call it work, for our delight." He grasped precisely, of course, Frost's sense of New England and, more surprisingly, Frost's way of "knowing what things are by knowing what they are like." In Lindsay, naturally, it was the "Gospel of Beauty" the old Altrurian liked best. When his chance came, the Dean in the Easy Chair showed that he had not forgotten how to respond to the real thing in American letters.

IV

The early strain of the new Harpers job was obviously heavy. Howells complained to Garland in the summer of 1901 that the Easy Chair and *North American* took up fully half his time between them. And no doubt *The Kentons,* 1902, and *Letters Home,* 1903, suffered from that drain on the novelist's energy. As the firm recovered, however, apparently it seemed better policy to give Howells more chance to do his own writing. By midsummer of 1902 he was free from his advisory work at Franklin Square. And though he carried a chatty column in the *Weekly* for 1903, he wrote only twice that year for the *North American.* He reacted to his freedom by the production, somewhat to his own surprise, of another major novel.

The Son of Royal Langbrith is another dark novel, another realist's tragedy, and it reverts with great success to the moods and mysteries from which *A Hazard of New Fortunes, The Shadow of a*

Dream, and *The Quality of Mercy* had sprung. Responding to ring-
ing praise of his novel's psychological penetration from the foremost American alienist of the age, Howells told S. Weir Mitchell
that he had worked the book out "less anxiously than usual, for the
notion had been at least 15 years in my mind, with the doctor, the
mother and the son pretty distinctly outlined, and some of the
dialogs already in their mouths." That is borne out by a pair of
entries in the familiar little pocket notebook Howells carried for
jotting down the germs of stories from *Indian Summer* forward.
One entry looks like a reminder: "Filial Love," it reads. "Son who
prevents his mother's second marriage." The earlier one is more
complete:

> 'Son who prevents his mother's second marriage from devotion
> to his father's memory whom he never saw. Man dies who wanted her.
> Then he falls in love himself and begins to ask himself questions. Talk
> with his mother when his father's true character comes out. "But it is
> all right." '

With the true character of Royal Langbrith and its significance in
the context Howells was to be acutely concerned in what proved to
be one of his most fruitfully Hawthornian moments. It was not
easy to name this novel. Howells wrote to Colonel Harvey to complete publishing arrangements and invited him to help choose a
title:

> 'As it is the story of an evil so long concealed that it is best for all
> the injured it should never be known, you will see the pertinence of most
> of the titles. I incline to "Reconciliation," as the shortest and best, after
> that, I like "The Law of Limitation." '

The list which followed contained an even twenty suggestions for
titles but not the one on which, whoever suggested it, Howells
finally fixed.

For private and obscure reasons, he had long played with a title
taken from a Tuscan proverb—*"Iddio non paga sabato"*—which he
translated *God Does Not Pay Saturdays* and listed to Harvey without in the least insisting on it. The title finally selected, apparently
rather bland on the surface, crackles with suggestiveness once the
novel is well begun. The title conveys the bitter Hawthornian irony
of the novel. "Royal" Langbrith was a despicable scoundrel. And
out of that irony proceeds the far more surprising profundity: only
to his son was the dead Langbrith royal—and James Langbrith's
use of his ideal of his father to domineer over his mother shows, in

the way the story works out, that Howells not only possessed but could wield imaginatively his own conception of the Oedipus complex.

As a whole, *The Son of Royal Langbrith* was a real triumph for Howells the novelist. The triumph of the totality rests on the clear success with which each of the levels within the novel functions. It is a triumph of action, simple but original and intensely dramatic. That opens the way for the triumph of the psychological studies of the beautifully defined characters. And that in turn leads organically into the ultimate triumph of the resolution of the moral tensions and "mysteries" which had exercised Howells from the beginning of his exploration into the tragic.

The opening scene of the novel was as original, and as defiant of the neoromanticists, as Howells could make it. A middle-aged couple, Dr. Justin Anther and Mrs. Amelia Langbrith, sit in her living room in the New England paper-mill town of Saxmills, and grimly face the fact that she is too weak to accept Anther's proposal of marriage. She has been widowed for nineteen years from a husband who tortured her physically and psychologically, kept a bigamous second establishment in Boston, and made a fortune by cheating and blackmailing others. She and Anther love each other dearly. But she is "afraid" of her son. She has let him grow up to cow her and tyrannize over her. She has never told him the truth about his father, and he has invented a father-image to love and revere. He holds his mother captive never to marry again, "Out of reverence for his father's memory."

The question then becomes, who shall "tell" James Langbrith? Mrs. Langbrith finds that she cannot. And Dr. Anther discovers that he, too, is effectively silenced. Arrogant and patronizing, James is not easy to tell anything to. And he is determined, with a *hubris* almost Greek, not only to worship his father-image but to compel everyone else to join. Returning to Saxmills on vacation from his senior year at Harvard, he hatches the scheme for a ceremony which will force the whole community to make obeisance. Carnegie-like, Royal Langbrith had willed a library to the town. James will have a memorial tablet to his father cast in bronze and dedicated on the Fourth of July as the center of the patriotic observance. That will nourish his father's ghost.

Brushing aside his mother's and Anther's reluctances, James rushes ahead with his plan. He also courts, with increasing seriousness, Hope Hawberk, the beautiful daughter of a man who was once Royal Langbrith's partner but has long been lost in the mental darkness of opium addiction. Neither James nor Hope knows that Hawberk had resorted to dope after being blackmailed out of the invention which created the prosperity of the Langbrith paper mill.

The day of the dedication forms the pivot on which the whole novel turns. Blindly feeding his arrogant illusion on the ceremony, James attains the pinnacle of his spoiled-child egotism. That same evening his salvation begins, however, because he is able for the first time to discover and confess his true, self-giving love for Hope Hawberk and make his engagement. When he returns home, he overhears his mother and Anther lamenting their love and is startled into bitter denunciation. But he finds that he cannot rage and rend them as one side of his mind demands. The sense of his own love inhibits. He takes his tragedy to Hope, wondering with her (self-enlighteningly) if he is not somehow mad. Though Hope cannot persuade him truly to forgive, she does successfully beg him to be reconciled with his mother and leave on those terms for his promised year in Paris to study playwrighting.

While James is off the scene, the moral tensions in Saxmills work themselves out. Sorrowfully, Anther finds that he cannot shake the incubi of the past; he may keep his love but must give up his marriage. He cures Hawberk and sends him back to work. With his mind clear, Hawberk too decides that no good can be served in blighting Hope's life by telling the truth about Royal Langbrith. At work at the mill, he slips into the pond, catches pneumonia, and dies. But there is one patient Anther cannot cure. James's uncle John Langbrith, a moral coward who has run the plant since his brother's death, has severe dyspepsia—nowadays we should say gastric ulcers. John despises James's patronizing airs and arty ambitions. He can take his first, and ineffectual, real vacation when Hawberk returns. But when Hawberk's death dooms him again to harness, John is exasperated. Meeting the returning James on a train from Boston, John is goaded into saltily telling James the full and exact truth about his father. A thunderstruck and penitent youth arrives home just in time to find that Anther has died of typhoid fever contracted from a patient. He will thereafter have to live with his own as well as his father's guilt.

Psychology and the mysteries of the subjective life had been featured in the best of Howells' fiction ever since *The Shadow of a Dream*. From childhood he had recurrently suffered through almost palpably vivid dream-experiences. And of course the tragedy of Winifred's death both harrowed the depths of his own psychic life and stirred up his intellectual interest in psychological phenomena. In Boston in 1891 he made contact with the Society for Psychical Research. In spite of himself, he was "badly rattled" for a moment at a farmhouse seance. Yet even though that and a session for "a sort of ghost-story swap" with members of the Society left him still convinced of "the final futility of all those things," his creative imagination recurred repeatedly to the pychological during the '90's and, in the next decade, to the psychic.

The psychic stories he enjoyed doing, basing "The Eidolons of Brooks Alford" and "The Memory that Worked Overtime" on experiences which were, he told Weir Mitchell, his own "save for the love business." But as the titles he gave his volumes collecting these tales show, he did not take them seriously. The first he called *Questionable Shapes*, 1903; the second was labeled clearly to warn the consumer: *Between the Dark and the Daylight: Romances*, 1907.

His psychological studies, however, quite properly became the objects of his most serious attention. He became conscious of the fact that he now did his best imaginative work through them. And, when he came to think of it, the same thing had become true of his great colleagues in serious fiction internationally. The fact made him modify his theory of realism.

In the midst of composing *Langbrith*, that "grimmish story," as he called it, Howells paused to reflect on its lesson in the June 1903 Easy Chair. The favorite game of the "Supreme Wisdom" with mortals, he began, "seems to be the simple action of the pendulum." The law of life is the perpetual oscillation of "knowledge" from one extreme to its opposite. "What really endures is mystery, which is the prime condition of existence, and will doubtless be its ultimate condition." With such books as John Bigelow's *The Mystery of Sleep* and "whatever Mr. William James writes upon his favorite themes" available, with the amazing case of Helen Keller to contemplate, with all the shift away from the old mechanistic assurances of "science" taking place, the pendulum seems swinging back toward elder questions of faith in the human soul and questions of its nature and functioning.

And nowhere is this more evident than in letters; "a whole order of literature has arisen, calling itself psychological, as realism called itself scientific, and dealing with life on its mystical side." And this, he emphasizes, is not mainly a matter of new writers—"it is not less evident in Tolstoy, in Gorky, in Ibsen, in Björnson, in Hauptmann, and in Mr. Henry James, than in Maeterlinck himself." Who could say "with which of these eminent authors the reaction from science, from realism, began? Which talent so strongly weighted the pendulum, then, when it began to slide from the scientific extreme, and gave it the momentum which carried it to the mystical extreme?"

Howells is not really, however, ready to let realism go. Agnosticism, after all, he maintains, "is not an unpromising or unhopeful frame of mind" and may help the "present psychologism" realize its potential. Whatever can be claimed for Maeterlinck, he is nowhere more mystical than "certain passages of Tolstoy, whose psychologism is rooted in a realism as rank and palpable as Gorky's own." The right conclusion suggests that the true novel should be the prisoner of no exclusive method: "We have indeed, in our best fiction, gone back to mysticism, if indeed we were not always there in our best fiction, and the riddle of the painful earth is again engaging us with the old fascination."

Wholly ignorant of Freud, Howells nonetheless understood his Saxmills Oedipus acutely. He used the psychological insights habitually available to him and improvised the new ones necessary to the case. In part Howells understood James Langbrith as a romantic egoist. Jim is so "patronizing," his college friend Falk reports, that at Harvard "a good many of the fellows think he's an ass." He is also in part a neoromantic egoist. He has delusions of baronial, of seigneurial splendor and importance in Saxmills. But most of all his arrogance stems from his lifelong power to walk over his mother and his allegiance to his compensating image of the lost, wonderful father.

Howells intended tragic redemption, not "cheap tragedy" for Langbrith, however, and he took care not to make him "the outright brute that Jeff Durgin was." That was why he delayed the occasion for Langbrith's Oedipal shock and outburst until after he had truly fallen in love himself. He comes away from the scene of his outburst bewildered: "He had meant to hurt Anther to death, so far as insult could kill; and he had meant to wither his mother with shame. But the cruelest blows he dealt then had seemed to fall like blows dealt in nightmare, as if they were dealt with balls of cotton or down. . . . His heart closed about the thought of his father with an indignant tenderness, which, somehow, could not leave his mother out. She had always been part of that thought, and he had an impulse to entreat her against herself, as if being a child she had struck him, and there was no one else to go to for comfort."

He is thunderstruck to find that when he tells the awful news to Hope she rejoices. And he finds suddenly that, to her clear and loving mind, he cannot explain. He tries to tell her:

‘ "No one can understand how I have always felt towards my father. You may call it superstition, if you like, but I have always felt him something sacred. I have felt as if he were a mysterious influence in my life, shaping it for the highest things. And at the same time it's as if he appealed to me, always, from his grave, for protection. . . . I thought my mother felt the same, and that was why she was so silent about him; and I thought that Dr. Anther— But if all the time they were conspiring to betray him —if they were thinking of themselves and each other, when they, of all people in the world, should have been truest to him—"

"Oh, oh, what *talk!*" Hope broke in. "Why James Langbrith, I should think you were insane."

"I am ! I am !" he choked out. "This thing is turning my brain. I try to realize it, and then when I realize it I feel that I must go mad. Oh, you don't understand; you can't ! you can't ! I feel so covered with shame for my mother." ’

As Howells promised Henry B. Fuller, however, Hope was able to "master" Langbrith and save him from final destruction. The reason why her success in persuading him to a reconciliation, however grudging, with his mother did save him lay in the ultimate moral development of the novel in which, as always, Howells' truest interest lay. It was inevitable that his effort in *Their Silver Wedding Journey* to go back to the dawn-methods of his fictional career should have disappointed Howells. After all his major work from *A Modern Instance* through *The Landlord at Lion's Head,* that first shallow method was bound to seem trivial. Only major moral issues confronted in psychological settings could really seem significant to him now. And the character through whom the author could pierce furthest into the moral depths of his fiction was Dr. Anther.

A man of entire personal and scientific probity, personally as well as professionally compassionate and self-sacrificial, mature, intelligent, ideally "civilized," Justin Anther finds it preposterous that his happiness should be denied him by these childish figments of James Langbrith's imagination. And when he considers the dreadful irony of the contrast between Royal Langbrith's actual character and James's image of a nobly reticent, austerely Puritanic hero-father, he finds it outrageous. When he sets about trying to remedy the situation, however, Anther finds himself maddeningly entangled in moral and psychic webs not dreamt of in his scientific, "civilized" philosophy. He painfully acquires an education in "the riddle of the painful earth."

For centered in the father-image of the son of Royal Langbrith, Justin Anther discovers the most Hawthorne-like of all the moral tensions in Howells' novels. The mysteries of how the evil men do lives after them are, in fact, no more profoundly explored anywhere in Hawthorne than here. And the reason why Howells had the courage so to handle them is the same as the reason for the ultimate great success of his novel. He could see both a way to create moral tensions of extreme tautness together with the means to resolve them.

Before we can understand the moral significance of James Langbrith's experience, we must understand that of Anther and Mrs. Langbrith. But the meaning of their experience in turn depends on the dramatic irony of the utter wrongness of James's image of his father, and so finally all other meaning comes to rest on the significance of wicked Royal Langbrith. Anther finds his every path blocked. Neither he nor Amelia Langbrith can tell James the truth. They have become vulnerable to his obvious impulse to suppose they are only compounding their "betrayal" of his father. Hawberk's dope addiction disables him as a witness. Public exposure of Royal Langbrith would expose Anther to unbelieving revulsion and suspicion. And even if successful, it would only corrupt the public morals. By the time Hawberk is restored to clarity, he and Anther agree that for James's and Hope's sakes the truth had better be suppressed. They must all live the lies of Royal's hypocrisy and his son's delusion until mere choler loosens John Langbrith's mouth.

Morally what shall be made of this maddening situation? In spite of himself, Anther is tempted to a sickening "superstition that doesn't believe in itself" that Royal Langbrith's evil is so diabolically potent as to be able to victimize the world from beyond the grave. Lucid at last, Hawberk agrees, "You might almost say that devil had planned it out to have his boy make it up with my girl, so as to stop my mouth for good and all." Even the well-tried Howellsian formula of complicity lacks proof against this devil. The good of the community conspires with Langbrith to keep his evil hidden and force his victims to bear it.

Against this counsel of Manichean despair are balanced, however, two hopes of resolution. One is the more congenial to Anther the scientist. It is an argument for moral law. The other, to which far more space is given, is a Howellsian sort of Christian argument, for the purposes of which he invents still another Episcopalian rector, the Rev. Mr. Enderby. Naturally, that is to say medically, Anther is cheered by the fact that one, at least, of Royal Langbrith's victims escapes his bondage to the devil. Hawberk, with his persistent opium vision of being buried alive by a moldy green demon, gets cured. Does Anther think this a true conversion, does he believe "in the supernatural"? asks his friend Judge Garley. " 'No,' Anther said, 'Only in the natural.' "

And so, reflects the narrator, defying the "dramatic method" for a paragraph, perhaps Anther's superstition of diabolism has some answer:

'Life is never the logical and consequent thing we argue from the moral and intellectual premises. There ought always to be evident reason in it; but such reason as it has is often crossed and obscured by perverse events, which, in our brief perspective, give it the aspect of a helpless craze. Obvious effect does not follow obvious cause; there is sometimes no perceptible cause for the effects we see. The law that we find at work in the material world is, apparently, absent from the moral world; not, imaginably, because it is without law, but because the law is of such cosmical vastness in its operation that it is only once or twice sensible to any man's experience. The seasons come and go in orderly course, but the incidents of human life have not the orderly procession of the seasons; so far as the sages or the saints are able convincingly to affirm, they have only the capricious vicissitudes of weather.'

From the point of view of the saints, however, Christian minister Enderby has more to say. There is a third way to look at Anther's dilemma. Men who "press for judgement," Enderby reminds Anther, "are in danger of becoming executioners." Justice is probably beyond the reach of man's mind, but mercy is not; "we have a duty to mercy." Therefore, Enderby counsels, "we must leave it all to

God now, as it has been left hitherto. . . . He will know how to do justice."

When James Langbrith hears the truth from his father's brother, he undergoes a very interesting and valid psychological experience. The truth seemed "to rage upon him like some war of the elements, and he was aware not only of the truth of what had been told him, but of its not being novel. He had that mystical sense of its having all happened before, long ago, and of a privity to it, in his inmost, dating back to his first consciousness." But he can hope to make amends until he arrives home to learn of Anther's death. Then he must face himself squarely: "No detail was missing in the retrospect of wilful arrogance, of blind conceit, of vain folly, of baseless illusion. . . ." Yet he is young. He can "as yet" believe "no error in life wholly irreparable." He will "undo" by "renunciation, sacrifice," by wrecking and exposing his own life for reparation. From this romantic folly Hope Hawberk's love and common sense save him. She will neither be renounced nor sacrificed. And she takes him to Enderby for guidance. At the last Enderby tells James that, while "it would be a relief to have all this known, and to take upon yourself the dishonor which the stupid and malignant love to visit upon the children of wrong-doers," he would, wisely speaking, "impose a more difficult, a heavier penance." James must live with his secret, must face and digest his self-knowledge, not reject it in prideful social suicide.

Eventually things do work out. Anther's natural law seems to function in that James's memorial celebration had the opposite effect in the community from that intended: "from the moment of the dedication of the votive tablet by the son, the myth of the father suffered a kind of discoloration, not to say obscuration." Shorn of arrogance, James made a good husband, and he and Hope were "radiantly happy, and more wisely happy for tasting the sorrow which has not passed down to their generation," Enderby observes.

But what about justice? Was Royal Langbrith's diabolism to go unrequited? And what of the real suffering of his victims? Mrs. Enderby, possessed of an inherited Puritan conscience, is hard for her husband to appease. He doubts that Royal Langbrith got away free: "Could there be fearfuller suffering than his consciousness in his sudden death that he could not undo here the evil he had done?" And Enderby has a daring surmise to suggest to his wife in which the mysteries of *A Hazard of New Fortunes, The Shadow of a Dream, The Quality of Mercy* and *The Landlord at Lion's Head* are unriddled. It is not proposed as gospel or doctrine: "in this it must be owned she never could follow him, great as her faith in him was." And so the author kept his agnosticism safe while letting his creature express the highest guess at the riddle of the painful earth he could reach after more than twenty years of trying in serious fiction. Enderby asks:

' "How do we know but that in the mystical legislation, as to whose application to our conduct we have to make our guesses and inferences, there may not be a law of limitations by which the debts over-due through time are the same as forgiven? No one was the poorer through their non-payment in Royal Langbrith's case; in every high sort each was the richer. It may be the complicity of all mortal beings is such that the pain he inflicted was endured to his behoof, and that it has helped him atone for his sins as an acceptable offering in the sort of vicarious atonement which has always been in the world." '

THE SUNSET ACADEMICIAN

NATURALLY ENOUGH, THE EXPENSE OF SPIRIT REQUIRED TO FINISH *The Son of Royal Langbrith* left Howells exhausted. He was in his sixty-seventh year, and he could not hope to rebound quickly. Unknowingly he fell into the pattern which would dominate his remaining years. With his daughter Mildred, herself a writer, for companion, he sailed for England in March. Until Mrs. Howells could join him in the summer, he would knock gently around England, storing up ideas and impressions. His fatigue was not "mental"—his eye was as alert to register, his mind to interpret as ever. That mysterious psychic power of the artist's creative imagination had now become almost permanently tired. It was so much easier to meet the demands of the world of chance by writing travel literature. He could do it expertly and just about endlessly. And the market was insatiable. It was just what Harvey wanted, and now with no major novel demanding to be written Howells had plenty of time.

I

England on Howells' closest scrutiny proved to be fascinating. From the gleanings there printed in *Harper's* through 1904, 1905, and 1906, he had in *London Films,* and *Certain Delightful English Towns,* 1906, his own interpretations of Britain to set beside Emerson's *English Traits.* And this peak of his travel-writing career he scaled because, to his no little surprise, he found himself suddenly reconciled with the English. There had been signs of reconciliation during much of the decade past. English criticism had been kinder. In Britain the neoromantics were calming down. Even Andrew

Lang had grudgingly made his peace. Recognition by the increasingly strong Fabians helped. And when Howells came there to reside for a period, he found the principalities and powers of British intellectual life delightfully eager to do him honor.

Though Howells carefully fought shy of the least suspicion of colonial Anglophilia, he had to own that the warmth of his new spot in the English heart was gratifying. He seemed to have won the Realism War. At least his approval of a writer could now be the making of him on either side of the water. Seven years after he had praised Leonard Merrick in the *North American Review* Merrick testified from England that "People speak to me about it still and it was, of course, the turn of the tide." Even better, Howells discovered that he had ardent fans among the leading minds of the nation. The great historian Sir George Otto Trevelyan wrote to thank him "for the enormous number of hours of keen and unmixed delight which I owe you. Almost all your books I have read several times. There are very few that I have not read aloud at least twice. . . ." That led to Trevelyan's entertaining Howells and a subsequent friendship. "What novels; and (alas,) how well I know them !" said Trevelyan afterwards.

At the same time, there were cordial relations with some of England's foremost writers. Though Hardy had now been forced out of novel writing, Howells' friendly correspondence with him dated from 1886. Rudyard Kipling during his American years had formed a friendship with Howells little short of reverential on Kipling's side. Though Howells had begun in 1890 by deploring Kipling's "knowingness and swagger" and never could care for his Imperial chauvinism, Howells grew quickly into hearty appreciation of Kipling's unique qualities, "intensely modern, conscious, and nervous." In 1897 he hailed Kipling as "laureate of the Larger England," praising "his uncommon quality as a poet," finding his work "purely dramatic" and thus truly moving, and distinguishing his quality as "heroic," not "romantic." Kipling's personal response showed him deeply touched, and the cordiality of their relationship survived his flight to England unimpaired. And of course Arnold Bennett thought of himself as almost an heir of Howells, boasted that he had grown up reading the Howells of "The Editor's Study," that he had feasted on Howells' novels and "stolen innumerable ideas" from them.

The obvious move under the circumstances was to recognize all this by presenting Howells with his second Litt. D. *honoris causa* (Yale had come first in 1901). Howells had become an Honorary Fellow of the Royal Society of Literature in 1901, and it was fitting to present him with the degree of England's great center of the humanities, Oxford. At the Encenia of June 1904 he was formally invested. His notebooks record his pleasant time of being dined and teaed in the colleges but scarcely mention the ceremony itself.

Nevertheless, that date and event will do to mark the onset of Howells' becoming, all despite himself, in America the first—and so far almost the last—great Academician after the French fashion. As his writing dwindled toward a suave but tired impressionism, and as his age and declining energies conspired with the deaths of more and more of his friends, he ceased gradually to be the leading man of letters or even the Dean of the faculty, and became a symbol of official culture. It was in some senses an enviable position. And yet, in the historical context, it was a dangerous one. Howells was spared neither the personal embarrassments of having the post thrust upon him nor the penalties of having occupied it by the fact that he would on the whole rather not have had it. Appointment as the Academician happened to him unsought.

It was confirmed by more doctorates: Columbia in 1905, Princeton in 1912. It was exploited by the Department of State, when Howells was high-pressured by the American Embassy in Rome to go to be "met" by the king of Italy in 1908. It was exploited by Colonel Harvey, who found occasions to throw huge dinner parties to the greater glory of the staggering House of Harpers. For Howells' seventy-fifth birthday party Harvey even corralled the President of the United States among his many distinguished guests.

All this sort of thing gave Howells much more trouble than pleasure. He hated crowds, spoke badly on his feet, though effectively if he could read a well-prepared manuscript, suffered nightmares of stage fright, and was not deluded by pomp and circumstance. Yet he had been a public figure for forty and fifty years; there was no use pretending that, though shy, he was too shy to appear. Becoming the Academician was one way to earn his salary from Harvey. And there remained, given all the facts of the case, a puzzling problem as to his responsibilities. It is a problem which remains for American artists and intellectuals. Until a man has done his creative work, he had obviously better steer clear of the ruinous effects of the popular celebrity system. There are far too many wrecks on that reef. But when his work is effectually done, what are his responsibilities to the constituents of a democratic culture who are mainly to be reached through the machinery of the celebrity system? Ought not some men to be standing clearly in the public view for the serious arts and the life of the mind? Can the nation afford to have its view wholly taken up by "celebrities" of the entertainment and athletic worlds?

That problem came to Howells most directly through the American Academy of Arts and Letters. It was perhaps all too easy to take the high, contemptuous ground of Charles Eliot Norton, who wrote in 1900 to inform Howells that he was resigning from the National Institute of Arts and Letters. Norton complained that Howells and Warner had "overpersuaded" him to join and that he could see no use in the Institute: "I dislike both the inclusiveness and the exclusiveness of its list, as I dislike all artificial distinctions. Nor am I fond of the self-celebration of mediocrity, or of the exaltation of the second-rate." In a democratic society where the unorganized is the unrecognized, Norton's first objection left the arts and letters out in the cold. As to the absolute exclusion of all but the great, perhaps only in Heaven could Mr. Norton be sure of associating exclusively with Socrates, Dante, and Shakespeare— supposing they associate.

In his own time and context, Howells had imposed on him the task of making something of the American Academy. As Hamlin Garland recorded in his journal, on December 2, 1904, the National Institute met and elected Mark Twain, St. Gaudens, Edward Mac-Dowell, John Hay, E. C. Stedman, John LaFarge, and Howells as the seven to form the American Academy. Howells was almost unanimously elected to head the group. The seven were to pick eight more, those fifteen a like number, and the resulting thirty to fill out this membership to fifty. At the first regular meeting of the fully constituted Academy, Howells was elected President and held that chair until his death.

Ironically, it seems to have been this very eminence which robbed Howells of his best and truest monument. That was a formal and official edition of his complete works. In 1909 he began to plan *The Writings of William Dean Howells, Library Edition,* considering how to arrange his volumes, and looking forward to a literary autobiography in which he should tell the story of each book. By the following winter all the details were arranged, and Duneka of the Harpers sent him a complete prospectus. Design was to be very deluxe and expensive, with large illustration for each volume. Howells was to revise each work, providing prefaces and introductions. There were to be complete indexes and a bibliography.

The final plan organized Howells' works into six categories: I. Criticism and Reminiscence—six volumes; II. Travel—six volumes; III. Studies, Sketches and Essays, and IV. Poems and Plays;—five volumes together; V. Fiction, and VI. Juveniles—twenty-three volumes together for a grand total of forty volumes. Accordingly, the Harpers put six volumes in work and, on July 26, 1911, issued *My Literary Passions/ Criticism and Fiction; The Landlord at Lion's Head; Literature and Life; London Films/ Certain Delightful English Towns; Literary Friends and Acquaintance;* and *A Hazard of New Fortunes.* There were never any more published. Henry Rood, who had worked out the design of the set and was "deeply disappointed" at the outcome, wrote that publishers' disputes "concerning details of copyright and adjustment of financial matters" had wrecked the enterprise.

II

If tragic experience had taught Howells not to forget death, 1910 could be said to be the year in which death remembered him. His great loss, of course, came in the death of his wife. But her sister Mary, who had come to Venice to take care of her when Winifred was born, had died in March. Mark Twain died in April; then Elinor Howells in May, and finally Larkin Mead in October. Twain had been Howells' most intimate and stimulating friend. The other Meads had been the playfellows of his most golden youth. But, as he said simply when the fact had achieved perspective, "My wife took the heart of my world with her." Time, philosophy, travel, work, the devoted companionship of his daughter, his measureless delight in John Mead Howells' children, whatever consolation there was in his celebrity—these could all dull the pain and cicatrize the wound. But nothing now could restore his world. He was doomed to make the stoical best, in a "cheerful despair," of a decade of exile to the faraway land of old age.

This was not, of course, exile from himself, and nothing could

separate him from the love of making literature. As he said in
"The Turning-Point of My Life," published in March 1910,

'From my
earliest remembrance, from the time before I could read when I made
up stories to match the pictures in the first book I ever looked at, "one
continuous purpose" of literature has run through my life. My work has
always been so "lief and dear" to me that now in my seventy-third year
a proof of the thing I have last written is as wondrously precious as that
which I printed from the types put together with my childish hands,
when I could have been about seven, in an essay on *Human Life*. The
theme is one which in manifold phases has engaged me since, and I suppose will flatter my notice to the end, with the perpetual chance of turning out a song or turning out a sermon.'

No amount of affection, on the other hand, could induce his creative
powers to flow. Working away at *The Children of the Summer*
(posthumously published as *The Vacation of the Kelwyns*, 1920),
he found that he just did not have the needed zest for the job. The
Altrurian ideals still seemed good, but like *Miss Bellard's Inspiration*, 1905, the novel slumped into tired failure. Other novels begun in this period were unfinishable. Only the Ohio roots of
Howells' boyhood seemed to reach deep enough to tap his sources of
imaginative vitality.

Around the figure of this aging Academician, ever decreasingly
vital and relevant in his production of literature as the second
decade of the new century marched forward, there was erected a
myth very repulsive to the new generations of young men. His
friends began, disastrously, to sentimentalize that "dear old saint,"
as Brand Whitlock called him. "From the depths of a store of a
mellow heart and the store of ripened artistic impressions Mr.
Howells has distilled his new volume of tales and sketches," said
the publisher's blurb on the dust jacket of his collection titled *The
Daughter of the Storage*, 1916. Even though there were good things
in the collection like the surprisingly Frostian poem "Black Cross
Farm," that sort of claim was calculated to infuriate the young
writer. It made Howells sound exactly like the "old coons" Stephen
Crane had hated.

Even worse, Howells' traditional generosity to the young was so
often attributed to him as virtue that he began to look patronizing.
Oliver Herford in his disingenuously titled cartoon-with-poem series

for *American Magazine* called "Celebrities I Have Not Met," for example, pictured Howells in 1913 as a balloonish Santa Claus with fur coat, top hat, cane and spats benevolently feeding the Central Park squirrels in the snow. And his poem ran:

> Not squirrels in the park alone
> His love and winter-kindness own.
> When Literary Fledglings try
> Their wings, in first attempt to fly,
> They flutter down to Franklin Square,
> Where Howells in his "Easy Chair"
> Like good Saint Francis scatters crumbs
> Of Hope, to each small bird that comes. . . .

That was doubtless well-intentioned, but it thoroughly misrepresented the real situation. In dealing with writers Howells had scrupulously avoided "charity," was never a Franciscan bird feeder. Yet more unfortunately, it had largely ceased to be true that he served as the finder and sponsor of new talent. He was passing out of touch, and the young men knew it. Or at least they knew that he was not in touch with them.

Actually, Howells, who had never been a hypocrite, was frank to confess, even publicly, that he was out of touch. And in private he complained of his loneliness: old friends were dead, scattered, enfeebled by age; and the new writers seemed to bore him. In turn, naturally, he began to bore them. "(Don't tell anyone . . .)," Brand Whitlock begged, but he found the "Easy Chair" easy to skip by 1906, ". . . of late, I confess, I have fallen asleep in that chair." Critics took note of a revolt against the Dean: the "younger generation makes rather free with Mr. Howells." But the worst fact was that this generation had almost ceased to read him.

It became a fashion to blast away critically at Howells without having bothered to read him. In England, Frank Harris concluded that Howells was "absolutely negligible" after reading "a couple of Tauchnitz volumes of sketches in Italy" and remained an inveterate enemy. Edwin Arlington Robinson dismissed him contemptuously, unread. Robert Grant listened to William Roscoe Thayer's delivery of an impassioned condemnation of the tediousness in Howells' novels. When Thayer paused, Grant interrupted to ask, " 'And how many of them have you read?' . . . He looked embarrassed . . . as though the question was a surprise. 'Only one,' he admitted with his usual frankness." Precisely parallel was the case of Van Wyck Brooks, who at the age of twenty-two or three went to interview Howells for *World's Work* in 1909. He found the novelist unpretending, plain, kind, and likable. Writing up his interview, Brooks praised the man and called him "a very great and choice artist" with a "picked and constant audience." But he undertook to explicate the novels in search of the reasons for their "lack of force" and proclaimed that Howells "has never surprised anybody, thrilled anybody, shocked anybody. His career and his works alike seem devoid of inspired moments." More than forty years later Brooks confessed that when he wrote that early piece he had read just one (was it *The World of Chance?*) of Howells' novels.

With his true career almost wholly over, that settled habit of ignorance in the young men made it impossible for the Academician to direct their view back toward his real achievement and meaning. With them he was left defenseless to his enemies. The neoromanticists remained virulent and had their effect. Young Sinclair Lewis went to Yale with the settled conviction that Howells was too unromantic to read—and apparently did not read him until the decade preceding his own death in 1951. And, as Howells had feared, the aristocratic romanticists, the romanticists of "Society" and "Culture," rose up against him with unprecedented power after the Spanish-American War.

A lady named Harriet Waters Preston discussed *The Kentons* in the January 1903 *Atlantic* in terms hardly credible. Its characters, she said, were not really human beings but "the scum and spawn of a yeasty deep,—the monstrous offspring of barbarous and illicit social relations." Treating them seriously in literature was "like riding in pink, and with winding of horns, to a hunt of cockroaches !" The point she wished to make was that in America you could not write the novel of manners, because real manners required a society "homogeneous and stable; a certain social creed and hierarchy accepted without question and almost without thought, together with a tyrannous tradition antedating but always coexistent with long codified laws of conduct. . . ." Clearly these conditions did not exist in the small-town and democratic world of *The Kentons,* and that was intolerable. It was equally so in the high-esthetic world into which the followers of Fra Elbertus Hubbard, the wistful little Bohemians, and the Harvard fugitives from

American Philisteria all yearned to escape. For the good of Howells' reputation entirely too many of the powers of American writing in the 1920's would come out of the Bohemian, but more especially out of that Harvard-esthetic school. Its assumption, as Van Wyck Brooks recalled, was simply that no artistic America existed.

Such objections Howells as realist and democrat had long experienced, however, and he could readily imagine defeating them in the long run. He could take courage from the fact that by no means all the younger people were alienated. There were always cases like that of Booth Tarkington. Hardly of the youngest generation, Tarkington was roughly contemporaneous with Crane and Norris. But he developed, especially from Howells' point of view, late. A lifelong admirer, reared from boyhood in the piety of Howells, Tarkington had nevertheless cashed in heavily on the neoromantic market with *Monsieur Beaucaire,* 1900, and plays in a similar vein. But he continued to regard Howells as the mighty iconoclast who had begun the reform of his nation's culture by smashing the shoddy idols of popular bad taste. He owed in substantial part to Howells the developing literary conscience which directed him toward his best achievement, the Middle Western trilogy, *Growth.* Howells' praise for the first volume, *The Turmoil,* 1915, and the second, *The Magnificent Ambersons,* 1918, of the trilogy set Tarkington glowing. "I share the opinion of all the writers I know that you are the only critic who *knows,*" he wrote Howells in 1915. ". . . Popularity, when I've had it, has been—or seemed—accidental: I've always tried for the other thing—and often got neither ! But I've got some of the 'other thing' this time, since you say so."

Even if, as Tarkington himself sensed, that was testimony from a second-stringer as compared with Crane or Norris, it meant that not everything was lost. The old battles might have seemed to go on in the old way. But it must have seemed really surprising to Howells—his reactions suggest bewilderment—to be exposed to attack from a wholly new source. He came to lose control of the very name of "realism" because, far from seeming too bold, crude, democratic, sociologically and psychologically daring, "common" even "vulgar," he now appeared to whole schools of the young writers too civilized, too timid, too, above all, "reticent," particularly about sex in literature. William Lyon Phelps did Howells dubious service in coining the term "Reticent Realism" for his outlook. And there was the true bittersweet flavor of historical irony to the fact that the presentation of the Gold Medal for Fiction (now the Howells Medal) of the American Academy of Arts and Letters was made to him by Hamilton Wright Mabie in 1915. Howells refused to appear for the ceremony, but it could not have escaped him that Mabie's tune had changed drastically in just thirty years. In 1885 Mabie had invited the public to rend the author of *The Rise of Silas Lapham* for "moral disease" and "atheism." Now he rejoiced in the great artist, "a realist, but never a literalist" who had "made Americanism synonymous with sanity, hope, the idealism of the clean hearth, and seriousness. . . ." Howells' fame would have been safer in the hands of the young writers with Mabie's blame (and Howells' books) of the bygone time.

The net result was the emergence of the young critic—who typically had read little or no Howells, was contemptuously ignorant of Howells' real achievement and contribution, knew only the Academician and was determined to destroy him—whose treatment of Howells often seems incredible. One of the earliest and most passionate of these was Gertrude Atherton of San Francisco. Originally an idolator of Howells, Atherton had discovered that she wanted to write "wild" romances and craved a freedom of impassioned treatment of subject matter which the Dean denied her. She exploded repeatedly into print, calling realism "Littleism," proclaiming that "American literature today . . . is the most timid, the most anemic, the most lacking in individualities, the most bourgeois, that any country has ever known. There is not a breath of American independence, impatience, energy, contempt of ancient convention in it." This she credited to a "tyranny" exercised "unconsciously" by Howells, but she asserted that nevertheless "books will be published in spite of the possibility that they might shock some old ladies and give bad dreams to girls."

Nor was Miss Atherton alone. One ostensible defender of Howells (thoroughly misreading the story in question) attacked his "romanticism" and "spinster-like intemperance" of "prudery" because the hero of the farce tale "The Pursuit of the Piano" blushed to recall from childhood the summer-tanned legs of a little girl who had now become a lady. (Howells thought that funny and so indicated in his handling of it within a light story.) John Macy, locating *The Spirit of American Literature*, 1913, condemned Howells for one of the last things he would have supposed about himself—

being "Europeanized and Bostonized" and being "stricken by the Dead Hand in Literature." Howells, said Macy, was no realist but "a feminine, delicate, slightly romantic genius, theoretically convinced that realism is 'the thing' . . . ," but without the art or the knowledge of life to work in it.

All this was bad enough, but it was capped by the weirdly rhapsodic and contradictory present Howells received for his eightieth birthday, the first book devoted to him, *William Dean Howells, a Study of the Achievement of a Literary Artist* by Alexander Harvey, 1917. Howells' own comment on the book was perfect: "After two-thirds," he wrote a friend, "I wouldn't have spoken to you; after the last third you wouldn't have spoken to me." Wholly an enthusiast, Harvey must have been somehow truly a lover of Howells. He was also, like many of the people of the postwar twenties, a dervish whose religion was "modernism." He thought passionately and in absolutes. All his ideas were extreme. He was violently anti-British, antibusiness, and a partisan of Poe.

In the same vein he began by pronouncing Howells "no less a precious portion of our national patrimony than Harvard or the Mississippi"—so that it were better to lose all the taxable value of New York City than a "national asset" like *The Rise of Silas Lapham*. Howells he rated the greatest living novelist in English, an incredibly thorough, penetrating, and distinguished portraitist of the American character, in style "one of the few lords of language," the master of "the mystery of woman," creator of women whose "strongly sexed . . . whole, passionate soul is naked before us," an artist whose work will endure "for centuries." And so forth for 177 pages of a 232-page text.

Just as violently, the book then turned about in its last third. Howells, Harvey now says, is the head of the "sissy school" of literature, accurately portraying the American world as feminized, his realism proceeding from "an attitude of receptivity, of passivity, the woman attitude." His war on romanticism is a battle, therefore, against masculinity. And finally, says Harvey, the new Freudian psychology has made it possible for the artist to know the souls of his characters accurately and unmistakably. Now "the great literary artist is he who plunges boldly into the subconsciousness of his heroine after the manner of Freud with the typical dream of the so-called 'Oedipus complex.'" And Howells is revealed as having done great damage to American letters by keeping "the American subconsciousness" sealed. His realism is totally discredited, and his criticism rendered pernicious. At the end Harvey will nevertheless have him a master genius and artist. "And what if Howells be a native American of Anglo-Saxon origin?" he asks, and answers in extenuation: "Homer was blind. Coleridge was a slave to opium. Poe drank." It ought probably to be added that Harvey's annotated index is the most gorgeously emancipated and funny set of anti-academic footnotes ever. His book made a stir, inspiring attacks but leading one reviewer to comment excitedly that his use of Freud's "amazing revelations . . . must attach discredit to the whole theory of realism" supported by Howells.

All this together constitutes the ground for that monstrous legend of Howells current in "modernist" circles of the twenties and thirties until Newton Arvin checked it sharply in 1937. The lines, old and new, of romanticistic revolt against Howells could be focused neatly in the charge, however developed, that he was not "virile." And their ecstatic half-understandings of Freud gave the rebels a strange and wonderful weapon. Howells so lost control of "realism" that it came to connote "Freudianism" (as in the thirties it would "Marxism" for a time). As early as 1917, contributors to Joyce Kilmer's symposium *Literature in the Making* felt compelled to face the new connotations. Rex Beach protested that, in saying "realistic," he did "not mean erotic or morbid" but "actual, convincing, clearly visualized." Robert Herrick, a regular member of Howells' Chicago School, set out deliberately to reform current modes of speech and found it necessary to begin by saying flatly that "realism" was not "sexuality."

More was involved in that revolt of the young than mere matters of realism, romanticism, and Freudianism, of course. It was perhaps Carl Van Doren, whose sensitivities to the total situation ranged very wide, who understood it best. "The whole movement of the world is involved," he wrote in 1923, "the movement away from an urbane liberalism with its balance and calm and delicate irony to a more insistent clash between extremes of temper which war on one another with an animus surpassed only by that with which they hew down the peace-makers of the middle ground. For twenty years Howells has been under judgement from such partisans."

III

In its own serene defiance of what was being said against him, Howells' creative imagination was much of this while hatching out a last, fine work of fiction the qualities of which denied major parts of the "modernist" legend. With considerable perspicacity, Mabie said in his Gold Medal presentation speech that Howells had remained "not only a man of his time and country, but of his section." Howells had begun in fiction in his youth with *The Independent Candidate* and *Geoffrey Winters* as an aspiring Ohio novelist. The speech, themes, and personalities of his postfrontier, village Ohio had remained fresh in his imagination, and he had often mined those strong memories for characters placed elsewhere. And he had always intended to go back and really "do" Ohio, without, somehow, quite getting around to it.

Nevertheless, he remained thoroughly a "Buckeye." He appeared gladly in Columbus for the Ohio Centennial Celebration in 1888. His autobiographical writings turned more and more homeward. He assisted with and ardently promoted his father's source book, *Recollections of Life in Ohio,* 1895, and by the end of the decade had at last wholly conquered the memories of his adolescent agonies in Jefferson. For the first time in forty years, he wrote Brander Matthews in 1898, he thoroughly enjoyed a visit in Jefferson. His reconciliation was complete, and he was in a mood to share Henry Demarest Lloyd's delight in a chance meeting with one of Howells' bluff, steamboating Dean cousins. The Howells boys? said the river Captain. Well, Joe was "very active," a hard worker. But not Will: "He did not have to be," Lloyd quoted, "He sat around, *and did nothing,* and did better !"

From the beginning Howells had cherished a dream of Ohio—a Jeffersonian, idyllic dream of the superiority of life in the village. "Wherever life is simplest and purest and kindest," he had Judge Kenton remind his daughter, "that is the highest civilization." For all that that dream was the source for Howells' repeated treatments of his "conventional-unconventional" fictional theme, it seems to have blocked him from direct study of Ohio life for its own sake. He started out in 1897 to write an "Ohio novel." Then, apparently, that idea was shouldered aside by the notion of *Their Silver Wedding Journey.* But while he worked on that "Discovery of Europe" idea, the Ohio novel forced its way back. And in 1900 Howells laid aside his *Heroines of Fiction* to write, as he told Aurelia, on a proposed "strong novel. I think of calling it A Girl's Heart." This would study "a serious, dignified girl" unfortunately in love with "a light man . . . a worthless fellow" who mistreats her so that "her problem is how to tear him out of her heart. . . ." This became *The Kentons*.

No matter how nauseating they might seem to the likes of Harriet Preston Waters, these people studied in "Tuskingum, Ohio," are fascinatingly American. Judge and Mrs. Kenton, Ellen (the Girl) and her brothers, and Bittridge, the cocky blackguard (again a reporter), in their customs, attitudes, emotions, and ideals are beautifully painted. It is almost maddening to have Howells pull the Kentons out of Tuskingum, send them abroad into the tired, old international set and another tired, conventional-unconventional love match with a sophisticated young minister from Brooklyn. Just as *The Coast of Bohemia* never regains its level after Pymatoning, Ohio, is left behind, *The Kentons* shrivels when away from Tuskingum. It seems obvious that the author's true creative impulse sprang from his Ohio memories and that he thwarted it by retreating into what had become his own convention.

Howells was, of course, not sentimentally blind to the faults of what was always the West to him. He applauded and boosted the young realistic critics of the West. And he knew that, if it ever had been true, the idyllic view of the West was outmoded. Frederick Jackson Turner read his famous paper on "The Significance of the Frontier in American History" before a meeting of the American Historical Association in July 1893. The previous December, Howells' Mr. Burton of Pymatoning, Ohio, had said in *The Ladies' Home Journal:* "We haven't got equality now, any more than we've got buffalo. . . . When I was a boy here, venison was three cents a pound, and equality cheaper yet. When they cut off the woods the venison and the equality disappeared; they always do when the woods are cut off." And on his lecture tour in 1899, Howells scented "intolerance in the air" of the West. "We are *freer* in the East, and say what we think. . . . People are freer *from West to East*" in matters of opinion, he concluded.

It might be guessed that, like Mark Twain, Howells found it hard to forgive the West for having become corrupted and that he could achieve enough perspective to deal with it imaginatively, artisti-

cally, only in the far distance of boyhood memory—where it could
be seen sometimes critically but sometimes idyllically, in a man-
ageable balance. He had to achieve full reconciliation with his
family before he could finish *New Leaf Mills*. But it was uniquely
a reconciliation with the West which had to be won before he could
take that last, fine gleaning from his pen, *The Leatherwood God*.

Writing to S. Weir Mitchell in 1904, Howells compared himself
to a circus performer. Getting older, he found in himself "a failure
of strength to do the old 'stunts.' I know how they are done better
than ever, but I haven't the intellectual muscles I once had."
Nevertheless, he thought he had "one good novel left" in him which
"involves some tremendous things." A year later Mitchell was asking if he was at work on "that final and too daring novel of which
we talked—oh long ago. . . ." In 1907 Howells told his brother
Joe that he still hoped to make *The Leatherwood God* "my last
great novel" and hoped Joe would (as he did) help him out with the
facts of the history and the legend.

There was more than sentiment to his turning to Joe in connection with this novel. From childhood he and Joe had shared enthusiasm for the exciting and richly varied history of their native
state. Old men often revert to the long-disused speechways and
recollections of their childhoods. Howells was turning, as he told
Mira Dock, a cousin on his mother's side, now to "our own kind of
backwoods ancestry," and that was a portion of his life uniquely
shared with Joe. Unfortunately, before the novel was done Joe was
dead in 1912. No part of their heritage of Ohio, historically true
yet so strange as to seem legendary, was more intriguing than the
story of the prophet of Leatherwood Creek, Ohio, who had convinced part of an Ohio frontier countryside that he was God.
Howells owned and read a copy of the one historical study which
had been made of the facts, and he found such previously inhibited
parts of his imagination loosed by contemplating the story that its
possibilities struck Mitchell as "too daring." Howells advised him
that some of the biggest things in it might only be treatable in-
directly. These "I can perhaps help the reader to imagine for me,
if I can't do it for him."

Where other fictional seed through these years fell on thin and
very stony ground, this struck root into fertile soil, matured beautifully, and bore such fruit as no other Howellsian plant ever had.
Plain, inelegant, and tough as the useful bark of the tree from

which their town took its name, the citizens of Leatherwood Creek lived in a Boeotian remoteness from the expansive political, commercial, and industrial concerns which boiled in the mainstream of American life in the 1820's. Most of their homes were still the log cabins of frontier days, and their sole cultural release from the routines of a simply prosperous farming came from the revivalism which their hairsplitting denominations shared tolerantly enough in the one big log church they called the Temple.

Into a fervid revival in this edifice one hot August night stepped a dramatic figure. Tall, elegantly dressed in Over The Mountains fashion, he tossed his great long mane of black hair over his neck, snorted strangely like a surprised stallion, and electrified the meeting with a great, annunciatory shout: "Salvation !" Upon invitation he mounted to the pulpit and in a long, rambling discourse revealed a letter-perfect memory for Scripture, and, almost wholly through the directional hints of his quotations, intimated that he was a prophet sent from God. Of course he created a sensation. And as the days wore on he was able successively to delude the Leatherwood folk into believing him prophet, Messiah, Savior, and, at last, God Himself. Tracing this, Howells is reminiscent of the Twain of "The Man That Corrupted Hadleyburg" or *The Mysterious Stranger*.

Dylks, the Leatherwood God, finds that all he has to do is give folks "the *chance* to play the fool." As he says, "Everywhere the people are waiting for a sign, just as they've always been." And, "It's been step by step with me: first exhorter, then prophet, then disciple, then the Son, then the Father: but it's been as easy ! You don't know how faith, the faith of the elect, helps along." One of Dylks's worst problems, in fact, arises from the confusion which comes to cloud his rascally mind—he doesn't after a while know whether to believe in himself or not. After all, the wealthiest and in general most respectable and influential of the local citizens are foremost in his cult. The easygoing miller, the richest, and the peppery little schoolmaster, one of the most honored, he has to make St. Peter and St. Paul.

Following the historical outline, Howells then has to confront the question: how could such things be? Introducing the book he acknowledged his historical source but added that many "details," and "the vital incidents, or the vital uses of them," and the characters "as to their psychological evolution" were "all invented." There had to be Dylks, and the most important thing about him had to be his interior history. Yet two scruples of honesty seem to have withheld Howells from "going inside" Dylks: it was not really imaginable what quirks of egoism, self-deceit, superstition, and scoundrelism could have motivated him (this was one of the things best hinted to the reader); and it was absolutely necessary that Dylks be prevented from assuming tragic stature. All was lost if this were not, however black and bitter, a tragicomedy.

So Howells began by imagining a local lawyer and country justice of the peace, Squire Matthew Braile (who could read in the dark?), who was a Tom Paine freethinker among the pious folk of Leatherwood. Braile is the novel's "register," its central observer to whom all things come, and at the crucial points its choral spokesman. To his eyes the ignorant folly of Leatherwood Creek is crystal clear. His good-humored, democratic calm, legality, skepticism, and responsibility erect the exact standard by which to measure the silly passions of his townsmen.

If Braile can oversee the overt drama, there must also be some window on the inward drama of the story. And for that purpose Howells invented Nancy Gillespie Dylks Billings and her family. Largely out of Braile's sight transpires the drama of poor tragic Nanny. Married to Dylks, she had been deserted by him at the birth of her son, had heard of his death, and had remarried. Now she must put away her second and true husband and suffer in silence while Dylks turns every word and association most sacred to her world to vicious travesty. Only she and her family, especially her Puritanic brother David, who hates Dylks with a Cromwellian fervor, know the whole truth about Dylks. And he can silence them with the threat of exposing Nancy's bigamy. Then they must suffer the torture of watching beautiful, willful, and intense Jane Gillespie, David's daughter, become one of Dylks's worshipers. It is more than they can bear. Both David and Nancy are forced to conclude that there is no God. If there were, He would never permit a Dylks.

Interestingly, it is freethinking Matthew Braile who answers them. God, he tells Nancy, "thinks it's best for mankind to let them have their swing when they choose to do evil. . . . He's made man . . . in His own image, and He's put him here in a world of his own, to do the best or the worst with it. The way I look at it, He doesn't want to keep interfering with man, but lets him play the fool or play the devil just as he's a mind to." But every now and then, in fine, pure persons, God sends man "Word made Spirit whenever there's a human creature comes into the world, all loving and all unselfish—like your Joey. . . ." (Dylks's son.)

But of course there is other opposition to Dylks in Leatherwood Creek. Dylks splits up families. His "Little Flock" drives the other sects out of their place in the Temple. And there are always "the Hounds," the brawny young mockers who have long hung on the edge of the revivals, exploiting their chances to spark the girls and heckle the exhorters. There is something about Dylks which particularly stirs up the Hounds—and not just the fact that he refers to them as "the Herd of the Lost." And it is in handling that something, that special *mana* which is the source of Dylks's power, that Howells especially relied on hinting and hinting at "tremendous things" which the reader must fill in for himself.

Howells knew of course that the path from evangelical excitement in camp meetings to powerful sexual stimulation was notoriously short and that the bushes around a revival full of "power" were likely to be well inhabited. And he suggests by every method short of open statement that the ground of Dylks's *mana* was sexual. He has David Gillespie, who knows Dylks through Nancy, defy him: "you turkey cock, you stallion ! . . . you can't prance *me* down. . . ." That is the point of the strange equine snort which is Dylks's trademark. It is the snort of the stallion. Matthew Braile reflects that "this god of theirs is a handsome devil, and some poor fool of a girl, or some bigger fool of a married woman, is going to fall in love with him, and then—"

"Did you just think of that?" his wife interrupts contemptuously.

The man most terrified by that prospect is David Gillespie. When he tries to reason, even to threaten Jane out of the "Little Flock," she turns on him ecstatically—and with significant reference to another stallion feature of her god. His long, glossy hair, dramatically tossed in histrionic moments, is always referred to as a "mane." Jane bargains defiantly: "If you touched him your hands would be withered. . . . If you will bring me a single hair of his head I will deny him." When word of that reaches Jane's suitors among the Hounds, the fall of the Leatherwood God is preordained.

Howells never had written such another series of picturesque, dramatic, and violent scenes as those which trace the downfall of Dylks. He promises a miracle in Hingston's mill and his failure to bring it off triggers a riot in which he is captured, has a whole lock of his hair snatched from his head, scalp and all, for Jane's benefit, is imprisoned in the Temple overnight while a "squalid travesty" of the early scenes of the passion of Christ takes place. When, instead of lynching him the Hounds take him before Braile for trial, however, the Squire is too intelligent to let him become a martyr.

Though Dylks begins with a brassy burlesque of Jesus before Pilate, Braile insists that there must be a regular legal charge against him. "Has he stolen anything? Like a mule, for instance? Has he robbed a hen-roost? Has he assaulted anybody, or set a tobacco-shed on fire? Some one must make a charge; I don't much care what it is." This makes the Hounds laugh, "and a kindlier spirit spread through them; they were beginning to see Dylks as a joke." The Squire concludes that, since there is no law against religious fanaticism and no punishable act is alleged against Dylks, he must be let go, and Dylks profits from the opportunity to race away into the woods. To the Little Flock the Squire says, "Go home, and look after your corn and tobacco; and you women, you go and get breakfast for them, and wash up your children and leave the Kingdom of Heaven alone for a while." And to the Hounds, "You let these folks worship any stock or stone they've a mind to; and you find out the true God if you can, and stick to Him, and don't bother the idolators."

In more fine scenes, Dylks hides out in a swamp for a week, consumed with self-pity and despair, then sneaks in to be succored by Nancy and by Braile. Eventually he announces to the Little Flock that he will take them Over-the-Mountains toward Philadelphia and the New Jerusalem. By the time he reaches Philadelphia with a starving, near-mutinous retinue and nothing has turned up, he despairingly lets himself roll into the nearby river. Only his loving-hearted son Joey, an unbeliever along for adventure, tries to save him; and it is Joey who sees him go finally down, a drowned man. Nevertheless, the Little Flock largely remained faithful. By the time they got home, some were sure they had seen Dylks translated into heaven.

Thirty years later the aged Squire Braile was visited by a scholar seeking information about the Leatherwood God. "Life is hard in a new country," he points out to the inquirer, "and anybody that promises salvation on easy terms has got a strong hold. . . . Somewhere, tucked away in us, is the longing to know whether we'll live again, and the hope that we'll live happy." But then why wasn't Dylks as successful as, say, Mohammed? asks the stranger. Because Dylks was a coward, answers Braile, "and perhaps he hadn't perfect faith in himself. . . . He was not ready to shed blood for his lie. . . ." He would run, not fight. "No liar ever had such a hold on them that believed his lie; they'd have followed him to any lengths; but he hadn't the heart to lead them."

When Howells, grasping the very last opportunity, at last wrote a true Ohio novel, he succeeded marvelously with it. His power to communicate the landscape, settings, backwoodsy atmospheres and folksy customs makes many of his historical novel followers seem pale. But then it should, he had lived that life and known such types as the wonderfully slipshod and vulgar Reverdys, with their soft, Ohio River talk; Jim Redfield, the colorful bucko leader of the Hounds; Laban Billings, the boy Joey, and all the rest during his own years of keenest sensibility. In point of fact, from the age of the First World War into which the novel was published it was as remote as a historical novel, available in its settings and textures only to the historical imagination of the general reader. That it was truly contemporaneous to Howells was only the measure of his years. But in its psychological and moral themes it was nowise obsolete, as any sufferer from the war propaganda about to deluge the heads of Americans might have testified.

The Leatherwood God is Howells' great unknown novel. It is his only true Western novel, unfortunately. It stands alone, a monument to a lifelong intention almost frustrated. But it stands together in the canon of Howells' first-rate fiction with the other nine of his ten best novels: *A Modern Instance, Indian Summer, The Rise of Silas Lapham, Annie Kilburn, A Hazard of New Fortunes, The Shadow of a Dream, The Quality of Mercy, The Landlord at Lion's Head,* and *The Son of Royal Langbrith.* It might be argued that *April Hopes* and *An Imperative Duty* should be added to make it an even dozen. But one can feel sure of those nine with *The Leatherwood God* to complete the canon at a decade.

IV

Before and after that final work of art, Howells toiled away at his "hated memoirs," gradually hammering out the materials for the luminous and graceful *Years of My Youth* and the never-finished *Years of My Middle Life* which was to have followed. Between his agedness and the onset of the War, travel, one of his greatest comforts since his wife's death, was cut off. There would be no more such unique moments as the excursion he loved to tell about taking into the Irish countryside with Pat Collins, the ex-Mayor of Boston. Howells had proposed to Collins that Irish wit was declining. Oh no, only in cities, in Dublin, Collins retorted. In the country it was as rich as ever. So they hired a car and drove out until Collins said this was the country and agreed to test the first person they met. Next came a boy driving pigs. Howells pointed a stern finger and asked, without parley: "If the devil appeared right this moment, which of us would he take—you or me?"

"Me, sir," came the quick answer.

"How do you figure that out?"

"Och—sure, he could get you anny time !"

Now he had to content himself with going to Florida winters and, no small consolation for a man who could never really care for horses, buying a Model T Ford.

"This old age isn't what it's cracked up to be. I'm going to write a sonnet about it and give it a black eye," Howells told a friend the day after his eightieth birthday. Nevertheless, he managed to keep a dignified and productive life going. In 1915 he had made a new compact with the Harpers by which they paid him $5,000 for the "Easy Chair" and occasional introductions to books, with other writings to be separately negotiated for, and that took considerable pressure from his shoulders.

With regard to the War, he became enthusiastically interventionist, and pro-Ally, of course. The anti-German propaganda convinced him, as he showed in the poem he wrote for *Le Livre des Sans-Foyer* edited by Edith Wharton, blasting "The master-spirit of hell. . . . The Anti-Christ of Schrecklichkeit." Yet when, in the spring of that same year, May 1916, the British government executed a group of Irishmen for nationalistic activities, Howells was quick to protest publicly against this "madness" of the English in copying "Schrecklichkeit." He endured the resulting storms of approval from Irish and condemnation from English patriots calmly. He had kept true to his principle—mercy is always better than "justice"—and the reaction must have seemed dim to the man who

had really risked and survived in the case of the Chicago Anarchists.

On February 28, 1916, Howells lost the last of his great and
intimate friends when Henry James died. In the two decades past
he and James had grown very close again in the special niche each
reserved for the other in his heart. Howells had continued to praise
James, ardently and discriminatingly, in print and to promote his
interests wherever he could. In the months of crisis which had
followed James's awful failure as a dramatist it had been Howells
who could most hearten him toward the new beginning in fiction
which resulted in James's greatest work. Howells continued to
receive the marvelous letters about the art for which James superbly lived, the letters James apparently could not quite write to
anyone else.

In 1911 Howells, joining a scheme launched in England by Gosse,
Edith Wharton, and Kipling, acted both personally and as President of the American Academy to try to persuade the Swedish
Academy to award the Nobel Prize in literature to James but was
not, of course, successful. He was entirely in sympathy with the
motives of James's demonstration in applying for British citizen-
ship in 1915. James died too late, too late that is for Howells'
remaining stores of energy, for anything like *My Mark Twain* to
be written for him. Yet when in 1920 Percy Lubbock's *Letters of
Henry James* appeared, Howells thought it not only a good occasion
for an "Easy Chair" on the letters but also the right moment to
correct the notion then current that James had somehow betrayed
his country in his expatriation and ceased to be a part of American
literature by living and working in Europe. As it turned out, the
last work Howells ever did was on those two unfinished pieces, and
he wrote on his deathbed of "The American James."

In the winter of 1920 the body which had endured so sturdily
through so many years and phases of American history began to
run down. Howells' winter at Savannah, Georgia, was largely un-
comfortable. He caught cold in April just before he left there and
could not shake it on returning to New York. According to the
New York *Times,* in the early minutes of May 11, 1920, John Mead
Howells saw his father stir quietly in his sleep. Not long after, he
died.

There were, of course, many tributes besides those long prepared in the newspaper "morgues." Woodrow Wilson telegraphed from the White House. Garland spoke for Howells' surviving followers. Other authors brought their praises. But perhaps the most striking and prescient of all was Rudyard Kipling, no man to compliment an American lightly or inadvertently. Kipling lauded at length "the essential power of the man and the craftsman, his equal gentleness." He recalled the impact of Howells read aloud during Kipling's boyhood in India. He found Howells' art and vision unique and permanently valuable. But, he concluded, he must not indulge too much in the "presumption" of "appraisal of one who for so long ranked without effort at the head of his country's literature and opened the road to so many and diverse intellects in his calling; for he is the father of a multitude of heirs who have inherited his treasures, but forgotten the paternity. Time will prove it so and your land's literature will acknowledge it."

BIBLIOGRAPHICAL NOTES

LIKE THOSE IN THE PRECEDING VOLUME *The Road to Realism,* these notes are selective rather than exhaustive. The key resources for the study of Howells remain: Mildred Howells, *The Life in Letters of William Dean Howells,* 1928 (hereafter referred to as *Letters*); William M. Gibson and George Arms, *A Bibliography of William Dean Howells,* 1948 (hereafter referred to as Gibson and Arms); Clara and Rudolph Kirk, *William Dean Howells, Representative Selections,* 1950; and Everett Carter, *Howells and the Age of Realism,* 1954. To these have been added at least two notable items: the supplement by Arms and Gibson to their bibliography in Kirk and Kirk which was mimeographed as "Books and Articles on W. D. Howells, 1950–1956"; and *Prefaces to Contemporaries (1882–1920) By William Dean Howells,* 1957, edited by George Arms, William M. Gibson, and Frederic C. Marston, Jr.

In the notes below, letters written by Howells to others are identified as "to John Doe," by date, and the present location of the document. Letters addressed to Howells identify the sender ("from Richard Roe") as well as date and location. The key to locations, when not obvious, is:

Brit. Mus.   The papers of Sir Edmund Gosse, British Museum, London, England.

Harvard   William Dean Howells Papers, Houghton Library, Harvard University.

Ohio   The Ohio State Historical Society Library, Columbus, Ohio.

Penn   The S. Weir Mitchell Papers, University of Pennsylvania Library, Philadelphia, Pa.

George S. Hellman, ed., "The Letters of Howells to Higginson," *Twenty-Seventh Annual Report of the Bibliophile Society,* 1929, pages 17–56, is referred to as *Hellman;* Percy Lubbock, ed., *The Letters of Henry James,* 1920, is referred to as *James Letters.*

Chapter One

I

Harpers Contract: see Howells' correspondence with Fairchild and Osgood (Harvard); to Gosse, October 26, 1885 (Brit. Mus.); Harper Contract in Howells Papers (Harvard); *Letters,* I, 369, 371–72; Joseph W. Harper, Jr. to Charles Fairchild, May 13, 1885; Fairchild to Harper, May 14, 1885; from Wolcott Balestier, January 14, 1891; from Alden, March 18, 20, 1890; January 31, August 20, 1891; from Alden, September 9, 1895 (Harvard). "Our New York Letter," *Literary World,* April 17, May 1, 1886; to Gosse, October 26, 1885 (Brit. Mus.); to Mrs. Fields, November 7, 1886 (Huntington).

II

To W. C. Howells, February 9, 1886 (Harvard); Robert Grant, *Fourscore,* 1930, 288; *Letters,* I, 371; to Mitchell, October 20, 1885 (Penn); see *"Indian Summer"* notebook (Harvard); cp. Howells, "Equality as the Basis of a Good Society," *Century,* November 1895; Garland, "Meetings with Howells," *Bookman,* March 1917, 2–3; *Letters,* I, 387.

III

For the dating of Howells' discovery of Tolstoi see E. H. Cady, *The Gentleman in America,* 1949, 200; an excellent summation can be found in Louis Budd, "William Dean Howells' Debt to Tolstoi," *American Slavic and East European Review,* December 1950, 292–301; on *Anna Karenina* see Howells to Higginson in Hellman, 19; cp. "Lyof N. Tolstoy," *North American Review,* December 1908; W. L. Phelps, *Autobiography, with Letters,* 1939, 504; see Arnold Fox, "Howells as a Religious Critic," *New England Quarterly,* June 1952. *Life and Letters of Edward Everett Hale,* 1917, II, 327–28; from Hale, September 17, 1887 (Harvard).

IV

To Higginson, August 31, 1886, Hellman, p. 44; Phelps, *Autobiography,* 502; to Gosse, January 24, 1886 (Brit. Mus.); from

Osgood, October 31, 1885 (Harvard) ; see E. H. Cady, "Armando Palacio Valdés Writes to William Dean Howells," *Symposium,* May 1948, esp. pp. 31–34. From J. W. Harper, May 16, 1887; from Ware, May 9, 1891; from Alden, August 21, 1888 (Harvard).

Chapter Two

The fine, pioneering article by Herbert Edwards, "Howells and the Controversy over Realism in American Fiction," *American Literature,* November 1931, still cries aloud to be expanded, confirmed, and elucidated in a full-scale study of the War.

I

To W. C. Howells, February 27, 1887 (Harvard) ; to H. B. Fuller, October 27, 1893 (*Letters,* II, 39) ; *Life* (undated clipping in Howells Papers, Harvard) ; H. C. Vedder, *American Writers of Today,* 1894, 54; Thayer, "The New Story-Tellers and the Doom of Realism," *Forum,* December 1894, 470–80; cp. Leonard Lutwack, "William Dean Howells and the 'Editor's Study,' " *American Literature,* May 1952, 200; see Stedman and Gould, *Life and Letters of E. C. Stedman,* 1910, III, 167, and *Letters,* I, 408–9; for Warner, see "Editor's Drawer," October 1890 and September 1891.

On Lafcadio Hearn, cp. E. Bisland, *Life and Letters of Lafcadio Hearn,* 1906, I, 332 (June 1884) quoting Hearn in the New Orleans *Times Democrat,* June 6, 1886; April 12, 1887; May 29, 1887 (cp. *Essays on American Literature*) ; and Bisland, *The Japanese Letters of Lafcadio Hearn,* 1910, 126, 214–15. On Thompson: see Thompson file of letters to Howells (Harvard) and *The Literary World,* July 23, August 20, and September 3, 1887; also Thompson, *Studies of Prominent Novelists,* 1887. Cp. unpublished interview of Howells by "Mrs. Gould," May 17, 1909 (Columbia).

II

The Critic, July 16, 1887, 2; *ibid.,* May 4, 1888, 255; from Alden, March 10, 1888 (Harvard).

III

From Curtis, March 5, 1887 (Harvard) ; "Editor's Easy Chair," *Harper's,* May 1889, 981; January 1890, 313; from Lowell, January 16, 1890 (Harvard) ; from Gilder, July 5, August 14, 1887 (Harvard) ; cp. Lutwack, p. 200; from Reid, November 8, 1887 (Harvard) ; for Brander Matthews, see "Recent Essays in Fiction," *Cosmopolitan*, November 1891, 124–26; "Mr. Howells as a Critic," *Forum*, January 1902, 629–38; and *infra;* W. P. Trent, "Mr. Howells and Romanticism," *The Authority of Criticism and Other Essays*, 1899; C. P. Woolley, "Mr. Howells Again," *New England Magazine*, December 1893, 408–11; Anna Laurens Dawes, "The Moral Purpose in Howells's Novels," *Andover Review*, January 1889, 23–36; for Boyesen, "The Great Realists . . . ," *Forum*, February 1895, 724–31.

IV

See from James, February 21, 1884, *James Letters* I, 103; from James, October 19, [1885] (Harvard); Henry to William James, October 15, 1887 in Ralph Barton Perry, *The Thought and Character of William James*, 1936, I, 399–400.

Howells' relations with Stevenson were unusual. He had printed pseudonymous verses for Stevenson in the *Atlantic* and received respectful letters from him (Harvard). Looking forward to meeting Stevenson in England in 1882, Howells was rebuffed by Stevenson's letter, to which he simply (and probably mistakenly) did not reply. On cooler reflection, Stevenson made cautious advances through mutual friends (see Caro Lloyd, *Henry D. Lloyd,* 71). But if Howells ever heard of them, he did not respond. Stevenson had become a major adversary in the Realism War. Not until Stevenson wrote in 1893, shortly before his death, from Samoa offering reconciliation did Howells respond—but then heartily (*Letters*, II, 37–38). But he apparently never reopened the literary question of Stevenson in his own mind.

Cp. W. Frierson, "The English Controversy over Realism in Fiction, 1885–1895," *PMLA* XLIII (1928), 533–50. Among Howells' defenders were Grant Allen [see from Allen, May 26, 1886 (Harvard); "Editor's Study," July 1890, 317–18; Sarah K. Bolton, *Famous American Authors*, 1887, 277–78], Gosse ("The Limits of Realism in Fiction," *Questions at Issue*, 1893, 216–24), Frederic Harrison ("The Decadence of Romance," *Forum*, April 1893, 216–24), W. Archer ("The Novelist as Critic," *Illustrated London News*, August 8, 1891, 175), A. T. Quiller-Couch ("A Literary Causerie," *Speaker*, August 1, 1891, 1143–44).

Andrew Lang: see F. L. Mott, *A History of American Magazines*, II, 399; Lutwack, *op. cit.*, 204; from Wolcott Balestier, July 12,

1890 (Harvard) ; for James on Lang, see *James Letters* II, 275–77;
see *The Critic,* April 16, 1892, 233; Lang's apology appears in
"The New Fiction," *Illustrated London News,* August 3, 1895, 141.

V

From Osgood, November 22, 1890; January 12 and March 27,
1891 (Harvard) ; Cp. Gibson and Arms, 39–40; Everett Carter,
"W. D. Howells' Theory of Critical Realism," *ELH,* June 1949,
151–66; and *Howells and the Age of Realism,* 186 ff.; Burroughs,
Critic, February 6, 1892, 85–86; Scudder, "Mr. Howells' Literary
Creed," *Atlantic,* October 1891, 566–69; Matthews, "Recent Essays
in Criticism," *loc. cit.,* see 124–26; to Matthews, October 21, 1891
(Columbia).

For Dostoevsky, see "Editor's Study," September 1886; for Verga
see Study for October 1890; from Clarence W. McIlwain, April 14,
1890, and Verga to Howells, October 28, 1874 (Harvard) ; for
speech see *Harper's Weekly,* March 9, 1912, 29.

VI

On *Trilby:* see Mott, *op. cit.,* II, 400; James D. Hart, *The Popular
Book,* carries a good account of the whole phenomenon of the neoromantic triumph; see also Mott, *Golden Multitudes.*

William Tindall, *Forces in Modern British Literature,* 18; to
Higginson, February 20, 1895, in Hellman, 53–54; Howells quoted
in Orcutt, *Celebrities Off Parade,* 1935, 128; Carl Van Doren,
"Howells, May, 1920, Eulogium," *The Roving Critic,* 1923, 73.

Chapter Three

To Gosse, February 24, 1889; to Gosse, October 26, 1885 (Brit.
Mus.) ; cp. to Mrs. Fields, November 7, 1886 (Huntington) ; see
"Indian Summer" notebook (Harvard) ; see Washington notebook
(Harvard) ; from Osgood, October 12 and 31, 1885 (Harvard) ; *The
Literary World,* April 17, 1886, 135, and May 1, 1886, 152.

To Conway, December 8, 1886 (Columbia) ; Gould interview,
May 17, 1909 (Columbia).

I

See Marion Wilcox, "The Works of William Dean Howells," *Harper's Weekly,* July 4, 1896, 655; to Garland, March 11, 1888, *Letters,*
I, 410; cp. Dawes, *op. cit.,* 23.

II

To W. C. Howells, February 20, 1887 (Harvard); P. H. Boynton, "William Dean Howells," *New Republic*, January 31, 1923, 256–57. The two major pioneers in this area have been Walter Fuller Taylor, *The Economic Novel in America*, 1942, and preceding articles dating back to 1930; and George Arms, see his New York University dissertation, *The Social Criticism of William Dean Howells*, 1939, and many subsequent publications, esp. "The Literary Background of Howells's Social Criticism," *American Literature*, November 1942, 260–76; from Roswell Smith, March 17, 1885 (Harvard).

See *Critic*, July 16, 1887, 32; to W. C. Howells, July 1, 1888 (Harvard); on Winifred, see Howells to W. C. Howells, July 17, August 7, September 18, November 13, 1887 (Harvard). Cp. Caroline Tickner, *Glimpses of Authors*, 1922, 170–71.

III

Ferris Greenslet, *Under the Bridge*, 1943, 29–31; from Gilder, February 18, 1885; from Roswell Smith, February 18, 1885 (Harvard). The Haymarket Riot and its aftermath form a part of every general history of this period; Miss Mildred Howells' account of it and her father's part in it is excellent, *Letters*, I, 393–403. On Howells and Pryor see *Letters* I, 393–98; and Percy MacKaye, *Epoch, the Life of Steele MacKaye*, 1927, II, 96; from Reid, November 8, 1887 (Harvard); N. Y. *Tribune*, November 6, 1887, 5 (cf. *Letters*, I, 398–99); to Francis F. Browne, November 4, 1887 (Harvard); from Browne, November 8, 1887 (Harvard); to Browne, November 11 (*Letters*, I, 401–2); cp. John W. Ward, "Another Howells Anarchist Letter," *American Literature*, January 1951, 489–90. From Curtis, August 12, 1887 (Harvard); from Whittier, "March 18" and "3rd. Mo. 23," 1886 (*Letters*, I, 380–81); from Whittier, September 21, 1887 (Harvard); to Whittier, December 10, 1888 (UCLA); from Whittier, December 12, 1888 (Harvard).

See the N. Y. *Tribune*, which reprinted many "exchanges" round the country in addition to its own items for this period, esp. November 5–12. Howells' own clipping file contains the *Life*, Cedar Grove, Me., and a number of other bits (Harvard). On *Puck* see Jensen, *Life and Letters of H. C. Bunner*, 1939, 119; Howells' mss. "A

Word for the Dead" is also in his Anarchist file (Harvard); from Alden, November 13, 1887 (Harvard); to Mrs. Achille Fréchette, November 18, 1887 (*Letters*, I, 403–4); Lloyd, *Lloyd*, 100–101; see Virginia Harlow, *Thomas Sergeant Perry*, 1950, 102; Matthiessen, *The James Family*, 622; *Selections from the Correspondence of Theodore Roosevelt and H. C. Lodge*, 1925, I, 501.

Howells' Anarchist file shows reactions in his favor. See Lowell to Howells, January 16, 1890; to W. C. Howells, December 1, 1887 (Harvard), and cp. *Letters*, I, 402–3; and A. L. Dawes, *op. cit.*, 35; from J. W. Harper, December 2, 1887 (Harvard). Caro Lloyd, *Lloyd*, I, 87, shows how alone Howells stood at this moment, and I am grateful to Professor Louis Wheelock, who has studied the Chicago period carefully, for corroborating and extending my information about this point. Joseph H. Harper to Mildred Howells, May 11, 1920 (Harvard). Cf. Everett Carter, "The Haymarket Affair in Literature," *American Quarterly*, Fall, 1950.

IV

To W. C. Howells, November 13, 1887 (Harvard); to Mrs. Fields, December 17, 1887 and January 20, 1888 (Huntington). For the Buffalo winter, see *Letters*, I, 403–8; "Mr. Howells' Socialism," *American Fabian*, February 1898, 2; to Garland, *Letters*, I, 407–8; to Perry, *ibid.*, 413–14. On New York see *Letters*, I, 413; on Buffalo, *ibid.*, 409. To C. H. Webb, April 7, 1888 (Library of Congress).

There are references to alcohol in many of Howells' letters. See to Comly, July 20, 1873 (Ohio); *Nation*, January 4, 1886, 5. See esp. from Joseph W. Harper, June 20, 1885 (Harvard). There is a photograph at Harvard showing Howells in the invitational act of pouring from a bottle of Scotch into a glass.

From Alden, August 24, 1888 (Harvard); from Hale, August 28, 1888 (Harvard); to Garland, *Letters*, I, 419; *The Diary of Rutherford B. Hayes*, IV, January 13, 1889.

Chapter Four

See to W. C. Howells, esp. April 15, June 17, and July 8, 1888 (Harvard); to Higginson, August 9, 1888, Hellman, 47; on the provenience of the New York novel, see *Letters*, I, 418–19.

On New York, see to W. C. Howells, February 19, April 1, September 19, and November 4, 1888 (Harvard) ; Henry Rood, "Howells at 75," N. Y. *Times,* February 25, 1912.

I

To Twain, *Letters,* I, 392; cp. to W. C. Howells, May 29, 1887 (Harvard). From Alden, September 14, 1888 (Harvard) ; on Basil March, to W. C. Howells, December 20, 1888 (Harvard) ; on Dryfoos, see fragment, "Unfinished Story Dealing with Pennsylvania Emigrants to Ohio" (Harvard) : typewriter face, paper, and handwriting look like about 1887; on Fulkerson, see to Stevenson, September 15, 1893 (*Letters,* II, 38) ; on Lindau, to W. C. Howells, April 6, 1890 (Harvard) ; cp. Rudolf and Clara Kirk, " 'Poems of Two Friends,' " *Journal of the Rutgers Library,* June 1941, 39, n. 6; see *"Indian Summer"* notebook (Harvard) entry of December [?], 26, 1888.

II

The best source is the memorial volume Howells wrote (and Aldrich edited?), *Winifred Howells,* 1891. Cp. Boyesen, "Mr. Howells at Close Range," *Ladies' Home Journal,* November 1893, 7–8.

On Winifred's death, see from Mitchell, about 1885 (Penn) ; to Mrs. Fields, November 18, 1888 (Huntington) ; to W. C. Howells, November 18, November 25, December 2, December 20, 1888; January 6, January 19, January 27, February 17, March 3, March 17, 1889 (Harvard) ; perhaps the key letter is to Mitchell, March 7, 1889; cp. to Mrs. Mitchell, November 18, 1919, when Howells had still not entirely forgiven Mitchell (Penn).

On Howells' reaction to Winifred's death: to W. C. Howells, March 22, March 31, April 23, 1889 (Harvard) ; to M. D. Conway, April 7, 1889 (Ohio) ; to Mitchell, April 2, 1891 (Penn). On effect upon his writing, see Clifton Johnson, "The Writer and the Rest of the World," *Outlook,* March 31, 1894, 580; to Higginson, January 30, 1891, Hellman, 48.

On Elinor Howells: to W. C. Howells, September 29, 1889 (Harvard), though evidence is widespread. On Mrs. Howells and Howells' work, see W. H. Bishop, "Mr. Howells in Beacon St. . . ." *Critic,* November 27, 1886; Boyesen, "Howells at Close Range," 8; to Mitchell, December 11, 1904, and February 9, 1911 (Penn) ; cp. *Letters,* II, 331.

III

For two excellent readings of *A Hazard of New Fortunes* which vary interestingly from one to the other and are both different from mine, see George Arms, "Howells' New York Novel: Comedy and Belief," *New England Quarterly*, September 1948, 313–25; George Arms, "Introduction," *A Hazard of New Fortunes*, Everyman's Library, 1952, vii–xx. Cp. Everett Carter, *Howells and the Age of Realism*, 201–24.

IV

See from Alden, October 29, 1889 (Harvard); to Storey, December 20, 1889 (Yale); *Endymion*, Book I, 11. 777–80, 853–57.

See Everett Carter, *Howells and the Age of Realism*, 145–52; "The Palpitating Divan," *College English*, May 1950, 423–28. Cp. Andrews, *Nook Farm*, 140–43.

See Howells' 1882 notebook (Harvard); for Howells' early training in sexual matters, see *The Road to Realism*, pp. 32–33; Gosse, "The Passing of William Dean Howells," *Living Age*, July 10, 1920, 98–100; on Cleveland, to W. H. Smith, June 16, 1886 (Ohio); cp. Andrews, *Nook Farm*, 115; Harlow, *Perry*, 101–2; A. Schade Van Westrum, "Mr. Howells on Life and Love," *Lamp*, February 1904, 26–31; E. Earnest, *S. Weir Mitchell*, 1950, 178–81; from Mitchell, June 4, 1885 (Penn); *Passages from the Journal of Thomas Russell Sullivan, 1891–1903*, May 6, 1891, 12–13; to T. C. Metcalf, March 13, 1893 (*Letters*, II, 34–35); Boyesen, "The Great Realists . . . ," 728; Owen Wister, "William Dean Howells," *Atlantic*, December 1937, 712–13.

On the limitations of fashionable literary Freudianism in the 1920's, see Frederick J. Hoffman, *Freudianism and the Literary Mind*, 1946. Cp. Norman Cousins, "Censorship and Bestselleritis," *Saturday Review*, November 2, 1946, 24.

V

To W. C. Howells, December 1, 1889 (Harvard); to W. C. Howells, June 15, 1890 (Harvard); for a fuller account of *A Boy's Town*, see *The Road to Realism*, 11–12, 22–23; to Aurelia Howells, January 6, 1890 (Harvard); from Mitchell, n. d.; to Mitchell, April 2, 1891 (Penn).

Harry Thurston Peck, "Mr. Howells as a Poet," *Bookman*, February 1896, 525–26; from Alden, December 26, 1894 (Harvard); Henry Van Dyke, *The Gospel for a World of Sin,* 1899, 18; Van Dyke, *Campfires and Guideposts,* 1921, 310–19; *Nation,* June 1890, 454; Morison, ed., *Letters of Theodore Roosevelt,* 1951, I, 410; "Mr. Howells' Views," *Critic,* January 2, 1897, 5.

Henry James' view of Howells' "incurable optimism" remained incurably the same throughout the years, e.g., "William Dean Howells," *Harper's Weekly,* June 19, 1886, 394; "American Letter," *Literature,* July 9, 1898, 18; "A Letter to Mr. Howells," *North American Review,* April 1912, 562; James' letters to Howells *passim;* Edith Wharton, *A Backward Glance,* 1934, 147. See E. H. Cady, "A Note on Howells and 'the Smiling Aspects of Life,'" *American Literature,* May 1945, 175–78; Carter, "Howells's Theory of Critical Realism," *loc. cit.,* esp. 157–60.

Robert Frost, "New Hampshire," *Collected Poems of Robert Frost,* 1942, 207; "Editor's Study," *Harper's Monthly,* March 1891, 641; August 1886, 477; Van Westrum, *op. cit.,* 27–28; for "Transfusion" see *"Indian Summer"* notebook (Harvard); cp. J. Donald Adams, "Speaking of Books," *New York Times Book Review,* March 13, 1949, 2.

Chapter Five

Rood, *Ladies' Home Journal,* 154; cp. Harlow, *Perry,* 139; from Alden, December 1, 1889 (Harvard); Perry, *William James,* I, 415; Matthiessen, *The James Family,* 333–34; *Letters of William James,* I, 298–99; *Letters of Henry James,* I, 163–66; Norton, *Letters of James Russell Lowell,* II, 399; Howe, *New Letters of James Russell Lowell,* 335–36; on Higginson, see undated clipping (*Boston Transcript?*) in Howells Papers (Harvard); to Higginson, January 29, and 30, December 14, 1891, Hellman, 48 ff.; *Autobiography of William Allen White,* 1946, 199; from Parton, December 30, 1889 (Harvard); Scudder, "New York in Recent Fiction," *Atlantic,* April 1890, 563–67.

I

Sylvester Baxter, "Howells's Boston" *New England Magazine,* October 1893, 133; M. A. D. Howe, *A Partial (And Not Impartial) Semi-Centennial History of the Tavern Club, 1884–1934,* 1934, 3, 5–7, 12, 14, 16, 52–53; to W. C. Howells, December 5, 1885 (Harvard) ; from Owen Wister, May 21, 1885; August 23, 1915 (Harvard) ; Alfred Lief, *Brandeis,* 1936, 30; cp. *Road to Realism,* 222–23.

On Hamlin Garland, see *A Son of the Middle Border, Roadside Meetings, Companions on the Trail, passim;* cp. Gibson and Arms, 163. I am particularly grateful to Dr. Doc. Lars Åhnebrink, Uppsala University, Sweden, for permitting me to consult his fine collection of Garland's correspondence with Howells. To Garland, October 21, 1888 (UCLA) ; to Baxter, October 22, 1890 (Huntington) ; to Garland, December 20, 1891; June 25, 1892; August 23, 1893 (UCLA). Garland, "Mr. Howells's Latest Novels," *New England Magazine,* May 1890, 243–50; to Garland, n. d. (about 1898) [UCLA].

The much which has been written on Herne has been brilliantly summed up and interpreted by Herbert Edwards, "Howells and Herne," *American Literature,* January 1951, 432–41; I am also grateful for certain insights to Professor Arthur W. Brown.

There is excellent material on Howells' contacts with these late Boston reformers in Louis Budd, *William Dean Howells's Relations with Politics,* unpub. diss., Wisconsin, 1949, 276 ff. See from Bellamy, April 10, 1884; to W. C. Howells, December 21, 1890 (Harvard) ; Arthur Morgan, *Edward Bellamy,* 1944, 249–50; to W. C. Howells, April 20, 1890 (Harvard), April 27, 1890, *Letters,* II, 3. Cp. James Dombrowski, *Early Christian Socialism,* 1936, 97; Arthur Mann, *Yankee Reformers in the Urban Age,* 1954. It is no doubt significant that in W. D. P. Bliss's, *Handbook of Socialism,* 1895, Howells does not figure, and that in Bliss's *Encyclopedia of Social Reforms* he gets the briefest mention as author of *A Traveler from Altruria.*

II

To William Cooper Howells, April 17, 1887 (Harvard) ; "A Letter from W. D. Howells," November 23, 1888, Anarchist file (Harvard) ; on Howells' developing socialism, see to W. C. Howells, January 22, 1888, October 25, 1891 (Harvard) ; see "Editor's Study" for April 1888, and cp. Arms, "The Literary Background of Howells's Social Criticism," *loc. cit.*; "Are We a Plutocracy?" *North American Review,* February 1894, 185–96; cp. to W. C. Howells, January 7, 1894 (Harvard).

On the Social Reform Club, from E. H. Crosby, November 18, 1895 (Harvard) ; Samuel Gompers, *Seventy Years of Life and*

Labor, 1925, I, 434. On strikes, see, *inter alia,* "Editor's Study," October 1889, 804; to W. C. Howells, July 19, 1892; April 1, 1894 (Harvard). On parties, to W. C. Howells, November 6, 1892; (Harvard); cp. Budd, *op. cit.,* 244.

On Howells' campaign contribution, Morris Hillquit, *Loose Leaves from a Busy Life,* 1934, 115–16. H. H. Quint, *The Forging of American Socialism,* 1953, provides excellent background for an understanding of Howells' relations, or lack of them, with the organized parties. From Edward R. Pease, December 12, 1890 (Harvard); "Mr. Howells' Socialism," *American Fabian,* February 1898, 1–2; *Life and Letters of Stedman,* II, 536–37; Lloyd, *Lloyd,* 198–99; from Eleanor Marx Aveling, n. d. (Harvard); from Theodore Roosevelt, August 28, 1906 (Harvard); Joseph Dorfman, *Thorstein Veblen and His America,* 1934, 196, 507; from W. H. Page, April 25, 1894 (Harvard); "The Nature of Liberty," *Forum,* December 1895, 401–9; C. H. Grattan, "Howells, Ten Years After," *American Mercury,* May 1930, 42–50; Boyesen, "Howells at Close Range," *loc. cit.,* 8; Arvin, "The Usableness of Howells," *New Republic,* June 30, 1937, 227–28; Richard Hofstadter, *The Age of Reform,* 1955.

III

See entry in *"Indian Summer"* notebook (Harvard); from Alden, September 8, 1890 (Harvard); to W. C. Howells, December 22, 1889 (Harvard); to Aurelia Howells, July 17, 1891 (Harvard). On Howells and the NAACP, see Louis Budd, *op. cit.,* 458–59; Calvin Kytle, "The Story of the NAACP," *Coronet,* August 1956, 142; on Dunbar, see *Life in Letters,* II, 67–68; from Dunbar, September 19, 1896 (Harvard); to Hitchcock, July 29, 1896 (Harvard); Dunbar quoted in Nevins, ed., *Letters and Journal of Brand Whitlock,* 1936, 25 (July 5, 1899); see also Alphonso O. Stafford, a Negro intellectual, to Howells, August 10, 1896 (Harvard); "Introduction" to *Lyrics of Lowly Life,* in Arms, Gibson, and Marston, eds., *Prefaces to Contemporaries (1882–1920) by William Dean Howells,* 1957, 65–72. Cf. James B. Stronks, "Paul Laurence Dunbar and William Dean Howells," *Ohio Historical Quarterly,* April 1958, 95–108.

IV

On relations between Howells and McClure, Mr. Peter Lyons has been helpful, esp. in quoting a letter of Mrs. McClure of April 11,

1890, in a letter to me of February 25, 1957; there is an outline proposal for *The World of Fiction* in the Howells Papers (Harvard) ; the two McClure contracts, the synopsis for *The Quality of Mercy*, and McClure to Howells, esp. April 21, 1890, are in the same place. On composition troubles with the *The Quality of Mercy*, see *Letters*, II, 13, 17; to W. C. Howells, February 8, March 1 and 22, July 5, 1891 (Harvard). From McClure, October 9, 1891; Scudder review of *The Quality of Mercy*, *Atlantic*, May 1892, 702. For an excellent analysis of *The Quality of Mercy*, see Arnold Fox, "Howells' Doctrine of Complicity," *Modern Language Quarterly*, March 1952, 58–60.

V

On leaving the Harpers: from J. W. Harper, Jr., September 17, 1889, April 18, 1890; from Alden, February 2, September 1, October 6, December 8, 1891 (Harvard). On going to *The Cosmopolitan:* from J. B. Walker, November 10, December 4, December 10, 1891; to W. C. Howells, December 7, December 13, 1891 (Harvard), December 20, 1891 (*Letters*, II, 20) ; to Norton, December 12, 1891 (*Letters*, II, 19–20) ; from Norton, December 19, 1891 (Harvard). Charles Wingate, "Boston Letter," *Critic*, January 16, 1892, 41. Cp. D. M. Rein, "Howells and *The Cosmopolitan*," *American Literature*, March 1949, 49–52.

Chapter Six

His problems of living in or out of New York Howells debated in his correspondence for many years. Quoted from or specially relevant are: to Henry James, September 25, 1890 (*Letters*, II, 7) ; to Aurelia Howells, May 12, 1895 (Harvard) ; to W. C. Howells, October 18, 1891 (*Letters*, II, 18) ; November 1, December 13, 1891 (Harvard) ; Johnson interview, *Outlook*, March 31, 1895, 580–82; Hector Charlesworth, *Candid Chronicles*, 1925, 99; to Aurelia Howells, May 5, 1895 (Harvard) ; "William Dean Howells at Home," *Current Literature*, May 1898, 402–3; Rood, "William Dean Howells," *Ladies' Home Journal*, September 1920, 154; Elinor Howells to Lucy Keeler, February 7, no year (Hayes Library) ; Garland, "Meetings with Howells," *Bookman*, March 1917, 7.

I

On provenience of *World of Chance,* to Alden, February 26, 1890;
to W. C. Howells, November 22, 1889, and September 20, 1891
(Harvard).

On Howells' own experience as the forerunner of Shelley Ray,
see *The Road to Realism,* 90; the mss. of *Geoffrey Winter* and the
letter from Macmillan's of London, December 27, 1862, declining
Geoffrey: A Study of American Life are at Harvard; cp. "The
Dream," *Knickerbocker,* August 1861, 146–50.

II

On *Cosmopolitan,* see from Walker, February 16, March 13, April
3 and 27, 1893 (Harvard); to W. C. Howells, March 6 and July 7,
1893 (Harvard); *Letters,* II, 24, 46; Charles H. Towne, *Adventures
in Editing,* 16, 25, 40; Arthur S. Hardy, *Things Remembered,* 1923,
275–76; Ellery Sedgwick, *Atlantic Harvest,* 1947, x–xi; cp. Rein,
op. cit., 53–55.

See from MacDowell, August 10, 1893; from T. Roosevelt, December 15, 1892 (Harvard); Garland, *Roadside Meetings,* 320; *Companions on the Trail,* 116; H. T. Peck, "Living Critics, XII-William
Dean Howells," *Bookman,* February 1897, 529–41; *The Americani-
zation of Edward Bok,* 191; G. S. Lee, *Critic,* XXXV, 1029–30.

Most of the fairly extensive personal financial records among the
Howells papers at Harvard would be relevant to nothing but an
exhaustive study of his business career. It seems essential only to
summarize his net-worth estimates as documenting the prosperity
which was one significant aspect of his position as the leading man
of letters. The list of prospects for 1893 is in the *"Indian Summer"*
notebook. The Houghton Mifflin agreement is dated May 15, 1889;
cp. Ticknor and Co. agreement, July 20, 1885; June 7, 1887; January 24 and April 16, 1889. On negotiations with the Harpers, see
John F. Phayre to Howells, February 18, 1892, and subsequent
correspondence with Phayre; from Alden, September 28, October 7,
October 10, 1892, and January 31, 1893; and, *inter alia,* June 2, and
October 26, 1899 (all the foregoing at Harvard). *The Americani-
zation of Edward Bok,* 202; F. C. Drake, "William Dean Howells
Helped This Young Man Write a Play," *Literary Digest,* June 19,
1920, 56. To Henry James, *Letters,* II, 133; to Aurelia Howells,
July 13, 1902 (Harvard).

Without supposing that he would at all necessarily agree with my findings, somehow here I should acknowledge my debt of gratitude to Professor William Charvat for helping me to think more seriously about, in the phrase I first heard from him, "the business of authorship."

III

To W. C. Howells, May 14, 1893.

On the Altrurian books: to W. C. Howells, December 21, 1892; January 10, 1893 (Harvard); to Sylvester Baxter, March 8, 1895 (Huntington). Cp. Gibson and Arms, items 94-B, 96-E, 07-B. *"Indian Summer"* notebook (Harvard).

Cf. Fox, "Howells as a Religious Critic"; on paganism, see "Editor's Study," February 1890, 485; S. Kirk, "America, Altruria, and The Coast of Bohemia," *Atlantic,* November 1894, 701; Howells' reconsideration of Swedenborg he recorded in a number of ways, but the conclusive statements seem to be those to W. C. Howells on January 12 and 19, 1890 (Harvard); on Mrs. Howells' Unitarianism see Mrs. George Fuller to Mrs. Howells, March 17, 1887 (Harvard); "CH" to Howells, March 1, 1900; Anon. to Howells, October 3, 1905 (Harvard); *Letters,* II, 4; to W. C. Howells, March 6, 1887, and especially June 14, 1891 (Harvard). For reviews see S. Kirk, *op. cit.,* and M. Wilcox, "W. D. Howells's First Romance," *Harper's Bazar,* June 16, 1894, 475. From Frances Willard, November 21, 1900. On letters, to W. C. Howells, October 15, 1893, and M. Wilcox, "Works of William Dean Howells," *Harper's Weekly,* July 4, 1896, 656; to W. C. Howells, December 24, 1893 (Harvard); *Letters,* II, 76; Quint, *op. cit.,* 264–65; cp. C. M. Destler, *American Radicalism, 1865–1901,* 1946, 20–22; Upton Sinclair, "A Utopian Bookshelf," *Saturday Review,* December 7, 1946, 20.

IV

For Birthday Speech, *North American Review,* April 1912, 551–52; to W. C. Howells, January 29, 1893 (Harvard), February 19, 1893 (*Letters,* II, 33), cp. April 2, 1893 (Harvard). To C. E. Norton, October 16, 1892 (*Letters,* II, 27; cp. 62). On *Flight of Pony Baker* see to W. H. Rideing, various letters of 1897–98 (Huntington); to T. B. Aldrich, June 10, 1900 (*Letters,* II, 129).

V

From T. N. Page, January 23, 1910 (Harvard); inscription, from Canby, in presentation copy of Henry Seidel Canby, *Our House,* 1919 (Harvard); to Robert Herrick, February 16, 1909 (*Letters,* II, 262); R. U. Johnson, *Remembered Yesterdays,* 1923, 354–55; *Autobiography of William Allen White,* 302, 383; from Alice French, December 27, 1887 (Harvard); from Brander Matthews, December 25, 1893; August 13, 1895 (Harvard); from Whitlock, August 23, 1906 (Harvard). Cp. Arms, " 'Ever Devotedly Yours'—the Whitlock-Howells Correspondence," *Journal of the Rutgers University Library,* December 1946, 1–19.

An excellent pioneering study of Howells and Frederic is in Everett Carter, *Howells and the Age of Realism,* 239–45, 296, n. 240. For Howells on *Theron Ware* see *Literature,* June 17, 1899 (English edition), 637; Roosevelt, October 20, 1890 (Harvard); to Baxter, July 11, 1890 (Huntington). From Frederic, December 11, 1890; June 16, 1898 (Harvard).

To Cora Crane, July 29, 1900 (Columbia). In the following correspondence Howells' letters are at Columbia, Crane's at Harvard: from Crane, March 28, 1893; to Crane, March 27, 1893; from Crane, April 8, 1893; to Crane, March 18 and October 4, 1894; to Crane, June 13, 1895; from Crane, January 1 [1896] (cp. *Letters,* II, 42); to Crane, January 26, 1896; from Crane, January 27, [1896]; from Crane, August 15, [1896]; to Crane, August 15, 1896; from Crane (again), "Saturday." [August 15, 1896]. Cp. Howells on Crane: to Ripley Hitchcock, February 29, April 24, July 13, 1896 (Columbia); to Garland, July 22, 1896 (USC); to Baxter, August 24, 1898 (Huntington). Though Crane's esthetic has yet to be explained, helpful insight on his relations with Howells and realism may be found in Corwin Knapp Linson, *My Stephen Crane,* 1958; Daniel G. Hoffman, *The Poetry of Stephen Crane,* 1957; Robert W. Stallman, *A Stephen Crane Omnibus,* 1952; John Berryman, *Stephen Crane,* 1950. See also Daniel G. Hoffman, ed., *The Red Badge of Courage and Other Stories,* 1957; William M. Gibson, ed., *The Red Badge of Courage and Selected Prose and Poetry,* 1950 and 1957; the "beautiful war" letter is in Melvin Schoberlin, ed., *The Sullivan County Sketches of Stephen Crane,* 1949, 19; the inscription in *The Red Badge* appears in Stallman, 620. For Howells' writings on Crane, see Gibson and Arms.

Frank Norris, *The Responsibilities of the Novelist,* 1903, esp. 3–10, 196, 213–20. Howells, "Some Recent Novels," *Literature,* December 17, 1898, 577; from Norris, December 31, 1898 (Harvard) ; Howells, "A Case in Point," *Literature,* April 8, 1899, 370–71; from Norris, (*Letters,* II, 102–3) ; "The Editor's Easy Chair," *Harper's,* October 1901, 824–25; "Easy Chair," January 1903, 327–28; cp. Paul H. Bixler, "Frank Norris's Literary Reputation," *American Literature,* May 1934, esp. 109–11; and Carter, 246–49. Howells, "Frank Norris," *North American Review,* December 1902, 769–78.

Chapter Seven

For Crane's disappointment, see Berryman, *op. cit.,* 248.

I

The Landlord at Lion's Head: see from Alden, January 24, 1895 (Harvard) ; from Barrett Wendell, April 16, 1897 (Harvard) ; Wister, *op. cit.,* 712; Mark Sullivan, *The Education of an American,* 1938, 136.

II

In anticipation of Professor Meserve's definitive edition of *The Plays of William Dean Howells,* the informational aspects of this discussion of Howells and the drama have been deliberately limited. Cf. Walter J. Meserve, "An Edition of the Plays of William Dean Howells," *The Howells Sentinel,* mimeo. ed. by Clara M. and Rudolph Kirk, III, March 4, 1957, 3–4. Booth Tarkington, *Pen Portraits,* n. d., 19–20; Wiggin, *My Garden of Memory,* 1923, 134; Augustus Thomas, *The Print of My Remembrance,* 1922, 178; Shaw, "Told You So," *Dramatic Opinions,* 1906, I, 265; from Daly, January 11, 1893 (Harvard) ; to W. C. Howells, November 21, 1886 (Harvard), cp. *The Critic,* November 27, 1886, 265; "Editor's Study," July 1887, 319; July 1889, 319; June 1890, 152; Henry James, "American Letter," *Literature,* July 9, 1898, 18.

III

On the return to the Harpers: W. F. Johnson, *George Harvey,* 1929, 70, 72, 77; J. H. Harper, *I Remember,* 1934, 15, 19–21, 53, 91; from McClure, October 24, 1899 (Harvard) ; *Letters,* II, 137;

from L. C. Page and Co., February 15, 1900 (Harvard) ; to Duneka, February 28, 1900 (Penn) ; to Mitchell, August 27, 1903 (Penn).

W. M. Gibson's "Mark Twain and Howells: Anti-Imperialists," *New England Quarterly,* December 1947, 435–70, leaves almost nothing to add. "Coaling-stations," *Letters,* II, 96.

IV

To Garland, June 27, 1901 (USC) ; *Letters,* II, 160.

On *The Son of Royal Langbrith:* from Mitchell, November 27–28, 1904; to Mitchell, December 11, 1904 (Penn) ; *"Indian Summer"* notebook (Harvard) ; to Harvey, July 28, 1903, in Johnson, *George Harvey,* 86–87; *Letters,* II, 169, 171.

On psychology: Cp. Cooke, *William Dean Howells,* 187–89; Arnold B. Fox, *The Progress of Thought in William Dean Howells,* unpub. diss., New York University, 1947, esp. 192, 200; and Ferris Cronkhite, "Howells Turns to the Inner Life," *New England Quarterly,* December 1957, 474–85; to W. C. Howells, February 15 and 22, 1891 (Harvard) ; to Mitchell, November 21, 1907 (Penn) ; *Letters,* II, 181, 186.

Chapter Eight

In most of its phases, this latter part of Howells' life is, for obvious reasons, far better documented by Miss Mildred Howells than it could be by anyone else: see *Life in Letters,* II, 181 ff.

I

From Leonard Merrick, May 29, 1914 (Harvard) ; from Trevelyan, March 31, 1904; May 1, 1912 (Harvard) ; on Kipling, see "Editor's Study," October 1890, 801; September 1891, 691–92; *McClure's,* March 1897, 454; from Kipling, March 8, 1897 (Harvard) ; from Bennett, March 1, 1911 (Harvard) ; cp. Johnson, *Harvey,* 90.

Oxford degree: from Lord Goschen, June 2, 1904 (Harvard). On American Academy of Arts and Letters, see *Letters,* II, 259, 290, 293, *et passim;* Garland, *Companions on the Trail,* 251–52. Howells' correspondences with such figures as Lounsbury, Stedman, and Garland, among others, contain many references to Academy affairs and his troubles over them.

On *Writings:* see esp. *Letters,* II, 267–68; from Duneka, February 28, 1910 (Harvard) ; Gibson and Arms, 64–66; Rood, *op. cit.,* 156.

II

To W. H. Rideing, March 14, 1912 (Huntington); *Letters of Brand Whitlock,* 80; Herford, *American Magazine,* March 1913, 95; Bliss Perry, *Richard Henry Dana, 1851–1931,* 1933, 198–99; *Letters of Brand Whitlock,* 80, 59; E. S. Chamberlayne, "Mr. Howells' Philosophy and 'The Son of Royal Langbrith,'" *Poet Lore,* Autumn 1905, 144–51; *Frank Harris His Life and Adventures,* 440; on E. A. Robinson see Sutliffe, *Untriangulated Stars,* 225–26; on Thayer, Robert Grant, *Fourscore,* 277–78; Van Wyck Brooks, "Mr. Howells at Work at Seventy-two . . ." *World's Work,* May 1909, cp. Arms and Gibson, "Five Interviews with William Dean Howells," *Americana,* April 1943, 283–87; Brooks, *Scenes and Portraits,* 111, 127, 153; see Sinclair Lewis, "My First Day in New York," in Maude and Crane, eds., *The Man From Main Street,* 1953.

H. W. Preston, "The Latest Novels of Howells and James," *Atlantic,* January 1903, 79; cp. Brooks, *Scenes and Portraits,* 108–10, 117–18; and Bisland, ed., *The Japanese Letters of Lafcadio Hearn,* 1910, 214–15.

On Tarkington, see James Woodress, *Booth Tarkington,* 1954; and Tarkington, "Introduction," *The Rise of Silas Lapham,* xx; *Pen Portraits,* 17, 21; from Tarkington, September 7, 1914; January 16, 1915 (Harvard); *Letters,* II, 115, 388–90.

H. W. Mabie, "William Dean Howells," *Outlook,* December 1915, 786–87; William Lyon Phelps, "William Dean Howells," *Essays on Modern Novelists,* 1910, 59.

Gertrude Atherton, "Why Is American Literature Bourgeois?" *North American Review,* May 1904, 771–74; "Gertrude Atherton Assails 'The Powers,'" *N. Y. Times,* December 29, 1907, V, 2; cp. *Current Literature,* February 1908, 158–60; and *Adventures of a Novelist,* 1932, 101–2; John Macy, *The Spirit of American Literature,* 1913, 281–83, 288; F. M. Colby, "The Casual Reader," *Bookman,* October 1908, 125; Alexander Harvey, *William Dean Howells,* 1917, esp. 1, 2, 16, 31–35, 38, 65, 104, 184–85, 194, 200–205, 209, 231–32; cp. *Letters,* II, 375; "Collapse of the Howells Realism in the Light of Freudian Romanticism," *Current Opinion,* October 1917, 270–71; Francis Hackett, "William Dean Howells," *New Republic,* April 21, 1917, supplement, 3–5; Kilmer, ed., *Literature in the Mak-*

ing, 1917, 64, 131; Van Doren, *The Roving Critic*, 1923, 17. Cp. Frederick Hoffman, *The Twenties*, 1954.

III

Mabie, *op. cit.*, 787; on Howells and Ohio: Hayes, *Diary*, IV, 404–5; to Matthews, September 6, 1898 (Columbia); from Lloyd, March 9, 1898 (Harvard), from Alden, April 28, June 30, July 2, 1897 (Harvard); to Aurelia Howells, July 29, 1900 (Harvard); *Letters*, II, 116; for praise of *Kentons*, see *James Letters*, I, 397–400.

Leatherwood God: to Mitchell, December 11, 1904; from Mitchell, December 17, 1905 (Penn); *Letters*, II, 235; to Mira Dock, April 16, 1916 (L. C.); to Mitchell, December 11, 1904 (*supra*).

IV

On "Memoirs": to Mira Dock, September 17, 1913 (Harvard); cp. A. S. Hardy, *Things Remembered*, 1923, 1; Orcutt, *Celebrities Off Parade*, 126; Hardy, 297; from Duneka, November 12, 1915 (Harvard).

Wharton, ed., *Le Livre des Sans-Foyer*, 1916, 17. On the Irish executions see *Letters*, II, 356–60, and the special file on the subject in the Howells Papers, Harvard. On Henry James and the Nobel Prize: Howells and R. U. Johnson to the Secretary of the Nobel Committee of the Swedish Academy, April 7, 1911; cp. Gosse and Benson to the same, "January 1911" (*Svenska Akademiens Nobelkommitté Sekreteraren* files, Stockholm); cp. from Edith Wharton, February 18, 1911 (Harvard); to Gosse, March 6, April 7, September 9, 1911 (Brit. Mus.); from Per Hallström, May 30, 1911 (Harvard).

N. Y. *Times*, Wednesday, May 12, 1920, 10, 11; cp. May 13, 11; May 19, 23; "Kipling on Howells—A Letter to the American Academy of Arts and Letters," *Literary Review*, March 5, 1921, 8.

INDEX

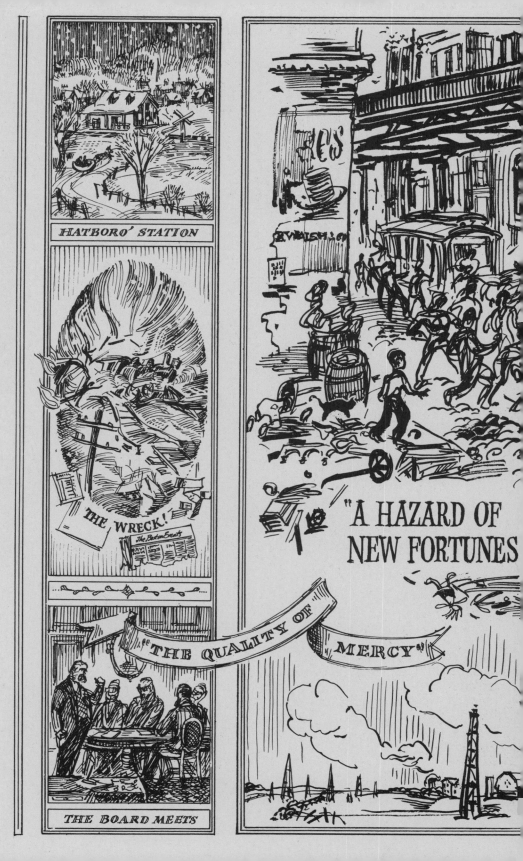

HATBORO' STATION

THE WRECK!

THE BOARD MEETS

"THE QUALITY OF MERCY"

"A HAZARD OF NEW FORTUNES